Every Tub Must Sit on Its Own Bottom

# Every Tub Must Sit on Its Own Bottom

## The Philosophy and Politics of Zora Neale Hurston

Deborah G. Plant

University of Illinois Press
Urbana and Chicago

*This book is printed on acid-free paper.*

An earlier version of chapter 1 appeared as "Narrative Strategies in Zora
Neale Hurston's *Dust Tracks on a Road,*" *Sage* 6 (Summer 1989): 18–23.
An earlier version of chapter 4 appeared as "The Folk Preacher and Folk
Sermon Form in Zora Neale Hurston's *Dust Tracks on a Road,*" *Folklore
Forum* 21, no. 1 (1988): 3–19.

Library of Congress Cataloging-in-Publication Data

Plant, Deborah G., 1956–
    Every tub must sit on its own bottom : the philosophy and politics
of Zora Neale Hurston / Deborah G. Plant.
        p.      cm.
    Includes bibliographical references (p.    ) and index.
    ISBN 0–252–02183–5 (cloth)
    1. Hurston, Zora Neale—Political and social views.  2. Hurston,
Zora Neale—Philosophy.  3. Politics and literature—United States—
History—20th century.  4. Women and literature—United States—
History—20th century.  5. Afro-Americans—Politics and government.
6. Afro-American philosophy in literature.  7. Afro-Americans in
literature.  I. Title.
PS3515.U789Z82      1995
813'.52—dc20                                                    4–47523
                                                                    CIP

To the memory of my mother
Elouise Porter Plant
and to my father
Alfred Plant, Sr.

# Contents

# Acknowledgments

I wish to express my sincere appreciation of my family, friends, and relatives for their nurturance, encouragement, and support. My circumference of daily life is there as well. My warmest appreciation goes to my dad, to my mother's spirit, to LeVita, Jean, June, Jackie, Ricky, Bobby, Dennis, Elaine, Meco, Auntie Jeannie, Cousin Izola, Iya, nieces and nephews, godchildren, the Carters, Lois Vaz, Laura Tohe, Glenda Johnson, and Phyllis McEwen Taylor (who loves her some Zora Hurston). My special, special thanks to and appreciation of Kim Marie Vaz for being there, for keeping vigil with me into the night, for discussing various points of the manuscript with me, and for tolerantly listening to me go on and on about Hurston and every new discovery I made in her works. I have the profoundest respect and appreciation for the New Jerusalem Baptist Church and Sunday School, in Baton Rouge, Louisiana, in whose bosom I was also nurtured. It was there that I received the knowledge and experience of the Black Southern Baptist tradition, which were fundamental to my writing of this book.

For reading and commenting on parts of the manuscript, I thank Jimmy Killingsworth of Texas A&M and my former chair, William O'Donnell of the University of Memphis, who also, in his offering of advice, rendering of assistance, and generosity of spirit, was very supportive of me and my work. For her reading of the manuscript in virtually every form it took and her advice and continued support, I thank my friend and mentor Linda Ray Pratt of the University of Nebraska–Lincoln. For her enthusiasm, support, and friendship, I thank Miriam DeCosta-Willis of the University of Maryland. For her moral support, her confidence in the publication of this work, and her special friendship, I thank Cynthia Tucker of the University of Memphis. And for her belief in me and my work, I thank my chair, Navita James of the University of South Florida.

I am grateful to the University of Memphis for funding that aided and facilitated my research. I was awarded a University Faculty Research

Grant for the summer of 1990 and a Tennessee Board of Regents Black Faculty Development Grant for the spring and summer of 1990 and 1991. I am also grateful to the University of Memphis Department of English for funding travel to a number of conferences at which I was able to present material on Hurston and receive valuable feedback.

I wish also to extend my gratitude to my editor, Karen Hewitt, for her insightful critical commentary and astute questions, her tenacity in seeing this project through, and especially for her calm reassurance. I am also appreciative of the keen eye and helpful suggestions of my copyeditor, Becky Standard. And I am certainly thankful to Zora Neale Hurston herself. Her work and her spirit have been an inspiration and motivation to me. I trust that her legacy lives on in these pages.

# Introduction: The Reclamation of an Intellectual Life

The world's most powerful force is intellect.

—"The Race Cannot Become Great
until It Recognizes Its Talent"

With four published novels, two collections of folklore, a collection of short stories, numerous essays and journal articles, and several musical and dramatic productions, Zora Neale Hurston was one of the most industrious and prolific writers of her day. Her achievement can be measured against her ability to survive engulfing poverty and to resist stereotypical images of Black womanhood. It can also be measured in relation to her determination for self-empowerment. Hurston's spirit of resistance is characteristic of women of Africa and the African diaspora who continually struggle against "racial," sexual, economic, and cultural domination. Because of her ability to negotiate adversity and succeed on her own terms, Zora Neale Hurston stands as a model of resistance.

Given women's centrality to the survival and liberation of African peoples, an examination of Hurston's strategies of survival and resistance and her struggle for self and self-empowerment, from every possible angle, is of vital importance. In this work, I examine Hurston's philosophy and politics. Since Black women's intellectual work is a fundamental component of Black women's resistance to domination and struggle for empowerment, understanding Hurston as a thinker as well as a doer is essential in an analysis of her as a model of resistance.[1] Through what is essentially a hermeneutic enterprise, I use a variety of critical approaches—narratological, biographical, archetypal, womanist, psychoanalytic, expressive, sociological, Black aesthetic—to explore Hurston's intellectual life and interpret its textual formulations.

Though Hurston's genius is now more widely recognized, the image of her as a folksy, smart-talking, "naturally" gifted individual yet obtains and undermines her intellectualism. She is rarely described as an intellectual and her intellectual life has been given minimal attention. This is due in part to "the secondary status afforded the ideas and experiences of African-American women," to the exclusion of Black women's thought from what is narrowly defined as intellectual discourse, and to conventional pedantic definitions that determine who qualifies as an intellectual (Collins 12–15). Hurston's informal writing style, marked by her use of the Black vernacular, though now celebrated and held as esteemed and authentic features of the African American literary tradition, formerly situated her work outside the elitist realm of intellectual, "serious" discourse. The breadth and depth of her intellectual endeavors were not only concealed by a seemingly effortless style of expression but were also rendered inconspicuous because of the author's reluctance to represent herself as an "intellectual," a class of people she held in contempt. In addition to a cultivated folksiness, Hurston's postures of naiveté and ambivalence, her provocative and questionable politics, and her art of dissemblance and silence resulted in a perception of the author as controversial, compromised, and nonserious.

The style and content of Hurston's work are generally attributed to her Eatonville experiences and to her formal training as a folklorist and cultural anthropologist. These influences explain certain surface elements of Hurston's literary production, but other aspects of her writing, such as her philosophical and political stances, have remained confusing and perplexing. As an intellectual, as a thinker, Zora Neale Hurston generated the individualist philosophy and politics upon which she based her activism and literary work. Her life in Eatonville and her formal academic training certainly informed her worldview. The intellectual standpoint from which Hurston interpreted and integrated her Eatonville and academic experiences into a coherent philosophical and political ideology and the constitution of that standpoint are aspects of Hurston's strategies of survival and resistance that I address.[2]

Though now viewed as a serious writer, Hurston is still described as enigmatic and unfathomable. Rather than quirks of character, however, these qualities are deliberate constructions of the Hurston persona. As Darlene Clark Hine has argued, the "dynamics of dissemblance" among Black women "involved creating the appearance of disclosure, or openness about themselves and their feelings, while actually remaining an enigma." Through a "self-imposed invisibility," "ordinary Black women accrue[d] the psychic space and harness[ed] the resources needed to hold their own in the often one-sided and mismatched resistance struggle" (915). Though they distrust society, Black women are compelled to negotiate it. So they disclose as little of themselves as necessary to obtain their ends, while safeguarding, as best they can, the interior world of their psychic and spiritual selves. This inner world in which so many Black women function is a hallowed locus, and as such, is the only sphere of freedom and security wherein they can live unmasked. I begin chapter 1, therefore, with an exploration of the only place in which Hurston felt secure—her self. Truly a woman who kept her own counsel, Hurston often referred to the source of her innermost thoughts as the only place in which she could escape societal limitations and censorship and freely express herself. There, in the inner regions of the self, she found affirmation, a place to heal, a place of restoration and recovery. There, she nurtured a spirit of resistance that enabled her to survive and continue. It is there that Hurston constructed alternative images of herself to stand in opposition to the controlling, stereotypical images of Black women, images that were devised in a society built on Black women's objectification and subjugation.

Hurston's autobiographical text, *Dust Tracks on a Road,* is analyzed as a configuration of the metaphors of self that sustained her. Generally disclaimed as a truthful account of her life, the autobiography, however, is the one text that traces Hurston's life as it unfolds in the only sphere of freedom available to her: the psychic, spiritual space of self. A mythic narrative, *Dust Tracks* is a glimpse into Hurston's interior world. Beneath the surface bravado and nonchalance and embedded in the text's deep structure lies the essence of Zora Neale Hurston.

"Sham and tinsel, honest metal and sincerity" are the controlling images in the *Dust Tracks* narrative. The honest metal and sincerity speak to Hurston's sense of herself as a woman of dignity, a self-reliant, resilient, and empowered individual. The sham and tinsel speak to her resourcefulness and her unwillingness to disclose and expose her essential self. Whether identified as masking, shamming, or tomming, the dynamic of dissemblance is an ingenious survival stratagem. In *Modernism and the Harlem Renaissance,* Houston A. Baker, Jr., analyzes masking as a modernistic enterprise brought to the "foreground of black intellectual history with the emergence of Booker T. Washington" (15). Because Washington mastered strategies of masking and put them to use in "the growth and *survival* of a nation," Baker reads Washington's dissemblance as a deft stroke (37). He notes, however, that consideration of Washington's dissemblance as liberatory and revolutionary is a novel stance (25). What is now considered subversive and empowering in Washington's expressive stratagems is yet viewed as duplicity or naiveté in Hurston's. But as Baker's reading of Washington's stances and standpoints situates Washington as a "modern" in Black intellectual history, a similar reading of Hurston's work situates her also as a "modern" and an intellectual. For, as a cultural anthropologist whose ethnographic writings resist and subvert Anglo-American cultural hegemony, Hurston's work also contributes to "the growth and *survival* of a nation."

Hurston was able to resist and subvert this cultural hegemony because of a powerful worldview. In chapter 2 I discuss the individualist underpinnings of Hurston's worldview and examine her family and community; Booker T. Washington's theory of self-help, industry, and personal responsibility; her anthropological study under Franz Boas and Ruth Benedict; the Spinozan philosophy of self-preservation, self-perfection, optimism, and pantheism; and the Nietzschean will-to-power, *amor fati,* and the Dionysian ideal as influences in Hurston's intellectual life. All of these factors culminated in a political philosophy of uncompromising individualism that helped her survive systemic sexism, racism, and classism, strengthened her will to resist negative controlling images, and empowered her to overcome Anglo-American cultural hegemony. Her individualist standpoint engendered and confirmed in her an autonomous sense of self, enabling her to negotiate a world particularly hostile to Black women. It reinforced her ambition to excel and her resolve to "wrassle up a living or die trying."

Hurston's philosophy of individualism was firmly rooted in an African American folk ethos, which is a "fundamental site of resistance." In chapter 3 I analyze Hurston's cultural politics in the context of the prevailing ideologies and politics of the Harlem Renaissance. Hurston understood profoundly the significance of African American culture as a vital component in the full political emancipation of African American people, individually and collectively. She understood cultural survival as a condition of liberation and cultural affirmation as an essential step in decolonizing the Black mind. Hurston saw that within African American culture lay the alternative images, self-definitions, and strategies necessary to resist Anglo-American cultural domination and to reclaim Black life. Central to the struggle was the vitality of the folk, which can be seen in Signifying, storytelling, indirect discourse, and humor—all instruments of resistance and self-empowerment Hurston used in her work.

Perhaps most central to the folk is the folk preacher, who figures as culture bearer and liberatory voice. In chapter 4 I look at Hurston's appropriation of the folk preacher's voice and the folk sermon form. Historically, the preacher's sermon stood in opposition to the dehumanization to which African Americans were subjected and served as a means of resistance to and rebellion against spiritual assassination and physical and mental enslavement. Hurston appropriated the style and tone of the folk preacher and the rhetorical devices of the folk sermon to express her individual standpoint and to oppose ideologies of domination.

Her ability to powerfully oppose ideologies of domination speaks to her intellectual acumen. In chapter 5 I challenge conventional notions of Zora Neale Hurston as an intellectual lightweight by assessing her political thought and analyzing it in terms of her philosophy of individualism. No greater manifestation of her thought can be found than *Moses, Man of the Mountain*. Critics have long identified *Moses* as Hurston's most ambitious novel and have praised her use of African American folklore in it. *Moses* has even been described as a masterpiece. Nevertheless, the critical attention given *Moses* has been negligible considering its true merit. *Moses* is a profound, mythic narrative that inverts, revises, and erases conventional social and political categories and ideologies. Because *Moses, Man of the Mountain* is Hurston's political manifesto, because it is illustrative of her intellectual brilliance, and because it has been neglected, it is the central focus of the chapter. Through a keen use of folk culture, Hurston redefines power in this novel and envisions a society based on individual merit and equal opportunity. Using parodic-Signifying language, Hurston makes incisive cultural critiques of African American and Anglo-American society, deconstructing conventional notions of power and authority and mocking the leadership of both. Her caricature of the folk offers penetrating insights into human nature as it explores the psychological and spiritual dynamics of an oppressed people. Her analysis is a commentary on the universal human will to survive and to resist oppression and exploitation.

Hurston's individualist standpoint recommends her as a self-reliant, self-determining, resilient, and autonomous individual. Her self-representation suggests that she was a pillar of strength, one who survived and negotiated adversity, and, like Dionysus, laughed in the face of it. Hurston was certainly a heroic figure. But her struggles were never so simple as she portrayed them, nor were they so easily overcome. She rarely spoke of the difficulties of growing up as a Black girl or of facing the world as a Black woman. Given the marginalization and devaluation of Black women in American society, her psychological and spiritual conflicts were inevitable. However, stories of the pain endured and the scars borne from continuous battle have been largely unattended to. In chapter 6 I examine some of those submerged stories of pain, including Hurston's "overwhelming complex about [her] looks." I analyze the effects of her experiences of "racial" discrimination in the larger society and those of sexism and alienation as female "other" in her family environment. I focus closely on Hurston's conflictual relationship with her father, John Hurston, exploring her father's rejection of her and her resulting feelings of unattractiveness, worthlessness, and woundedness. Never a victim, Hurston was able to resist being overwhelmed by her feelings of inferiority because of a strong sense of self nurtured by her mother and, paradoxically, by her father.

By emphasizing the patrilineal line of descent in Hurston's personality and her literature, I argue for the importance of recognizing and acknowledging the significance of the paternal factor in Hurston's psychospiritual development. In chapter 6 I also focus on sexual dualism in Hurston's work and her difficulty in reconciling contending notions of the masculine and feminine, a difficulty that stems from her childhood experiences. The sexual dualism apparent in Hurston's writing makes more evident Hurston's emotional scars and submerged stories of pain. A reading of Hurston's life that considers the problem of sex role socialization and sexual dualism brings to the surface those submerged stories as it helps to explain stereotypical notions of sex roles in Hurston's texts. The assumption that Hurston was somehow unaffected by sex role socialization has resulted in the discursive formation of a Hurston canon that ignores these aspects of Hurston's life and that excludes one of her major works, *Seraph on the Suwanee*. In chapter 6 I retrieve this text and analyze it in the context of Hurston's sexual politics.

Hurston transcended the paralyzing polarities of sexual dualism as a matter of practice in her own life. Her androgynous character was a major factor in her ability to do so. In the Conclusion I analyze this aspect of her character in terms of resistance and (self) empowerment while emphasizing the need to recognize and reconcile the feminine and masculine principles of human nature. As Toni Cade contends, "The usual notions of sexual differentiation in roles is an obstacle to political consciousness" and that cracking through the veneer of society's definition of "masculine" and "feminine" is essential to total self-autonomy (101, 108). As an ardent individualist, Hurston practiced a politics of self that defied stereotypical conventions of sex and sex roles. In her personal life, she was able to embrace both masculine and feminine principles in a way that empowered her to achieve what she did. Hurston is not an anomaly, but rather part of a continuum of "manly women" that can be traced from the United States and other parts of the African diaspora to the African continent itself.[3] As African women of antiquity and modernity are models of resistance, they also are models of the androgynous character and spirit necessary for self-actualization and continued resistance and progress. As we can draw inspiration from women of Africa, we can also look to Zora Neale Hurston as a model of empowerment.

# 1

## Metaphors of Self, Language, and the Will-to-Power

Women forget all those things they don't want to remember and
remember everything they don't want to forget. The dream is the
truth. They act and do things accordingly.

—*Their Eyes Were Watching God*

The adjustments and adaptations Zora Neale Hurston made in
her struggle against stereotypical images of her life as a poor, southern,
African American woman create the discursive formation that marks
her autobiography, *Dust Tracks on a Road,* as a discourse of resistance.
To combat received controlling images of the African American woman
as objectified "other," Hurston constructed a history of her life based
on empowering metaphors of self. This self-representation served to
assert the author as a willful, speaking subject. A teleology of the self
at a given point in time, her autobiography is a documentation of the
author's ordering of the world in accordance with her particular
standpoint. It is an account of the "unitary self" and its "daimon" as
well as a history of the events and circumstances that created that self
and to which it responded. As James Olney explains in *Metaphors of
Self: The Meaning of Autobiography,* the autobiographer is motivated
by an "impulse to order," to control the phenomena and noumena of
her existence. That existence is ordered by the creation of a metaphorical construction—the autobiography—that functions to satisfy the
autobiographer's feeling and need for order (8). Olney defines this
metaphorical construct thus:

Something known and of our making, or at least of our choosing, that
we put to stand for, and so to help us understand, something unknown
and not of our making;...[it is] that by which the lonely subjective
consciousness gives order not only to itself but to as much of objective

reality as it is capable of formalizing and of controlling. The focus through which an intensity of self-awareness becomes a coherent vision of all reality, the point through which the individual succeeds in making the universe take on his own order, is metaphor: the formal conjunction of single subject and various objects. (30)

The cosmology created, the metaphor, is reflective of the individual standpoint and of the individual will that created it. Metaphors projected from the autobiographer's unitary and personally unique point of view are created to express the subjective self rather than imitate the outer world (33–34). An understanding of the "intimate relation of self-knowledge and cosmology," the "becomingness of the self," and the will-to-power,[1] which is the human impulse to create, order, and control its world—its most profound act—is essential in understanding *Dust Tracks* as a testimony of survival and an act of resistance and in understanding Zora Neale Hurston as a "strong-willed resister."

Negative readings of *Dust Tracks* as untruthful, contradictory, and irrational assume a mimetic criteria for the interpretation of autobiography. Critics have considered it compromised and judged it an incomplete, if not false, picture of Zora Neale Hurston's life and her representation of the African American experience.[2] Accordingly, the focus has been less on the *bios* than on the history, the "truthful" rendering of events in the external world. In his foreword to the autobiography, Darwin Turner describes *Dust Tracks* as perhaps the best fiction Hurston ever wrote. And in a sense it is. The original published version of *Dust Tracks* did not candidly deal with the racist, sexist, and classist world that other sources tell us confronted Hurston. But when the autobiography is viewed as a documented teleology of the self and as a creation of the will, the fictional quality undergoes a transformation wherein it becomes truth—about the *bios*. Jacqueline de Weever, in *Mythmaking and Metaphor in Black Women's Fiction,* is insightful on this point:

> Black-American writers are part of the "return to myth" in the general and the specific sense, especially the women writers. The experiences of black people in the New World, into which they have been forcibly thrust against their will, cannot be told or treated in realistic or naturalistic traditions in which much American literature has been cast—the pain of the results of three centuries of oppression is too great to be faced and confronted in a realistic mode. Such experience demands another mode for which the mythic narrative is most appropriate. If fiction establishes lines to a world other than the real one . . . , the mythic narrative establishes lines to a world that is not only beyond the real world but that, at the same time, transforms it. Such narrative gives the

writer greater control over the material since it distances both writer and reader from the very harsh primal experience. (4)

Just as the autobiographer constructs a self-satisfying, mythic cosmology, she or he also constructs a persona, the unitary self, that obviates conflicts with the world beyond the author's creation. Both constructions are mutually protective systems that reflect "an aggressive, creative expression of the self, a defense of individual integrity in the face of an otherwise multiple, confusing, swarming, and inimical universe" (Olney 15). In view of the multiple dualities with which Hurston was confronted, a reading of *Dust Tracks* from the standpoint of the author-narrator is particularly useful. How did Hurston order her "inimical universe"? What does her particular pattern of order reveal? What strategies of coping, survival, resistance, and empowerment are found therein?

Shaped by the prevailing ideologies and the material circumstances of the author's existence, the persona narrating *Dust Tracks* appears to have been constructed by an individual who refused to accept the "thou-shalt-nots" of her external world. Born around the turn of the century, Hurston grew up in an unreconstructed South, in a separate and unequal society in which Jim Crow was the unabashed order of the day. Not quite a second-class citizen because of gender and ethnicity, neither respected for her genius nor wealthy despite her success, not a paragon of anybody's standard of beauty, she was placed, decidedly, on the margins, in a position of relative powerlessness vis-à-vis white, patriarchal America. I suggest that these marginalizing factors and the author's resolve to resist and overcome them determined the "daimon" of the unitary self or persona in Hurston's narrative. The daimon, that is, the driving motivation, is the empowerment of the self. The author, therefore, constructs a mytho-narrative wherein the persona created transcends the oppressive conditions of society and holds power over self and world.

• • •

In the early chapters of the autobiography young Zora is portrayed as a spirited and defiant child who must fight against repression and domination in the social spheres of home and community. Given to talking back, she is often at odds with her father and grandmother. Her father cared nothing for her high-spiritedness and "sassy tongue." "Let me change a few words with him—and I am of the word-changing kind—and he was ready to change ends" (27–28). He did not believe "Negroes" should have too much spirit, so he threatened to break hers or kill her in the attempt (21). Nor was he tolerant of her fantasies and wishes. Driven by the "inside urge" to travel to the horizon and "see what the end of the world was like," she asked her father for a riding horse as a Christmas present: " 'I want a fine black riding horse with white leather saddle and bridles,' I told Papa happily."

> "A saddle horse!" Papa exploded. "It's a sin and a shame! Lemme tell you something right now, my young lady; you ain't white. Riding horse! Always trying to wear de big hat! I don't know how you got in this family nohow. You ain't like none of de rest of my young 'uns."
>
> "If I can't have no riding horse, I don't want nothing at all," I said stubbornly with my mouth, but inside I was sucking sorrow. My longed-for journey looked impossible. (38–39)

This scenario paints a picture of the narrator as persistent in her desires and defiant in the face of those who would deprive her of or prevent her from attaining them. Significant in the narrative is the distinction between the outward show of things and the inward reality. *Inside* she sucked sorrow, and *inside* is where she journeys to realize her desires and where the external world is powerless to control her. When the saddle horse is vehemently denied her, the narrator creates her own: "Since Papa would not buy me a saddle horse, I made me one up. No one around me knew how often I rode my prancing horse, nor the things I saw in far places" (39). No one knew, so no one had the power to deny her. No one had the power to control her.

Like the father, the grandmother is portrayed as a figure of parental authority bent on subduing the willful and outspoken child. She desires, for instance, to break her grandchild of storytelling, an activity the grandmother considers abominable: " 'Why dat lil' heifer is lying just as fast as a horse can trot. . . . I bet if I lay my hands on her she'll stop it. I vominates a lying tongue' " (72). Shielded from her grandmother's wrath by her mother, young Zora evinces little concern for the grand-mother's threats. "I knew that I did not have to pay too much atten-tion to the old lady and so I didn't. Furthermore, how was she going to tell what I was doing inside? I could keep my inventions to myself, which was what I did most of the time" (72–73). The narrator again portrays herself as defiant in the face of parental authority. Retreating within the private psychic space of self, she is beyond external censor and control.

The community, symbolic of sanctioned custom and tradition, is depicted as another coercive power that must be resisted and nullified. In following instructions received from her mother shortly before her death, Zora attempts to prevent the community's traditional rituals of death. "I was called upon to set my will against my father, the village dames and village custom" (86):

> "Don't," I cried out. "Don't take the pillow from under Mama's head! She said she didn't want it moved!"
> I made to stop Mrs. Mattie, but Papa pulled me away. Others were trying to silence me. . . .
> "Don't cover up that clock! Leave that looking-glass like it is! Lemme put Mama's pillow back where it was!"
> But Papa held me tight and the others frowned me down. (87–88)

The imperative statements in this passage and the frustrated action reflect Zora's determination to set her will against established authority as well as to keep her solemn promise to her mother. It also reflects her sense of her own authority, control, and power, though it was unheeded.

In these chapters, negative figures and scenes are counterbalanced by more positive ones that explain how the narrator as a youth is able to negotiate attempts by adult figures to silence and repress her. In opposition to her father and grandmother, her mother is portrayed as nurturing and protective. The mother's image of her daughter as one who would "come out more than conquer" opposes negative images of her as a lying "lil' heifer" who is nothing like her siblings. Her mother "never tried to break" her and didn't want to "squinch [her] spirit too much." She creates a protective haven for her daughter wherein her self confidence is encouraged and her self-esteem is nurtured.

In opposition to tradition and communal mores stands the old white man who served as a midwife at Zora's birth. He is imbued with all the roughness and self-sufficiency of the strident individualist of frontier life and justice. The "lessons" she learned from him are intended to explain aggressive, individualistic actions on her part. If she does battle, it is because battle must be done. And if she battles anyone or anything, it is because she is courageous and is either facing down a lie or standing up for the truth.

Those figures the narrator portrays in a positive light are unfailingly depicted in mythic dimensions. For instance, the old white man "was supposed to be so tough, it was said that once he was struck by lightning and was not even knocked off his feet, but that lightning went off through the woods limping" (43–44). Even though the father is characteristically portrayed in a negative light, he has qualities the narrator admires, praises, and mythologizes. She loves his poetry and, particularly, his physical strength: "He was two hundred pounds of bone and muscle" (22). She and her siblings are "certain of Papa's invincibility" even in the face of God (91). As she renders godlike the people or qualities of people she loves or admires, she also suggests her own mythic dimensions. As a child, the narrator was anguished because her soul was with the gods, but her body was in the village, and the people about her "just would not act like gods" (56). Portraying herself as godlike, she proposes to follow in the footpaths of Hercules, with whom she identifies. Her imaginative consort with the gods of Greek and Roman myth and the biblical men of God, along with the prophetic visions she recounts, foreshadow the emotional and spiritual distance that gradually becomes a reality for the narrator.[3]

As the narrator invests herself with divine qualities, she describes herself as an iconoclast. She respects neither the idols people build for themselves nor "the gods of the pigeonholes" (33). Whether by questioning those who set themselves up as gods or by revealing their clay feet, the narrator shows herself as having no qualms about unveiling what she considers to be false gods and confounding the "truths" and values they consider sacred. "I was full of curiosity like many other children, and like them I was as unconscious of the sanctity of statuary as a flock of pigeons around a palace" (34). This image of the narrator as an iconoclast, early on in the narrative, anticipates the controversial position she takes later on in relation to race, "Race Leaders," religion, religious leaders, and their traditions.

That Hurston narrates her story in the mythic mode suggests that her experiences, both as a child and an adult, were difficult and painful. The emotional distance created by virtue of writing in the mythic mode enables Hurston to recount harsh primal experiences without seeming affected by them. This narrative distance empowers Hurston, giving her control over self and world and the agency and authority to interpret both from her own standpoint. Hurston also revises a situation from an empowered angle of vision, transforms negative situations or events into positive ones or ones that cast the narrator in a favorable light, changes the subject or redirects the focus, usually from the narrator to others, and uses silence to construct a persona that can tell Hurston's own story from a position of strength and power while avoiding self-disclosure.

Hurston's relationship with her father was probably one of the most hurtful relationships she experienced. In this narrative, however, that relationship is revisioned as one that she determined and controlled, even from the very beginning. As the second girl born into the family, the narrator writes that her father disliked and dismissed her. "Plenty more sons, but no more girl babies. . . . I don't think he ever got over the trick he felt that I played on him by getting born a girl" (27). The narrator's assertion of power over her own birth and her father's wishes places his rejection of her in her control. If her father was distressed by another girl baby—"I did hear that he threatened to cut his throat when he got the news" (27)—it was not because he fathered a girl baby, but because the girl baby got herself born that way. The narrator renders herself powerful and wily in that even as an infant it is possible for her to "trick" her father.

The narrator interprets her father's refusal to acknowledge her and his lack of affection toward her as marks of her distinction and intellectual superiority. Such interpretations are intended to explain the narrator's nonchalant pose. Yet, hurt feelings and resentment are implicit in her statements. "I know that I did love him *in a way*"; "It did not matter *so much* to me that Sarah was Papa's favorite. I got my joys in other ways, and so, did not miss his petting. *I do not think* that I ever *really* wanted it" (91, 100; emphasis mine). What comes across in the tone of the narrative voice is a wistfulness for a relationship denied. The statements are qualified and calculated to diminish the hurt, create an emotionally imperturbable persona, and foster a positive self-perception in the face of rejection and powerlessness.

The narrator gives a cursory description of what must have been another painful experience. After her mother's death, Zora is abandoned and thus orphaned by her father, who relinquishes his guardianship to the Jacksonville school: "I kept looking out of the window so that I could see Papa when he came up the walk to the office. But nobody came for me. Weeks passed, and then a letter came. Papa said that the school could adopt me" (108–9). The reader might expect an analysis of a child's disappointment, confusion, and pain. But the narrator examines her devastation over this "crumbling news" by showing the moment through another's eyes. Instead of her own feelings, she examines those of the assistant principal, who related the letter to her: "It was crumbling news for me. It impressed every detail of the office and her person on my mind. . . . I had always been afraid of her sharp tongue and quick hand, but this day she seemed to speak a little softer than usual . . . as if she had her tender parts to hide" (109). The narrator immediately shifts attention from herself to the assistant principal. The focus through an objective observer allows the narrator to distantly view herself rather than intimately confront the meaning of her feelings. The pathos of her situation is measured by the soft tone of the usually harsh tongue of the other.

Even her response to her mother's death is portrayed in a matter-of-fact manner. Having observed a woman who resembled her mother, the narrator resolves to find her. "But before I did, the hope that the woman really was my mother passed. I accepted my bereavement" (96). And the narrator silences herself about her relationship with her brother, who, the narrative suggests, misused her. The situation is never fully discussed: "There was much more, but my brother is dead and I do not wish even to risk being unjust to his memory, or unkind to the living" (129–30).

Abrupt endings of discussions, shifts in subject or focus, and silence create the disruptions and surface incoherence that characterize the text. They also make manifest Hurston's intention to exclude from her own immediate consciousness, and from the awareness of her audience, the effects of any suffering she may have experienced in her struggles to become the figure she was. Acknowledged pain, fragility, timidity, and fear are all considered forms of weakness and impediments to self-empowerment. Suppressed discussions of unhappy childhood experiences parallel suppressed discussions of adult experiences of racism, sexism, and classism in the latter chapters of the autobiography. What is discussed is to be interpreted in light of the persona constructed from these early chapters: the archetypal, undaunted, questing figure who can deal with the world on its own terms and emerge unscarred and unscathed.

The metaphorical construction of the persona is reinforced by specific metaphors in the narrative. A look at a few of the more striking metaphors of self the narrator uses shows how, on every level of the narrative, the cosmology is reinforced. *Dust Tracks* opens with a telling metaphor:[4] "Like the dead-seeming, cold rocks, I have memories within that come out of the material that went to make me" (3). At once a mythic dimension is set. Rocks are enduring and timeless. "Dead-seeming, cold rocks" suggest hardness, isolation, indestructibility, imperviousness. The narrator implies that she is primeval. Though difficult to understand, she is not unfathomable since, like the rocks, she only seems cold and impenetrable. "So you will have to know something about the time and place where I came from, in order that you may interpret the incidents and directions of my life" (3). By telling the reader something of the time and place and the "material that went to make me" the narrator influences the reader's appreciation of the author's own standpoint, her own interpretation of the incidents and directions of her life. These initial passages project the overall narrative structure: The persona, a metaphorical construct created in the early chapters, interprets incidents portrayed and directions taken in the later chapters.

This persona is best described by these metaphors of self the author uses: "I am a bundle of sham and tinsel, honest metal and sincerity that cannot be untangled. My dross has given my other parts great sorrow" (347). The sham and sincerity "that cannot be untangled" are the overriding metaphors by which the author wants to be perceived. Through linguistic transcendence, the self created in *Dust Tracks* escapes an imposed marginal existence. This self is grounded in language and is redeemed and made whole through language.[5] When the author of *Dust Tracks* recreates herself through words, through metaphor, she (un)names the "chaos and disconnection" of her external oppressive existence and sets in motion a process of symbolic action akin to Kenneth Burke's notion of dramatic determinism. Hence, the author-narrator is at once propelled and compelled by her own language. "Like the dead-seeming, cold rocks," she is distant, isolated, and explainable only in terms of the persona she has created. She is also a "bundle of sham and tinsel, honest metal and sincerity." These contradicting metaphors of self create the narrative tension that sets the rhythm and pattern of *Dust Tracks on a Road.*

* * *

As the keystone of the narrative, the persona created in the early chapters is the standpoint from which typically questionable and controversial ideas and events related in later chapters are to be viewed. Chapters 9 through 11 of the autobiography chronicle the author's accomplishments and the circumstances surrounding them. In chapter 9, "School Again," the narrator illustrates her orientation toward achievement. Though confronted with poverty and ill health, she realizes her ambition to acquire a formal education. Making little money as a waitress and tired of "jumping up and down in my own foottracks ... I just went" to school (146). Although the narrator's struggle to realize her goals is evident, her remarks are such that they diminish the significance and complexity of her struggle: "I just went." The language and the action implied are simplistic. "I just went" emphasizes the power of the self and negates any external influences. It narrows the purview, taking the narrator out of the racial melee, and severs racial bonds. Simultaneously, this oversimplified representation of the struggle to achieve deemphasizes the author's experiences vis-à-vis systemic inequities in American society. The narrator creates the image of the ideal, industrious individual who, in accordance with Booker T. Washington's philosophy, lifts herself up by her own bootstraps. By emphasizing her courage and tenacity, the narrator tends to mitigate the impact of oppressive forces in the lives of African Americans in general and her own life in particular.

The simplistic rendition of her personal struggle for academic achievement, in this instance, adumbrates the narrator's reductionist treatment of a controversial situation also described in "School Again." After attempting to be served at a Jim Crow barbershop where the author-narrator worked as a manicurist, a Black man was thrown into the street. The narrator writes that, theoretically, she and the other employees were supposed to resist Jim Crow practices; however, the incident "made me realize how theories go by the board when a person's livelihood is threatened" (162). The narrator interprets the incident, foremost, as a matter of job security: The barbers, porters, and manicurists were "all stirred up at the threat of our living through loss of patronage" (164). Even though she concluded that she "was giving sanction to Jim Crow," she continues to focus attention on and condemn the individual Black man: "There is always something fiendish and loathsome about a person who threatens to deprive you of your way of making a living. That is just human-like, I reckon" (165). "You" could very easily be the reader, and the narrator assumes the reader's sympathy and admiration while ignoring the likelihood that her response to the incident really would cost her her living. Described in malignant terms, the anonymous Black man is transformed into a sacrificial victim—the mythic scapegoat. His being thrown into the street becomes a purifying ritual drama that cleanses the employees of the blight of racist practice and the guilt of their sanctioning it. The point of view that rationalizes this action keeps intact the philosophy of individualism and the notion of ethical capitalistic competition while it perpetuates the convention of blaming the victim. It allows the narrator to avoid confrontation with her malevolent external reality and to maintain the order of her constructed cosmology. A focus on this single "threat" instead of on the larger one of a racist society also serves to limit the sphere of conflict and allow the narrator more personal control of the situation, which enhances her own sense of power. "I did not participate in the mêlée, but I wanted him thrown out, too," she writes (164). Her restraint from action signifies her potential power while at the same time it creates the image of "the innocent bystander" that intimates her humility as well as her lack of sympathy with "troublemakers."

The humble persona surfaces again and again in the narrative. To what extent the narrator's humility was sincere or spurious is debatable, given the entanglement of sham and tinsel, honesty and sincerity. The question is particularly problematic in regards to the narrator's relationship with Charlotte Mason as described in "Research," chapter 10. Mason is portrayed as "mother-love," an "extremely human" individual with whom the narrator shared a "psychic bond." Though sensitive and generous toward her charge, Mason is also dictatorial. The narrator must address her as "Godmother" and submit to her scolding: "'Keep silent. Does a child in the womb speak?'" (176). As the early chapters reveal, the narrator chafes under the restraints and restrictions of authority figures. This characteristic restiveness is not apparent in the relationship with Mason. Here, the narrator identifies with Mason: "I was her only Godchild who could read her thoughts at a distance," for "she was just as pagan as I" (176). Scoldings received at Mason's hands are represented as deserved: Mason would rebuke "anything in you, however clever, that felt like insincerity to her. . . . Her tongue was a knout, cutting off your outer pretenses, and bleeding your vanity like a rusty nail. She was merciless to a lie, spoken, acted or insinuated" (177). By granting Mason a higher wisdom, the narrator does not present Mason's dictates and fiats as directed by an imposing authority that must be resisted. Approving of Mason and suggesting that they are alike allows the narrator to accept what seems to be a displaced self-discipline. She portrays Mason as right when she scolds and astute in her judgments instead of tyrannical, bigoted, and patronizing. Given this view of Mason, it is almost a moral duty to accept her rule. The narrator invests Mason with such powers that any instance of falsity—such as "tomming"—on the part of the narrator would be easily detected. This portrayal of Mason implies that either the narrator is utterly sincere or shrewdly deceptive.

In another passage, the narrator manifests a willingness to subject herself to external authority in order to relieve her economically oppressed condition. After submitting to "a proper straightening" from Mason and her friends, "I would be wrapped in love. A present of money from Godmother, a coat from Miss Chapin, a dress from Mrs. Biddle" (176). The passage implies an altogether pragmatic narrator. Rather than outwardly rebel against authoritative and repressive forces, she circumvents them. Deception, deference, and dissemblance, or "tomming," are among the strategies used. The narrator states that she finds merit in "'tomming' if it's done right. 'Tomming' is not an aggressive act, it is true, but it has its uses like feinting in the prize ring" (295). Whether her obsequious self-representation was authentic or an act of subversion, the narrator's ambition for self-empowerment through the attainment of financial and material necessities, which allowed her the means to continue her work, is evident in the narrative pattern.

In "Books and Things," the narrator's restiveness under perceived coercive forces surfaces again. Frustrated over what ideological perspective to take in *Jonah's Gourd Vine,* she writes, "What I wanted to tell was a story about a man, and from what I had read and heard, Negroes were supposed to write about the Race Problem. I was and am thoroughly sick of the subject" (206). The narrator rationalizes her controversial statement by taking recourse in her philosophy of individualism: "My interest lies in what makes a man or a woman do such-and-so, regardless of his color. It seemed to me that the human beings I met reacted pretty much the same to the same stimuli. Different idioms, yes. Circumstances and conditions having power to influence, yes. Inherent difference, no. But I said to myself that that was not what was expected of me, so I was afraid to tell a story the way I wanted, or rather the way the story told itself to me. So I went on that way for three years" (206).

In the last statement of this passage, the narrator implies her patience, humility, and her willingness to conform to what she views as narrow race-serving expectations that contradict the larger claims of human reality. For three years she refrains from following her own, superior inclinations. Although she insinuates her deliberate consideration of literary expectations and conventions, she does not bow to them. Three years' consideration—a number significant in Christian symbology— validates her decision as judicious. Moreover, the narrator writes that she is obliged to a higher authority. The Sublime is invoked: "Anyway, the force from somewhere in Space which commands you to write in the first place, gives you no choice. You take up the pen when you are told and write what is commanded" (212–13).[6] The language here, marked by biblical allusions, casts the gift of the artist in a mystic light. The narrator, thus, is transformed into the reverent and obedient prophet of God; she is a divine oracle. The books she writes are sacred texts. The narrator, therefore, is not reactionary and is not a rebel who refuses to fulfill imposed expectations or racial obligations. She is a servant of a higher power expressing higher wisdom.

Her decision to reject the expectations of the Black intelligentsia and follow "the force" or "the inner urge" distinguishes her from the common lot who blindly follow the dictates of others. The incidents and situations discussed in chapters 9 through 11 depict a narrator of deliberate and uncompromised action: she "just went" to school; she risks her life to accomplish research goals; and she writes the story she chooses. The narrator tells us that whatever direction she takes, she is compelled by an "inner urge" that is not responsive to external reality. These chapters, in their turn, foreshadow the last chapters. A recounting of what the narrator considers uncompromised and deliberate action sets the stage for the progressively more radical statements and opinions made in the last part of the narrative.

• • •

"My People! My People!" "Two Women in Particular," "Love," "Religion," and "Looking Things Over," chapters 12 through 16, speak to issues of race,[7] community, friendship, marriage, sex, and religion. With the exception of her view on friendship, the narrator's perspectives on these issues are decidedly negative. They are characterized as impediments or barriers to the development of the individual. In chapter 12 the narrator ridicules superficial class distinctions drawn in African American society. She satirizes "My People": the "humble Negro," the "upper-class" or "dicty Negro," and the "better thinking Negro." The one phrase that describes them all, she contends, is "My People! My People!" "It is called forth by the observations of one class of Negro on the doings of another branch of the brother in black" (215). When the "humble Negro" and the "dicty Negro" contend, the "humble Negro" is the undisputed victor:

> The educated Negro may know all about differential calculus and the theory of evolution, but he is fighting entirely out of his class when he tries to quip with the underprivileged. The bookless may have difficulty in reading a paragraph in a newspaper, but when they get down to "playing the dozens" they have no equal in America, and, I'd risk a sizable bet, in the whole world. Starting off in the first by calling you a seven-sided son-of-a-bitch, and pausing to name the sides, they proceed to "specify" until the tip-top branch of your family tree has been "given a reading." No profit in that to the upper-class Negro, so he minds his own business and groans, "My People! My People!" (217)

The narrator implies the superiority of the oral tradition because it can silence those who make pretenses to power by virtue of their formal education and socioeconomic status. Though the narrator can read—and write prolifically—she identifies with "the bookless." Her identification with them suggests that, like them, she feels the pangs of class distinctions drawn by the "upper-class Negro." And, like them, she resents it. The narrator recognizes in the folk the power of language, and she uses language as a weapon in her defense against elitism. Although the narrator joins forces with the "humble Negro" in the verbal warfare directed against the elite, her identification as one is only partial. The strategy's real design is to place her in an outside but superior position to both. For even though she is one of the folk, she is not "bookless." The metaphor she uses to describe the folk creates a distance between them and her. Ultimately in the narrative, this created distance becomes fixed. However, in the first part of the chapter, the narrator bridges that distance with a display of her intimate knowledge of "My People" in order to undo the category of class. She unites with them on a common front against a common foe: the "dicty," "educated Negro" who, gradually in the narrative, crystallizes as the "Race Leaders" for whom the narrator expresses resentment and contempt. She characterizes Race Leaders as self-righteous, dictatorial assimilationists who attempt to impose themselves on the people and judge them—and her. The narrator first speaks as a Signifying mediator between the two groups, but as her identity with "the bookless" fades and her own agenda emerges, the battle becomes personal.

In the following passage, the narrator *is* the "humble Negro" she describes. The tirade she levels against Race Leaders, under the guise of the "humble Negro," recalls the narrator's initial confrontation with the Black intelligentsia in chapter 11: "What that educated Negro knows further is that he can do very little towards imposing his own viewpoint on the lowlier members of his race. Class and culture stand between. The humble Negro has a built-up antagonism to the 'Big Nigger' " (216). The narrator's agenda becomes clear: justification of *her* controversial position and empowerment of the self through the nullification of external control. The "educated Negro" who cannot verbally subdue the "humble Negro," the narrator explains, has little power to do anything else. She, and the folk with whom she shares the same culture, will resist any imposition of viewpoints. She describes the presumed power of the "educated Negro" as a pretense and an illusion. Through Signifying language, she conquers her antagonist by naming him: " 'Big Nigger.' " The phrase is intended to level class distinctions and silence pretenders.

The narrator's antagonism against "so-called Race Leaders" is evident in her deconstruction of epithets associated with the "Race Problem": " 'Race Pride'—'Race Prejudice'—'Race Man'—'Race Solidarity'—'Race Consciousness'—'Race' " (217). She (un)names Race Leaders and their ideologies. She defines their epithets as impotent folk labels and treats their ideas as so much insignificant verbiage.

> "Race Prejudice" I was instructed was something bad that white people used on us. It seemed that white people felt superior to black ones and would not give Negroes justice for that reason. "Race Pride" was something that, if we had it, we would feel ourselves superior to whites. . . . A "Race Man" was somebody who always kept the glory and honor of his race before him. Must stand ever ready to defend the Negro race from all hurt, harm and danger. Especially if a white person said "Nigger," "You people," "Negress" or "Darkies." It was a mark of shame if somebody accused: "Why, you are not a Race Man (or woman)." People

made whole careers of being "Race" men and women. They were champions of the race. (217–18)

This passage recalls again the narrator's resistance to pressures that she write in accordance with the dominant discourse, which valued analyses of the "Race Problem." Having dropped the veneer of the "humble Negro," the narrator outwardly renews her personal struggle with the Black intelligentsia. The sense that she is yet imposed upon by them and their ideologies is reflected in the statement that she "was instructed," that is, pressured, to think in terms of "Race Prejudice." The pressure she feels is that the intelligentsia will judge her and find her wanting. She responds by rendering the phrase fictive. It only *seemed* that this prejudice existed. The claim that she "was instructed" that prejudice did exist implies that she had not experienced it. The solipsistic stance she takes gives her viewpoint the only reality. "Race Pride" is cast in a subjunctive mood, and the "Race Man" is a foolish sentinel, guarding "the Race" against something that does not exist. The narrator rejects the badge of shame associated with not being a "Race Woman." She not only ridicules Race Women and Men but also shows her utter contempt of the imposition she feels by referring to "Race Champions" in the same disparaging terms they perceived as contemptible.

The narrator's coup d'etat against the "so-called Race Leaders" is to deconstruct their rallying point—*the Negro:* "But maybe, after all the Negro doesn't really exist. What we think is a race is detached moods and phases of other people walking around. What we have been talking about might not exist at all. Could be the shade patterns of something else thrown on the ground—other folks, seen in shadow" (304). She expresses an existential metaphysics that renders "the Negro" nonexistent and reduces the beliefs, hopes, and aspirations of "the Race" to mere fiction. Group solidarity becomes a myth, "good only at the political trough," and "Race Men" only feckless con artists. She wields language to vanquish all perceived antagonists. As she negotiates power and self-respect, she makes a mockery of the African American experience. She denies African America's suffering and Anglo-America's control and privilege. Her apparent determination to annul race as a factor in her life and to castigate Race Leaders shows her ardent struggle against being defined by external powers that would narrow her individual power of self-definition and self-determination. To accept ideologies of race and accord them any significant influence would compel her to redefine her own life as well as render her morally responsible to take up the "Race Problem" and work to resolve the dilemmas of "thirteen million people," a responsibility she refuses to accept on the terms laid down by the Black intelligentsia.

Though the narrator presents her opinions as honest and her feelings as sincere, she masks her responses to the call of the Race Leaders by assuming a naive, deferential pose—a variation of the sham and tinsel. She contextualizes many of her statements with allusions to her childhood. This strategy establishes the naivete and innocence of the narrator that, in turn, is designed to disarm the audience and mitigate harsh criticism of her controversial statements. Through the voice of the seeking, questing "child" speaks the adult who explodes reverently held ideals and values as figments of other people's imaginations. The voice of the child in this chapter echoes that of the child in early chapters who, "like many other children . . . was as unconscious of the sanctity of statuary as a flock of pigeons around a palace."

The naive voice is reinforced by a projection of bewilderment and consternation that further obscures and shows as unfounded the ideas of the "so-called Race Leaders." It points out the contradictions between what African Americans say and what they do. As the narrative progresses, the target of attack gradually comes to include all of "My People." Their actions stirred up confusion in "the child": "Everybody would laugh at [jokes comparing a monkey with Blacks], and the laughter puzzled me some" (222). "What was all the talk about? It certainly was puzzling to me" (232–33). Amid humorous anecdotes and bewildered inquiry, the naive voice attempts to undermine the discursive foundations of dominant arguments articulating the oppression of African Americans and their struggle to overcome oppressive forces. Speaking through the mask of the child, the narrator appears tentative about the controversial remarks she makes. The tentativeness is marked by her consistent display of humor and her persistent use of interrogative statements. The humor disarms and the questions serve to protect the narrator from backlash. They also function as much to create self-doubt in the reader as to project self-doubt in the narrator: "Since the race line has never held any other group in America, why expect it to be effective with us?" (218). "Were Negroes the great heroes I heard about from the platform, or were they the ridiculous monkeys of everyday talk? Was it really honorable to be black?" (226). "What was this about white and black people that was being talked about?" (232).

Question posing and feigned self-doubting are typical strategies women use to assert themselves and to assert counterarguments while maintaining a pose of intellectual inferiority and an appearance of submission and deference in the face of presumed male dominance. Race Leaders, in the forefront, were male. So were most of the dominant figures on Joe Clarke's porch. The narrator's duplicitous stance is indicative of her sensitivity to and defense against sexist, condescending attitudes of African American men (as well as the paternalistic attitudes of white Americans). In "Negotiating Respect," Roger Abrahams illuminates the dynamics involved in the narrator's struggle to assert herself:

> If a woman places herself in a public situation, she is in jeopardy of having to contend with men and their *jive*. . . . What is a serious variety of communication in the enclosed settings of home or church becomes a playful one in the more open context of porch and road and country store. If a woman's sense of respectability is challenged in such a situation, she may fight fire with fire, becoming as verbally open and aggressive as her contenders, resorting to a very tendentious sort of *smart talking*. . . .
> "Talking smart" routines develop in male-female interactions in a range of situations—from the totally public badinage . . . to the dyadic interaction between two already deeply involved participants in which the smart talk is intended to produce strategic advantage (and thus to modify the behavior of the man). (75–76)

Naivete, innocence, and humor are aspects of sweet talk. Controversial remarks, "name calling," and "finger pointing" are variations of smart talk. A woman negotiates these two modes of discourse in an offensive-defensive stratagem against "anyone who might threaten her self-image" (62). The conflicting messages of boldness and deference result in a narrative that appears contradictory. But seen as an inherent and integral aspect of Black women's strategy to negotiate with (male) contenders, the element of contradiction becomes an authenticating feature of a discourse of resistance.

· · ·

By the logic of the cosmology of *Dust Tracks* the narrator is compelled to renounce her familial, cultural, and historical past. The notion of friendship, however, is salvaged. Rather than threaten the cosmology of *Dust Tracks,* the idea of friendship reinforces it. "Two Women in Particular" is a symbolic microcosm of the egalitarian ethics of the narrator's created world. In this chapter, the narrator attempts to illustrate the meaninglessness of race as a social index. Focusing on her friendship with Fannie Hurst, a white author and former employer, and with Ethel Waters, a Black recording artist, she insinuates her ability to get along with whites as well as Blacks. What social problems there are, are caused by individuals, not races. Such a perspective does not threaten the autonomy struggled for and does not conflict with the narrator's individualist enterprise.

In the absence of conflict, the narrator shows herself to be totally affable. When her world is threatened or off kilter, she maneuvers to set it aright. Chapter 14, "Love," exemplifies the narrator's determination to balance her cosmology. In this chapter the narrator focuses on conflicts between personal relationships and career. She reveals herself as a woman who, though capable of great passion, is at bottom rational, objective, and self-possessed. Here, she expresses her Spinozan aversion to emotional excess—the chains of human bondage. When a relationship conflicts with her career, the relationship is modified or terminated. And sometimes her career is an escape from failed emotional commitment. Evident in the narrator's discussion is a judgment against stereotyped gender roles and sexist treatment. Men are portrayed as authoritative figures who want to subdue and dominate her. Though she pretends a desire to submit and conform, a contradicting discourse in the narrative reveals otherwise. The narrator writes that her lover, A.W.P., "wanted to do all the doing, and keep me on the receiving end. He soared in my respect from that moment on" (253). Since American social conventions at that time dictated that women were supposed to be "taken care of" and feel grateful to find a man willing to assume that responsibility, the narrator must express her gratitude, especially since her man is willing to perform this duty so enthusiastically. His choice to do for her suggests that she, in reality, is a typical, traditional woman with typical, womanly desires and expectations. If the relationship does not work, she is not to blame. If she does not submit, as she states she wants to, it is not because she willingly resists male domination. The narrator claims to be pleased by her lover's "great desire . . . to do for me," but she finds his "great desire" to be egotistical and problematic: "That very manliness, sweet as it was, made us both suffer. My career balked the completeness of his ideal. I really wanted to conform, but it was impossible. To me there was no conflict. My work was one thing, and he was all of the rest. But, I could not make him see that. Nothing must be in my life but himself" (253–54).

The persona who says that she "really wanted to conform" strongly contrasts with the nonconformist of earlier chapters. The narrator writes that it is not her unwillingness to submit that is a problem, but rather her lover's "very manliness." Perhaps because the relationship was still active as the narrator wrote her story, she mixes "sweet talk" with her persistence in negotiating her autonomy. The narrator's desire to be submissive is contradicted by the portrayal of her lover and their relationship. A.W.P., though described as intelligent, is depicted as an insecure, diffident individual who doesn't know his own assets (256). Though described as "manly," he is depicted as indecisive and incapable of looking after his own interests. The narrator assumes control of the relationship and determines its direction: "I began to feel that our love was slowing down his efforts. He had brains and character. He ought to go a long way. I grew terribly afraid that later on he would feel that I had thwarted him in a way and come to resent me. . . . Even if I married him, what about five years from now, the way we were going?" (259–60). The lover lacks control of himself and his situation, nor does he have foresight. Therefore the narrator must do what is best for him. Having received her Guggenheim Fellowship, she decides, "This was my chance to release him, and fight myself free from my obsession" (260). Though "hog-tied and branded," the narrator keeps her wits about her, showing herself more rational, reflective, and focused than "her man" and more capable than he of self-control and level-headedness: "the telephone or the doorbell would ring, and there would be my career again. A charge had been laid on me and I must follow the call" (256, 259).

Since women were expected to happily neglect self and renounce their work for men, the narrator finds it necessary to attribute her dedication to her career—and her determination to do as she pleased—to a force beyond her, a force that would not allow her to fulfill her traditional woman's desires. Her resistance to external control is always accompanied by an invocation of the Sublime, by a call from some higher power. In "Love," the higher power is her work. Under the guise of allegiance to her work, the narrator again maneuvers herself to the seat of power. The chapter is a testimony not to love, but to the rational, objective persona and her career commitment. Reason overcomes emotion as the narrator declares that "the oath of Hercules [to shun pleasure and follow duty] shall always defeat me in love" (261).

Whatever else might have transpired in her relationship with A.W.P., or the other affairs she briefly mentions, is silenced by the narrator's control of information. The narrator clearly articulates and justifies the authorial intentionality that determines the discursivity of this chapter: "Ladies do not kiss and tell any more than gentlemen do," so "I have no intention of putting but so much in the public ears." Besides, "I am supposed to have some private business to myself" (249, 261). The narrator's prerogative to withhold information is also a device to conceal anything that might upset the equilibrium she has created. It is also, perhaps, a flaunted indication of her power as narrator and as the controlling force in her world. Moreover, withheld knowledge establishes an air of mystery. And as the narrator asserts in chapter 6, "You cannot have knowledge and worship at the same time. Mystery is the essence of divinity. Gods must keep their distances from men" (93).

In "Religion" the narrator makes complete her demiurgic transformation. From a consort of the gods in chapter 4 to a servant of God in chapter 11, the narrator, through a metaphysics that culminates in pantheism, ultimately becomes a reigning god herself. As the mythic narrative establishes lines to a world beyond the real and transforms that world, as Weever has suggested, so the narrator as mythmaker is also transformed. Thus, the mythic dimension comes full circle. As the narrator finds community and culture burdens to be dismissed, love—that is, emotion—is also considered a liability that impedes her bid for self-creation and autonomy. Likewise, institutional religion is considered a challenge to the narrator's sense of authority. It, too, is rendered insignificant. Although she was "pitched head-foremost" into the Missionary Baptist Church where her father was the minister and her mother the superintendent of the Sunday school, the narrator pretends to know nothing about religion. Some of the same rhetorical strategies displayed in "My People! My People!" are used here. The narrator assumes a naive posture that recalls childhood confusion and questioning. As early as she could remember, she "was questing and seeking" clarity about religion. "It mystified me" (267). Though she listened to the songs and sermons and the congregation's acceptance of all that was said, "somehow it left a lack in my mind" (267). Under cover of the naive voice, the narrator questions the believers, their beliefs, and the idea of God itself. "I wanted to know, for instance, why didn't God make grown babies instead of those little measly things that messed up didies and cried all the time? What was the sense in making babies with no teeth? . . . Why did God hate for children to play on Sundays? If Christ, God's son, hated to die, and God hated for Him to die and have everybody grieving over it ever since, why did He have to do it? Why did people die anyway?" (267–68). The question-posing stance and the use of puerile language renders almost innocuous what might otherwise be considered a blasphemous passage. The narrator trivializes Judeo-Christian doctrine by depicting God as an incompetent creator. She poses questions that initially are fatuous but subtly become more pointed. This pattern characterizes the chapter and reflects the controlling metaphors of the *Dust Tracks* narrative.

After undermining the solemnity of the church with childish questioning, humor, and finger pointing, the narrator clears space to make her personal observations about religion and the idea of God. Though assertions are prefaced with tentative phrases like "it seems to me to be true"—the sham and tinsel—the narrator's authoritative voice speaks. The honest metal and sincerity come into play. According to the narrator, "People need religion because the great masses fear life and its consequences. Its responsibilities weigh heavy." Those who are weak "seek an alliance with omnipotence to bolster up their feeling of weakness, even though the omnipotence they rely upon is a creature of their own minds" (277–78). The persona created is not weak and does not fear life but meets it head on. Unlike the great, timorous masses, she sees only futility and cowardice in transacting an alliance with a nonexistent supreme being through prayer. For her, prayer is "a cry of weakness," "an attempt to avoid . . . the rules of the game as laid down" (278). But the narrator avoids analysis of "the rules," the dictates, and the influences of an unjust, prejudiced society. She simplifies and minimizes their effects by interpreting "the rules" in accordance with her doctrine of individualism and self-determination. The denunciation of the practice of prayer is less an attack on religious tradition than another argument in support of a determination for self-direction and personal responsibility. Just as the narrator states that no one should expect special blessings on the basis of race, she believes that no one should expect or depend on special blessings from God through prayer. The desire for prayer and the hope for God's blessing is a character flaw. She accepts the means at her disposal for working out her destiny. Having been "given a mind and will-power for that very purpose[,] I do not expect God to single me out and grant me advantages over my fellow men" (278).

Rebaptized by the fire of individualism, the narrator recreates herself in her own image and challenges anyone or anything that threatens to alter her self-image or prevent her own personal conversion. As she dethrones the notion of an omnipotent, omniscient, and intervening God, she renders herself omnipotent creator. The supreme being who oversees the affairs of humans is cast out in favor of an indifferent universe. "Life, as it is, does not frighten me, since I have made my peace with the universe as I find it, and bow to its laws" (278). On those terms, the narrator can reign supreme. To bow to universal laws is tantamount to bowing to herself since she has recreated the universe and sees that she is "one with the infinite" (279). Boundless, "ever changing, ever moving," she is a part of all life. She concludes that "nothing is destructible; things merely change forms. When the consciousness we know as life ceases, I know that I shall still be part and parcel of the world" (279). Ubiquitous and eternal, she is part of the constant reformulations of Spinozan metaphysics and part of the

Nietzschean "eternal recurrence." The narrator wrests power from the ultimate source of all power and creation. A modality of divine substance, she is Alpha and Omega. On a fine black riding horse, the child, symbol of new beginnings, travels to the distant horizon, an image of illusive boundary, of end and future time. Part and parcel of this mythic junction of earth and sky, she is elemental. Escaping the strife of her temporal existence through the alchemy of mythic transformation, she is empowered and sublime.

In "Looking Things Over," the transfigured creator who has "stood in the peaky mountain wrappen in rainbows, with a harp and a sword in [her] hands" gives a summary look over the world she leaves behind (280). It is full of "human self-bias" and void of universal justice, an ideal impossible to bring about since "justice, like beauty, is in the eye of the beholder" (281). The narrator, here, allows for the complications of external influences. But just as she refrains from describing the pots in Sorrow's kitchen, she continues to avoid close examination of her external world. And since there is not nor ever will be "some disinterested party to pass on things" as she might wish, the narrator renounces the external world for her own internal one. Her leave-taking is marked by the typical ceremonial closure that asserts a believer's determination to make it to some unearthly paradise: "So I give you all my right hand of fellowship and love, and hope for the same from you" (286).

· · ·

*Dust Tracks* is an indictment against Zora Neale Hurston's external world. The narrative's inhibited and halted expression suggests that her primal experiences in the world outside the *Dust Tracks* cosmology were indeed harsh, such that the author is compelled to distance herself from those experiences. *Dust Tracks,* then, documents how repressive and oppressive social forces can yield a language of illusion that leaves inarticulate and invisible the historical woman. Darlene Clark Hine problematizes this phenomenon of invisibility in her discussion of the inner lives of Black women. She argues that the "inclination of the larger society to ignore those considered 'marginal' actually enabled subordinate Black women to craft the veil of secrecy and to perfect the art of dissemblance" (915). She questions the ramifications of this "veil of secrecy": "Yet it could also be argued that their secrecy or 'invisibility' contributed to the development of an atmosphere inimical to realizing equal opportunity or a place of respect in the larger society. . . . In other words, stereotypes, negative images, and debilitating assumptions filled the space left empty due to inadequate and erroneous information about the true contributions, capabilities, and identities of Black women" (915). However, given the fact that "Black women did not possess the power to eradicate negative social and sexual images of their womanhood," Hine sees Black women's dissemblance as a mode of resistance essential to their survival. She states that "it was imperative that they collectively create alternative self-images and shield from scrutiny these private, empowering definitions of self" (916). Therefore, as *Dust Tracks* bespeaks the objective reality of an inimical external world, it also illustrates the power of subjective thought and interior life. The inner self, as a site of resistance, is where alternative self-images and self-definitions are created. *Dust Tracks,* as a metaphor for Hurston's inner self, serves to protect its author as it mediates between the author and a hostile society. The discursivity of the *Dust Tracks* narrative gives us an individual larger than life who, though restrained, was autonomous; though fragile, strong; though compromised, independent; and though hurt and scarred, resilient and indomitable. A mythic narrative, the text illustrates the transformative power of myth. Zora Neale Hurston's ability to survive in a world that denied her existence and her ability to control her own destiny were possible to the extent that she believed in these possibilities. Who she was was possible to the extent that she could create, value, and define herself. Her autobiography recounts her abiding faith and belief in herself.

Yet, questions and criticisms abound concerning *Dust Tracks* and its author. Did Hurston, in her autobiographical narrative, damn African America to save herself? Did she renounce public responsibilities and obligations to nurture herself? In her attempt to subvert the system by recreating it, did she also undermine her own life and career? In his literary biography of Hurston, Robert Hemenway writes that the autobiography "can be a discomfiting book, and it . . . probably harmed Hurston's reputation" (276). The many questions her book left unanswered rendered her a questionable literary and political figure: "How can Zora Hurston express herself as both one of the folk and someone special? How can she admit that discrimination may occur, but argue that it does not signify? How can her autobiography describe the drive to success of a black woman and not explain how she overcame the institutional racism and sexism of her society? How can Hurston claim identity with the masses, yet affirm the supremacy of the individual?" (283).

These questions point up the dialectics of Hurston's literary career and her private and public life at the point of writing *Dust Tracks*. In a letter that Hemenway quotes, Hurston writes of the autobiography:

"I did not want to write it at all, because it is too hard to reveal one's inner self" (278). Ironically, it is the deepest "inner self" that is revealed in *Dust Tracks*. And the author's "inner self," her ego, is the angle of vision in the narrative that must be brought to bear on any assessment of how she negotiated the antagonisms of race, sex, class, and culture in her society. Her struggle with oppressive forces was often submerged or silenced, but it was as often disguised. The narrative patterns in *Dust Tracks* speak to the author's conscious act of self-reliance, of turning in to her self for a trusted and safe space for self-recovery, transformation, and creativity. They speak to her conscious decision to negotiate the "multiple jeopardy" she encountered with strategies of silence and dissemblance.[8]

The "truth" Hurston sought and presented in her autobiography was one different from what most readers expected. Not what *was*, necessarily, but what ought to be—the dream, the vision. Ultimately, an autobiography must meet the needs of the autobiographer—Hurston's need for order, control, self-worth, security, and self-empowerment. In the case of *Dust Tracks*, critics have tended to judge the surface text against a standard of mimetic reality, and the submerged text, which gives a more accurate documentation of the author's life, has gone unexamined. If the submerged text had been made explicit we would have been given a totally different autobiography. But it would necessarily have reflected a different personality, a different standpoint, and a different means of dealing with the world. Then, too, what would it have cost the author to make explicit all that is implied in *Dust Tracks*? In *Talking Back* bell hooks writes that "there are some folks for whom openness is not about the luxury of 'will I choose to share this or tell that,' but rather, 'will I survive—will I make it through —will I stay alive'" (2). There are no easy answers or definitive responses to the questions *Dust Tracks* raises. Nevertheless, we can trace from its patterns a great deal about the author and the standpoint from which she perceived the world. We see the psychological strategies that characterized Hurston's struggle in the face of a culture of domination. To have a view of one's self and one's world that opposes controlling images and ideologies and that, moreover, is empowering is a fundamental act of resistance and liberation. Such a view is imperative in the lives of Black women and in the lives of all who resist domination.

# 2

# "Every Tub Must Sit on Its Own Bottom": A Philosophical Worldview

I know that I cannot accept responsibility for thirteen million people. Every tub must sit on its own bottom regardless.

—*Dust Tracks on a Road*

Though community, as a site of resistance, and collective action, as a strategy of resistance, are highly valued among African Americans, Zora Neale Hurston's site of resistance, though grounded in the community, was located within herself. Hurston perceived the individual, not the group, as the basic social and political unit and the point of origin for sociopolitical change.[1] A staunch individualist, Hurston believed in personal industry, individual merit, and self-empowerment. Her orientation toward individualism and achievement[2] combined to create a third and even more compelling orientation: a power imperative, or a "will-to-power," that expressed itself as a determination to achieve self-reliance, self-definition, and self-direction, an autonomy conceived as nothing short of a mastery of self.

Hurston wrote in "Seeing the World as It Is" that the "solace of easy generalization was taken from me, but I received the richer gift of individualism. When I have been made to suffer or when I have been made happy by others, I have known that individuals were responsible for that, and not races" (*Dust Tracks* 323). By the same token, whether she had succeeded or failed, Hurston held no one accountable but herself. She refused to give too much weight to systemic inequities in American society, thereby implying also that even if individual African Americans were not so much responsible for their conditions and situations, they were responsible for changing them. Though a preserver and continuer of African American cultural heritage and oftentimes the voice of Black nationalism, Hurston declared her independence from the folk and everyone else. She would carry her own weight, but not the weight of "the Race": "I know that I cannot accept responsibility for thirteen million people. Every tub must sit on its own bottom regardless" (324–25).

Hurston's philosophical worldview evolved out of an idealistic vision wherein individuals would be considered according to their behavior and accomplishments. Moreover, individuals would not necessarily be equal, but would enjoy equal opportunity. "I am all for the idea of free vertical movement," she wrote, "nothing horizontal. Let him who can, go up, and him who cannot, stay there, mount down to the level his capabilities rate." Those desirous of and capable of achieving and acquiring should not—could not—be held back. As she put it, "The able at the bottom always snatch the ladder from under the weak on the top rung. That is the way it should be" (345). Nevertheless, arbitrary, though very real, factors of ethnicity, class, gender, and culture all too often are powerful variables that influence or determine individual destiny. These variables have no play in Hurston's simplistic vision. Hurston, nonetheless, was painfully aware of the impact of these forces. Her idealistic vision, then, is less a denial of the complexities of human existence than a reactionary response to a very complex political reality in which individuals were and are circumscribed by forces outside the self.

Though her vision can be described as idealistic, Hurston's awareness of complex social and political forces and her own standpoint in relation to them were often pointedly expressed. Her remonstration against those who would indulge in anything other than fair play and who would subscribe to anything other than individual merit as a standard of measure is one example:

> And then I know so well that the people who make a boast of racial, class, or national prejudices do so out of a sense of incapability to which they refuse to give a voice. Instead, they try to be ingenious by limiting competition. They are racial cardsharps trying to rig the game so that they cannot lose. Trying to stack the deck. If I choose to call these cardpalmers poor sports, then the burden of proof is on them. I give the matter the corner of my eye and smile at the backhand compliment, for I know that if I had been born where *they* were born and they had been born where *I* was born, it is hardly likely that we ever would have met. So I smile and not bitterly, either. For I know that Equality is as you do it and not as you talk it. (331)

Hurston's individualist orientation propelled her beyond the boundaries prescribed by social prejudices and unfair competition. The world in which she lived was the antithesis of her ideal world, yet her ideals became firm praxis. For what may not be possible for humankind as a whole may be possible for individuals.

To realize the ideals she fostered, Hurston had more than a healthy dose of self-assurance. She believed in herself thoroughly and was strongly motivated by self-interest. Her accomplishments, of course, reinforced her good opinion of herself: "If you are better than I, you can tell me about it if you want to, but then again, show me so I can know. . . . And then again, if you can't *show* me, don't bother to bring the mess up" (331). An irrepressible self-confidence and a combative spirit were at the foundation of Hurston's individualistic philosophy. In view of the influences on her life, it is not likely that Hurston's ardent sense of self was simply an overcompensation for an inferiority complex. It seems, rather, having learned early on that she and African Americans, generally, were quite capable of achieving whatever they envisioned, that her very strong sense of self became more ardent as she "proved" herself to others and as she struggled against negative external forces. Within the matrixes of family and community were the incipient formations of Hurston's self-perception, her value orientations, and her intellectual standpoint. Other predominant influences on her philosophical worldview were the legacy of Booker T. Washington, associations with Franz Boas and Ruth Benedict, and the philosophies of Benedict de Spinoza and Friedrich Nietzsche.

• • •

Hurston's orientation toward personal responsibility and industry were engendered by her childhood experience in all-Black Eatonville. Incorporated and run by Blacks, Eatonville was a model of Black ingenuity. Her own father, John Hurston, was thrice mayor and a prominent minister. Hurston's obvious pride in the history of her hometown and the part her family played in its development are reflected in her writings. She dramatized the town's history in her first novel, *Jonah's Gourd Vine,* and in her second novel, *Their Eyes Were Watching God.* Through the character of John Pearson in *Jonah's Gourd Vine,* Hurston highlighted the contributions her father made as civic and spiritual leader. *Their Eyes Were Watching God* emphasized the role of Eatonville's founder, Joe Clarke. Cast as Joe Starks in the novel, Clarke is depicted as strong, determined, self-reliant, industrious, and productive. An individual with a positive psychology, unbounded by self-restricting notions, he is one who neither acknowledged nor accepted externally imposed limitations. Regarded as the quintessential individualist, he became the prototype upon which Hurston based her ideal male characters.

In *Their Eyes* Hurston also voiced an impatience with "average mortals" who were unduly concerned with what "de white folks ain't goin' tuh 'low." As well, she decried those who were not only diffident about African Americans' ingenuity and capability but who also indulged in malicious and petty criticism of their efforts. Here and elsewhere Hurston foregrounded the internecine conflicts of African Americans who, as the narrative suggests, can at times be their own worst enemies. The image of Hurston's ideal individual and the theme of the conflict-ridden, back-biting individual or group who would bring *him* down recur in Hurston's *Seraph on the Suwanee, Moses, Man of the Mountain,* and "Herod the Great."

What Hurston saw in the actual accomplishments of Eatonville's citizenry was complemented by the local lore she imbibed from the old white man who "grannied" her. She figured him as a "hard-riding, hard drinking, hard-cussing, but very successful" individualist who was the embodiment of frontier law and who transmitted its truths to her. He took it upon himself to nurture in her a spirit of fearlessness and to coach her in the ways of self-defense. Accordingly, his counsels and the example of his life taught her that "personal strength and courage were the highest virtues." "You got what your strengths would bring you" (*Dust Tracks* 44, 62). Hurston depicted him as the ideal frontiersman who met life head on and taught her to do the same.

"As in all frontiers," Hurston observed, "there was the feeling for direct action," which required strength of body and mind (44). The former she inherited from her father. "Extra-strong" like him, she could battle boys and even "take a good pummelling without running home to tell" (39). The latter she learned from her mother, Lucy Potts Hurston. Her mother encouraged her mental tenacity and her spirit of resistance. Though she exhorted all her children to "jump at de sun," she gave Hurston particular encouragement. She declared, " 'Zora is my young'un,' " and predicted she would " 'come out more than conquer' " (21). The pride and confidence expressed in her mother's words no doubt went a long way in nourishing Hurston's ego and buoying up her spirit.

The effect of her mother's words can be seen in Hurston's depiction of herself in *Dust Tracks*. Hurston described herself as a precocious schoolgirl whom others enviously referred to as "Old Smarty." She recounted her school days in a manner designed to showcase her superior intelligence and capabilities. The school she attended, however, was much more than a stage for her youthful flamboyance. Hurston wrote of a Mr. and Mrs. Calhoun, who were strict disciplinarians preoccupied with the impression their students made on white northern visitors. The history of the school and its purpose are not considered in Hurston's account. Omission of this history obscures the significance of Booker T. Washington's legacy as a central force in the development of Eatonville and in Hurston's own development. The anthropologist Eleanor Ramsey and the architect Everett Fly point out the connection: "Two years after the town of Eatonville was incorporated, the Hungerford Normal and Industrial School was founded by Roger F. Hungerford. Russell and Mary Calhoun, the school's first and second principals, patterned the school after Booker T. Washington's Tuskegee Institute. . . . The school was designed to teach students the work ethic, sound moral and human values and the proper social graces" (123–24). Anna Lillios, in *Zora in Florida,* documents that Hurston attended this school that emphasized vocational as well as academic education. It may not have been the "heart and spring of the town" in Hurston's evaluation, but the school played a vital role in the development of the town and the townfolks' sensibilities and mores. Like Tuskegee, Hungerford was self-sustained. Members of the administration and faculty instilled in their students and in the townsfolk the virtues of industry, self-pride, self-help, and individual merit. That could only have reinforced Hurston's ideas about how personal and group autonomy were to be achieved.

Hurston omitted discussion of Hungerford's history, but she referred to Washington in her autobiography. She tempered an accounting of her academic success with this allusion: "Booker T. Washington said once that you must not judge a man by the heights to which he has risen, but by the depths from which he came" (172). In "My People! My People!" she decried the "better-thinking-Negro" who shunned all things Black and believed "Booker T. Washington was absolutely vile for advocating industrial education" (233). In unpublished versions of "My People! My People!" Hurston declared her allegiance to Booker T. Washington as she cursorily delineated ideological contentions between Washington and W. E. B. Du Bois.

On the point of industrial education, as with many other issues, Hurston's ideas are almost carbon copies of Washington's. Although she experienced the advantages of a college education, she also saw the wisdom in teaching "a thousand men to stand upright." Hurston's autobiography, in fact, stands in a Signifying relationship with Washington's work.[3] *Up from Slavery* sets forth Washington's philosophy of Black education and foregrounds strategies to achieve it. Washington regarded hard work as an essential component of a solid education.

"Nothing ever comes to one, that is worth having, except as a result of hard work" was his experience and doctrine (135). Tuskegee students were to perform agricultural and domestic work and learn to see beauty and dignity in labor as well as utility (109). Washington believed in the redemptive quality of (manual) labor and its capacity to transform the laborer into a confident and self-reliant individual.[4]

Hurston also praised hard work and did not see herself, even when a successful writer, as above manual or domestic labor. In one explanation for her work as a maid when she was a renowned author, she stated, "You can only use your mind so long. Then you have to use your hands" (Hemenway 325). Whether as waitress, "lady's maid," manicurist, researcher, folklore collector, or writer, Hurston worked all her life. Like Washington, she viewed work as the essential element of a rewarding life. "I don't know any more about the future than you do," she wrote in *Dust Tracks*. "I hope that it will be full of work, because I have come to know by experience that work is the nearest thing to happiness that I can find. No matter what else I have among the things that humans want, I go to pieces in a short while if I do not work" (285).

For Washington, industry would result in the kind of productivity and achievement that would free African Americans from a posture of dependence. It would be a clear indication of the capability of newly emancipated African Americans to be productive and, therefore, valued members of a booming industrial society. It would convince whites of the sound integrity of African Americans, and it would foster in an erstwhile enslaved people a self-esteem that would allow all to rise above a history of enforced servitude and overcome a psychology of servility and inferiority. Proud, they could resist the tyranny of racist propaganda. Confident, they could survive and overcome it.

To talk about the potential of African Americans irritated Washington: "I have always had more of an ambition to *do* things than merely to talk *about* them" (143). This expedience manifested itself in his self-help brand of education and in his racial politics: "I have found, too, that it is the visible, the tangible, that goes a long ways in softening prejudices. The actual sight of a first-class house that a Negro has built is ten times more potent than pages of discussion about a house that he ought to build, or perhaps could build" (113). In *Dust Tracks* Hurston portrayed herself as a woman of action as well. Her rise to literary acclaim from humble beginnings is a shining example of Washington's ideal of pulling one's self up by the bootstraps. Her glib discussions of her achievements emphasize what she accomplished rather than why or how she accomplished them. She, too, was impatient with all talk and no action, thus her rejoinder to those who presumed themselves superior to her: You told me, now "show me so I can know."

Washington held it a universal law that the ability of the talented and industrious would overcome all odds. Individual merit was the bedrock of his philosophy: "Every persecuted individual and race should get much consolation out of the great human law, which is universal and eternal, that merit, no matter under what skin found, is in the long run, recognized and rewarded" (40). His ideas anticipate Hurston's: "I do not share the gloomy thought that Negroes in America are doomed to be stomped out bodaciously, nor even shackled to the bottom of things. . . . It would be against all nature for all the Negroes to be either at the bottom, top, or in between. . . . It is up to the individual. If you haven't got it, you can't show it. If you have got it, you can't hide it. That is one of the strongest laws God ever made" (*Dust Tracks* 236–37).

Washington's ideas infused Hurston's optimism that the individual who wills it can and will rise above arbitrary forms of social discrimination. Such optimism underlay her tendency, and Washington's, to accentuate the positive and deemphasize the negative. These tendencies were part of an intricate web of survival strategies that helped both to resist succumbing to despair and inertia. Self-confidence, self-sufficiency, and self-dependence were all aspects of and strategies to success, resistance, and empowerment. Having pulled themselves up by virtue of their desire to achieve and their capacity for the hard work achievement requires, they were proud of their accomplishments and proud, moreover, because they surmounted obstacles that were designed to impede their progress. Though proud of their ethnicity, neither claimed for themselves special recognition based on their race, and each spoke disparagingly and pityingly of those who did. Washington wrote to that effect:

From any point of view, I had rather be what I am, a member of the Negro race, than be able to claim membership with the most favoured of any other race. I have always been made sad when I have heard members of any race claiming rights and privileges, or certain badges of distinction, on the ground simply that they were members of this or that race, regardless of their own individual worth or attainments. I have been made to feel sad for such persons because I am conscious of the fact that mere connection with what is known as a superior race will not permanently carry an individual forward unless he has individual worth, and mere connection with what is regarded as an inferior race will not finally hold an individual back if he possesses intrinsic, individual merit. (40)

Hurston repeated Washington's argument against social determinism, making a stylistic revision marked by African American vernacular expression:

> So Race Pride and Race Consciousness seem to me to be not only fallacious, but a thing to be abhorred. It is the root of misunderstanding and hence misery and injustice. I cannot, with logic, cry against it in others and wallow in it myself. The only satisfaction to be gained from Race Pride anyway is, "I ain't nothing, my folks ain't nothing, but that makes no difference at all. I belong to such-and-such a race." Poor nourishment according to my notion. Mighty little to chew on. You have to season it awfully high with egotism to make it tasty. (*Dust Tracks* 326–27)

Individual merit was the rule by which Washington and Hurston wished to be measured and by which they chose to measure others. Thus, each renounced the practice of racial prejudice. Washington testified, "With God's help, I believe that I have completely rid myself of any ill feeling toward the Southern white man for any wrong that he may have inflicted upon my race. . . . I pity from the bottom of my heart any individual who is so unfortunate as to get into the habit of holding race prejudice" (120). Washington's words resonate in Hurston's declarations that she harbored "no race prejudice of any kind" and in her description of "Race Pride" and "Race Consciousness" as sapping vices (*Dust Tracks* 285, 325).

Several times in his autobiography, Washington declared himself free of any bitterness or ill will: "I have long since ceased to cherish any spirit of bitterness against the Southern white people on account of the enslavement of my race. No one section of our country was wholly responsible for its introduction, and, besides, it was recognized and protected for years by the General Government" (24). Hurston reiterated this sentiment in *Dust Tracks:* "What I had to swallow in the kitchen has not made me less glad to have lived, nor made me want to lowrate the human race, nor any whole sections of it. I take no refuge from myself in bitterness" (280). "I am not bitter" is a refrain that resounds throughout Hurston's writings.

Washington and Hurston both portrayed themselves as morally superior to the "cardsharps" and "cardpalmers" who would stack the decks against them. Their ultimate moral stance is not only to absolve whites, past and present, of any wrongdoing, but also to claim some value in the experience of enslavement. Washington stated that when we "look facts in the face, we must acknowledge that, notwithstanding the cruelty and moral wrong of slavery, the ten million Negroes inhabiting this country . . . are in a stronger and more hopeful condition, materially, intellectually, morally, and religiously, than is true of an equal number of black people in any other portion of the globe" (24). Hurston made a similar concession in "How It Feels to Be Colored Me": "Slavery is the price I paid for civilization, and the choice was not with me. It is a bully adventure and worth all that I have paid through my ancestors for it" (153).

The rationalization and reconciliation Washington and Hurston made with a history of oppression and dehumanization operate as much as a cathartic as a manifested generosity of spirit. In order to work as arduously as they did, each had to believe that industry would be rewarded and each had to cast off the weight of an oppressive history that was potentially self-defeating. Their temperaments required them to create an emotional distance from the past that would allow them an emotional and intellectual space in their present. Both believed that too much contemplation of the past was just so much time taken from present endeavors, thus their ahistorical stance and their willingness to "settle for from now on."

Hurston repeated and revised key elements in Washington's narrative. She focused intently on Washington's ideology of individual merit. Washington proclaimed that his attention to individual worth and merit was "not to call attention to myself as an individual, but to the race to which I am proud to belong" (40). Whereas Washington's ideology was proclaimed to be an instrument of "racial uplift," a collective enterprise, Hurston found in his ideology a philosophical context that affirmed and validated her individual self and her individualistic outlook. Her attention to individual worth and merit *was* to call attention to herself—as an individual.

· · ·

The pride Hurston felt in the ingenuity and capability of the Eatonville folk that was seconded by the self-help philosophy of Booker T. Washington was further strengthened by her work in anthropology. As a student and a protégé of Franz Boas, Hurston learned to see even more clearly and appreciate more fully the cultural wealth of her community and the rich legacy bequeathed her. What she intuitively felt about the genius and humanity of African America was corroborated and validated through her anthropological research. Her studies and fieldwork armed her with the knowledge and skill to prove and show to white America and elitist Black America the native genius and authenticity of African America, traceable to an African, as opposed to a European, tradition. Appreciating her cultural heritage enabled Hurston to better appreciate herself. The essentially self-reflexive enterprise of interactive fieldwork afforded Hurston the uncanny opportunity to objectify the "other" and discover the "other" as "self." To the extent that she could validate and demonstrate the value of African American cultural traditions, she felt her own self-worth and self-esteem. Secure in the realization that her authentic self was part of an authentically *African* American culture, Hurston underwent a transformation from healthy self-confidence to bodaciousness.

Franz Boas was instrumental in this transformation. In *The Character of the Word*, Karla Holloway emphasizes how Boas's approach to cultural anthropology through sociolinguistics gave Hurston a meaningful context in which to examine and explore her linguistic community and herself. As Robert Hemenway suggests, the intent of much of Boas's research was to challenge racist assumptions and stereotypes and establish a scientific basis from which to advance his belief in the equal capabilities of all social groups (Hemenway 88). He endeavored to document the cultural sophistication of so-called primitive and marginalized groups and delineate the continuity of their cultural traditions in modern society. In relation to his general concern with the survival and continuity of ancient traditions in the Americas, a phenomenon he referred to as the "peculiar conditions of society," Boas demonstrated particular interest in African Americans: "The investigation of the ideas and beliefs of the American Negroes throws an interesting side-light on these conditions. Unfortunately this subject has received very slight attention, and it is hardly possible to state definitely what the conditions are in various parts of the continent. It is quite clear, however, that the Negroes, owing to their segregation, have retained much of what they brought from Africa" (*Race, Language, and Culture* 22).

In 1926, Hurston began fieldwork for Boas. Her task was to document African survivals among African Americans in the United States (Hemenway 88). Her documentation of these survivals was guided by Boas's sociolinguistic perspectives. In "Language," Boas theorized that "language is a reflection of the state of culture and follows in its development the demands of culture." Words, phrases, and linguistic usage such as metaphorical expressions and allusions, he stated, "are symbols of cultural attitudes" (142–43). Her linguistic investigations informed by those theories, Hurston was to find language to be a powerful cultural indicator. Her observations led her to conclude that the medium through which African Americans recreated and transformed themselves and their world was the spoken word, imbued with an African sensibility and expressive of an African worldview. In "Characteristics of Negro Expression," Hurston wrote that drama permeated the African American sensibility, which demanded action and beauty. That drama was central to the culture was apparent in the language: The "very words are action words. [The] interpretation of the English language is in terms of pictures. One act described in terms of another. Hence the rich metaphor and simile" (49).[5] Hurston reasoned that this urge to dramatize, to display thought and feeling, was birthed in the cradle of African communal life. "There is no privacy in an African village," she writes. "The community is given the benefit of a good fight as well as a good wedding. An audience is a necessary part of any drama" (60).

Hurston claimed the use of metaphor and simile ("Regular as pig tracks"), double descriptives ("Kill-dead"), and verbal nouns ("Sense me into it") as "the Negro's greatest contribution to the language" (51–52). These elements exemplify what Hurston called the "will to adorn," "the second most notable characteristic in Negro expression" (50).[6] She explained this will to adorn as a creative impulse infused in all manners of cultural expression, whether linguistic, domestic, artistic, or religious. Angularity and asymmetry, salient features of this aesthetic, were expressed in the deep angles in which pictures are hung, furniture is set, and dances are danced. "Everything . . . becomes angular," Hurston observed, recognizing again the African origins of this aesthetic: "In all African sculpture and doctrine of any sort we find the same thing. . . , the sculpture and carvings are full of this beauty and lack of symmetry" (54).

Hurston adduced a blues poem by Langston Hughes as evidence that the African American predilections for angularity and asymmetry were also "present in the literature, both prose and verse" (54–55). One stanza of the poem reads, "I ain't gonna mistreat ma gal any more, / I'm just gonna kill her next time she makes me sore." These characteristics were repeated in the folklore. As in blues songs and dances, a rhythm is created in the verse from the "abrupt and unexpected changes" consequent to an angular and asymmetrical style. Jack, for instance, is "the greatest culture hero of the South." He always does the unexpected and outsmarts mortals and immortals alike, including God and the Devil. Hurston tells us that Jack, like his blood-brother the rabbit and other culture heroes—the bear, the lion, the buzzard, the fox—is "the trickster-hero of West Africa [who] has been transplanted to America" (56–57).

The theories of cultural and linguistic relativism that Boas expounded influenced and confirmed Hurston's belief that in African American folklore she had discovered "the greatest cultural wealth of the continent." Notably, Hurston chose to examine African American folk culture through the prism of language, the one mode of cultural expression by which African Americans were judged deficient and condemned as culturally inferior. However, Hurston had absorbed Boas's ideas on cultural diffusion—which recognized those cultural forms and traits generated in one culture but dispersed over diverse culture areas—and cultural integration—which recognized the defining cultural configurations of one specific culture. She was therefore able to approach her study of the language and culture of the folk through comparative analyses that acknowledged the interdependence of cultures while allowing for an evaluation of folk expression on its own terms.[7] Hurston states that the African American idea of ornament perhaps "does not attempt to meet conventional standards, but it satisfies the soul of its creator" (50). Hurston thusly centers African Americans in their own African-centered traditions. Things European are described in contradistinction to those African and African American, not as universal standards of measure. The descriptive speech of African Americans is seen in contrast to the "stark, trimmed phrases" of European Americans. The suggestive motions of African American dancers are "achieved by the very means which a European strives to avoid." And the religious expression of African Americans, who are not "Christian[s] really," sets in relief the bleak prayers of whites. "We each have our standards of art, and thus we are all interested parties and so unfit to pass judgment upon the art concepts of others" (53–55).

Hurston's anthropological perspectives also guided her fieldwork in the Caribbean. Her research in Jamaica and Haiti underscored her ideas on cultural relativism as they confirmed her belief in the African roots of African diasporan cultures in the United States and the Caribbean. "Through her investigations of the primal black communities of the Americas, those whose links to the motherland were least culturally diffused by the slavers," Holloway points out, Hurston "was assured that the source of the culture she celebrated was truly African" (102). Holloway notes that among the people of Haiti, Hurston found the same "will to adorn." "The ornate trappings of Catholicism appealed to the African's 'urge to adorn,' and the networks of saints in this religion was a convenient vehicle in which to store the multitude of spirits that inhabited the African view of the world" (108). In "Voodoo and Voodoo Gods" in *Tell My Horse,* Hurston writes that Voodoo, the religion of the Haitian people, "is the old, old mysticism of the world in African terms" (113). She cites Dahomey, Congo, and Guinea as points of origin of Haitian deities (116). She relates that the stories about the deities, the songs and orations that celebrate them continue and are continually transformed as the "unlettered" create new local demigods (114).

By studying the creative powers of Haitians, Africans, and African Americans, Hurston gained profound insight into her own abilities. These insights were, Holloway proclaims, the source for "Hurston's view of language as creator" (102). Hurston's training and her own acute sensibility allowed her to discover in the various modes of linguistic expression, in the songs, stories, sermons, and speeches she heard all her life, the primacy of oral tradition as the foundation of African American cultural expression. As she (re)discovered her community through its linguistic expressions, she discovered and defined herself. Her introduction to *Mules and Men* indicates that Hurston's enthusiastic study and exploration of "the folk" was always, simultaneously, a journey of self-discovery and self-recovery:

> I was glad when somebody told me "You may go and collect Negro folk-lore."
>     In a way it would not be a new experience for me. When I pitched headforemost into the world I landed in the crib of negroism. From the earliest rocking of my cradle, I had known about the capers Brer Rabbit is apt to cut and what the Squinch Owl says from the house top. But it was fitting me like a tight chemise. I couldn't see it for wearing it. It was only when I was off in college, away from my native surroundings, that I could see myself like somebody else and stand off and look at my garment. Then I had to have the spy-glass of Anthropology to look through at that. (3)

In *Mules and Men* and in her writings collected in *Sanctified Church,* Hurston retrieved treasures of African American oral culture. These texts offer insight into that which the African American soul lives by and that which Hurston's soul lived by. The lore, replete with survival and resistance strategies, adaptation skills, and coping mechanisms, also conveys the lessons of hope that renew the spirit and sustain the soul.

From the cultural heroes of African American folktales, African Americans imbibed a tenacity of mind and spirit and the paradigms of behavior needed to negotiate a hostile environment. The patterns of behavior recognizable in Hurston's life and work—silence, shamming, tomming, Signifying, masking, and posturing—are all patterns of behavior exhibited in archetypal African American trickster figures like John, High John de Conquer, and Jack. In several tales collected in *Mules and Men,* John, the slick slave, invariably makes a fool of "Ole Massa." Whether through John's shrewdness or Massa's cupidity or stupidity, John prevails. In one tale, John throws Massa into the river to his death because Massa believes he can make money that way (45–49). In another, instead of arguing with Massa about whether or not he was "a nigger," John "consumed on wid his bag" and kept on steppin' to Canada—to freedom (97–98). Illustrated in this tale is the struggle of African Americans to exist in a society bent on their obliteration. It shows the iron will needed to resist domination and dehumanization. In this story, language is used as an instrument of domination. By persistently defining John as "a nigger," Ole Massa attempts to render John a linguistic cipher. Each time Ole Massa yells to John, " 'Member youse a nigger,' " John responds, " 'Yassuh.' " John is well aware of the intended message as well as the perlocutionary effect desired by its sender. What the sender is not aware of is that John's response is coded and the code is decipherable only by John, who more realistically understands the situational context. Ole Massa needs to hear that John acquiesces to an existence of nothingness. He wants to believe that John continues to be submissive and that, consequently, he, Ole Massa, remains dominant. John's speech act leaves in place, for Ole Massa, a false reality that allows John the figurative and literal distance to be spiritually as well as physically free.

The dynamics of John's communication with Ole Massa plays up the Du Boisean notion of double consciousness and the double-voiced discourse characteristic of the African American trickster figure. Perceived ideas and images of the powerful and the powerless are overturned. Truth and falsity are inverted. Such stories communicate to the teller and listener—who, unlike Ole Massa, can extract a meaning from the multiplicity of meanings or the ambiguity inherent in the language used—the significance of linguistic astuteness. Such stories show language as creator and strategy in the constant battle for existence, resistance, and self-definition. Posturing as the servile, self-debased slave and knowing what to say and when to say it are "school lessons" embedded in the tales. John oftentimes drops this mask of submission and servility. Knowing when, where, and with whom to drop the mask and express oneself authentically is as important as mastering language or, more aptly, an essential aspect of mastering language. Punishment or death could be the result of indiscrete language usage. This is the moral of "Dat Lie 'Bout Big Talk." In this story, one slave says to the other that he had given Ole Massa "uh good cussin' out," and Ole Massa "didn't do *nothin'*." Feeling bully, the second fellow decides he would do the same the next time Ole Massa made him mad. The following day, after Ole Massa reprimands him for some infraction, he gives Ole Massa "one good cussin'," after

which "Ole Massa had 'im took down and whipped nearly tuh death."
Confused, he asks the first fellow, " 'How come he never did nothin'
tuh yuh? Ah did it an' he come nigh uh killin' *me.* ' "

> "Man, you didn't go cuss 'im tuh his face, didja?"
> "Sho Ah did. Ain't dat whut you tole me you done?"
> "Naw, Ah didn't say Ah cussed 'im tuh his face. You sho is crazy. Ah
> thought you had mo' sense than dat. When Ah cussed Ole Massa he
> wuz settin' on de front porch an' Ah wuz down at de big gate." (83–84)

In her life and work, Hurston implemented lessons learned from
John, the dissembler, and from Jack, the "over-noble hero," whom the
devil compliments as being " 'Almos' as wise as me.' " In one tale, Jack
loses a card game to the Devil (51–58). Having bet all his money, Jack
bets his life and loses. The Devil promises Jack, " 'If you git to my
house befo' de sun sets and rise agin Ah won't kill yuh.' " The Devil
lives "across de deep blue sea" and knows the journey to be an impossible one, but it's one Jack makes. The Devil reneges on his promise
and, instead, imposes on Jack a number of equally impossible tasks.
Through Jack's ingenuity, will, and luck, and with the assistance of
Beatrice, the Devil's daughter, Jack accomplishes impossible tasks and
escapes from the Devil. In hot pursuit of Jack, the Devil is thrown
from his bull-drawn buckboard and is killed. Jack never looks back
and bemoans his having played cards with the Devil or that the Devil
continuously stacked the deck against him. Though he cries at the
thought of losing his life, he does not consume his energies in self-
pity. Nor does he deplore the disadvantage of a mortal pitted against
a supernatural and seemingly overwhelming force. Instead, he takes
advantage of every opportunity to change his circumstances, to relieve his oppression, and to free himself. The game is not fair, but Jack
wins.

The card game is a recurring leitmotif in Hurston's work, particularly as it symbolizes unfair play in American sociopolitical life. But
like Jack, Hurston prided herself on beating the odds. Winning against
a stacked deck indicated her superiority: "It seems to me that if I say a
whole system must be upset for me to win, I am saying that I cannot
sit in the game, and that safer rules must be made to give me a chance.
I repudiate that. If others are in there, deal me a hand and let me see
what I can make of it, even though I know some in there are dealing
from the bottom and cheating like hell in other ways. If I can win
anything in a game like that, I know I'll end up with the pot if the
sharks can be eliminated" (*Dust Tracks* 346). Courage in the face of
seemingly insurmountable obstacles was essential for self-preservation.

The ability to see one's advantages and negotiate a path through less than favorable circumstances was crucial to survival.

Laughter "in the face of things" was another lesson conveyed through these stories. Hurston writes in *Mules and Men,* "The brother in black puts a laugh in every vacant place in his mind. His laugh has a hundred meanings. It may mean amusement, anger, grief, bewilderment, chagrin, curiosity, simple pleasure or any other of the known or undefined emotions" (67–68). Of the many functions of laughter, Hurston saw its curative and purgative powers as its most important ones. One cultural hero Hurston particularly identified with is High John de Conquer; "he was a whisper, a will to hope, a wish to find something worthy of laughter and song" ("High John de Conquer" 69). Figured in Hurston's characterization of High John are aspects of Hurston's own character: "Playing his tricks of making a way out of no-way. Hitting a straight lick with a crooked stick. Winning the jack pot with no other stake but a laugh. Fighting a mighty battle without outside-showing force, and winning his war from within. Really winning in a permanent way, for he was winning with the soul of the black man whole and free" (70–71). High John represented for Hurston and the folk the subtle power of love and laughter. "It is there to help them overcome things they feel that they could not beat otherwise" (78).

Hurston's presentation and analysis of folktales highlight an ethos of pragmatism, emphasizing self-preservation and individualistic action. This foregrounding of individualism is evident as well in her analysis of other forms of folklore. Although the religious experience is a communal activity as is the telling of tales and "lies," Hurston's representations invariably emphasize the role played by the individual. This is evident in her description of the spirituals in "Spirituals and Neo-Spirituals": "The real Negro singer cares nothing about pitch. The first notes just burst out and the rest of the church join in—fired by the same inner urge. Every man trying to express himself through song. Every man for himself. Hence the harmony and disharmony, the shifting keys and broken time that make up the spiritual" (80–81).

The communal effort is a background of sorts for "the glorious individualistic flights that make up their own songs" (81). This same pattern describes the prayer. When the pastor calls on "the greatest prayer-artist present" to pray the communion prayer, "a lively something spreads over the church as he kneels, and the 'bearing up' hum precedes him" (83).

> There is in the body of the prayer an accelerando passage where the audience takes no part. It would be like applauding in the middle of a solo at the Metropolitan. It is here that the artist comes forth. He adorns

the prayer with every sparkle of earth, water and sky, and nobody wants to miss a syllable. He comes down from this height to a slower tempo and is borne up again. The last few sentences are unaccompanied, for here again one listens to the individual's closing peroration. Several may join in the final amen. The best figure that I can think of is that the prayer is an obligato over and above the harmony of the assembly. (84)

"Sermons, prayers, moans and testimonies have their definite forms," but individual expression is encouraged, and "any new and original elaboration is welcomed" (83).

Hurston's participant-observer method of collecting the folklore published in *Mules and Men* creates an excellent vantage point from which the reader can view the theatrical dynamics of storytelling in the African American folk community. Her descriptive analysis of the religious expression of the folk illustrates the characteristic "will to adorn" as it exemplifies the anthropological concept of cultural integration. Further, Hurston's interpretation of data collected bespeaks an identifying pattern of thought in her. Her emphasis on the respect of and value of individual performance, whether in tales, songs, or prayers, reflects her own individualist orientation. It appears that the perspective of cultural relativism through which Hurston identified the unique expression of African Americans correlates directly with the discovery of her own uniqueness, which she at once valued and embraced.

· · ·

Hurston's orientation toward individualism, achievement, and empowerment and her cosmological perceptions seem bolstered by the ideas and formulations of Benedict de Spinoza. Hurston cites history and philosophy as the disciplines through which she obtained a broader and more objective appreciation of concepts surrounding God, nature, and humanity. In *Dust Tracks on a Road,* she specifically referred to the works of Spinoza: "When I get old, and my joints and bones tell me about it, I can sit around and write for myself, if for nobody else, and read slowly and carefully the mysticism of the East, and re-read Spinoza with love and care" (285). Hurston wrote that she would *re*-read Spinoza, indicating, of course, that she had read him. She would re-read him "with love and care," I imagine, because his writings affirmed her feelings, thoughts, and actions, thus validating her "self" and her worldview. Hurston's ideology of individualism, as influenced by the individualistic fervor and frontier lore of Eatonville, the self-help doctrine of Booker T. Washington, the anthropological direction of Franz Boas and Ruth Benedict, and the lessons of self-preservation manifested in African American folklore can also be found in the philosophy of

Spinoza.[8] Spinoza wrote in *The Ethics* that "virtue is nothing else but action in accordance with the laws of one's own nature" (Part IV, Prop. XVIII, Note, p. 201). "Self-preservation is the first and only foundation of virtue," and the attainment of virtue is the acquisition of power (Part IV, Prop. XXII, Corollary, pp. 203–4). Virtue, which is power, is acquired through self-perfection, and self-perfection is having "knowledge of the union existing between the mind and the whole of nature" ("Improvement" 6).

Spinoza reasoned that God is the first cause and only substance of the universe. Existence, divinity, infinity, and eternity are God's attributes (*Ethics*, Part I, Props. X–XI, pp. 50–51). Since there is "but one substance in the universe," God or Nature, every form or modality issuing from it is necessarily endowed with the aforementioned attributes. Humankind, as a modality of God, must understand the nature of God in order to understand itself. This requires awareness that "all things which come to pass, come to pass according to the eternal order and fixed laws of nature" ("Improvement" 6). Hurston subscribed to an eternal order and believed in playing "the rules of the game as laid down" just as she considered herself an extension of the first cause. Like Spinoza, she believed in the "indivisibility of substance" and the ever-changing-same that characterized existence. Spinoza stated in Prop. XIII, *"Substance absolutely infinite is indivisible"* (*Ethics*, Part I, p. 54). Further, in Prop. XXI, *"All things which follow from the absolute nature of any attribute of God must always exist and be infinite, or, in other words, are eternal and infinite through the said attribute"* (Part I, p. 63).

Spinoza's natural law of continuance and change prefigured Hurston's deliberations in *Dust Tracks:* "I know that nothing is destructible; things merely change forms. When the consciousness we know as life ceases, I know that I shall still be part and parcel of the world. I was a part before the sun rolled into shape and burst forth in the glory of change. I was, when the earth was hurled out from its fiery rim. I shall return with the earth to Father Sun, and still exist in substance when the sun has lost its fire, and disintegrated in infinity to perhaps become a part of the whirling rubble in space" (279). To this constant and continuous change there is an "invisible harmony." James Olney describes it as "the unitary self." Spinoza describes it as reason. For Nietzsche, it is the ego or "will-to-power." And for Hurston, it is the "inner self," "internal drive," or "inside urge."[9]

Neither Spinoza nor Hurston believed in a teleology of nature, thus, both shunned institutionalized religion predicated on such a doctrine. Spinoza believed "nature had no particular goal in view, and that final causes are mere human figments":

All such opinions spring from the notion commonly entertained, that all things in nature act as men themselves act, namely, with an end in view. It is accepted as certain, that God himself directs all things to a definite goal (for it is said that God made all things for man, and man that he might worship him). . . . [This] general credence . . . has given rise to prejudices about good and bad, right and wrong, praise and blame, order and confusion, beauty and ugliness, and the like. . . . Hence also it follows, that everyone thought out for himself, according to his abilities, a different way of worshipping God, so that God might love him more than his fellows, and direct the whole course of nature for the satisfaction of his blind cupidity and insatiable avarice. Thus the prejudice developed into superstition, and took deep root in the human mind. (*Ethics,* Part I, Appendix, pp. 75–77)

This passage from Hurston reflects Spinoza's argument: "As for me, I do not pretend to read God's mind. If He has a plan of the universe worked out to the smallest detail, it would be folly for me to presume to get down on my knees and attempt to revise it. That, to me, seems the highest form of sacrilege. So I do not pray. . . . Why fear? The stuff of my being is matter, ever changing, ever moving, but never lost; so what need of denominations and creeds to deny myself the comfort of all my fellow men?" (*Dust Tracks* 278–79). Just as Hurston described as weak those who pray for divine favoritism, Spinoza wrote that those who take refuge in "the will of God," in actuality, take refuge in "the sanctuary of ignorance" (*Ethics,* Part I, Appendix, p. 78). Since nature had no particular end in view, humans, then, were responsible for themselves, which should compel them to seek self-knowledge and knowledge of natural law.

Given Spinoza's conclusions that substance is governed by the fixed laws of motion and cause and effect, human beings must also be governed accordingly. Therefore, the human body acts and is acted upon, its particular modality affected by various external forces or modifications: *"If the human body is affected in a manner which involves the nature of any external body, the human mind will regard the said external body as actually existing, or as present to itself, until the human body be affected in such a way, as to exclude the existence or the presence of the said external body"* (Part II, Prop. XVII, p. 98). Any body that is persistently acted upon by negative bodies and forces must necessarily make negative impressions upon the mind. This idea is crucial in understanding Hurston's egotistical character and her insistence on minimizing the effects of negative external forces. In a society in which she was made to know she was "a little colored girl," in which she felt like "a dark rock surged upon and overswept, in which "no black could ever forget his [or her] race," and in which no woman could forget her sex and gender, Hurston stubbornly decided, "I am not tragically colored. There is no great sorrow damned up in my soul, nor lurking behind my eyes" ("How It Feels to Be Colored Me" 153). The not too distant past of enslavement and Reconstruction and the racism, prejudice, and discrimination she encountered were all forces, ideologically or actually, present to Hurston. These were all potentially destructive forces that she, through a will to self-preservation, was determined to "exclude the existence" of or at least mitigate.

Hurston chose not to "fix blame for the dark days of slavery and Reconstruction," and she chose not to tell "lurid tales" about her experiences of racism, though she "had met it in the flesh." She apparently chose to focus rather on her achievements and possibilities since *"whatsoever increases or diminishes, helps or hinders the power of activity in our body, the idea thereof increases or diminishes, helps or hinders the power of thought in our mind"* (*Ethics,* Part III, Prop. XI, p. 138). Her successes impressed upon her that recognition of individual merit was, indeed, a universal law.

Further parallels in the philosophy of Hurston and Spinoza can be seen in what each viewed as a hindrance to the virtue of self-preservation and self-perfection: envy; pity; hate; unrestrained indulgence in "Riches, Fame, and the Pleasures of Sense"; and human weakness. Emotional excess and lack of reason were the chains of human bondage according to Spinoza. Freedom was self-determination: "That thing is called free, which exists solely by the necessity of its own nature, and of which the action is determined by itself alone. On the other hand, that thing is necessary, or rather constrained, which is determined by something external to itself to a fixed and definite method of existence or action" (Part I, Def. VII, p. 46).

• • •

Figured prominently in the intellectual standpoint that sustained Hurston's struggle for self-determination is the philosophy of Friedrich Nietzsche. Though Hurston never mentions or directly alludes to Nietzsche in her work, it is highly probable that she studied him as well as discussed him in her intellectual circles. The ideas of Nietzsche, like those of Freud and Marx, had wide currency during the first decades of the twentieth century. They proferred much food for thought for America's "lost generation," many of whom were associates of Harlem's Black intelligentsia. Nietzsche's undressing of rationalism and the Christian ideal had a great impact on the United States during a period when its intellectuals were faced, simultaneously, with their own struggle for identity as Americans and with the pronounced "decline of the West," which ushered in a skepticism of the very concepts of European civilization and culture. Nietzsche's ideas infused philosophical, psychological, sociological, anthropological, and literary thought in the United States.[10] Nietzsche's influence on Ruth Benedict's ideas and works is readily apparent. Benedict read and assimilated Nietzschean philosophy, particularly as it is set forth in *The Birth of Tragedy* and *Thus Spoke Zarathustra*.[11] She appropriated Nietzsche's ideas of the Apollinian and Dionysian personalities as anthropological concepts, which she used to describe and distinguish cultural configurations among Native American nations.[12]

Hurston states in her autobiography that as a student at Columbia University, she "began to treasure up the words of Dr. Reichard, Dr. Ruth Benedict, and Dr. Boas" (170). During Hurston's matriculation at Barnard from 1925 to 1927, Ruth Benedict, herself a former student of Boas, had become, in Margaret Mead's words, "Boas' Left Hand." She was "a kind of second self," says Mead, who, sharing Boas's "sense of responsibility to ethnology, its students, its problems, its methods," gave opening lectures of courses for him, discussed field problems with his students, and helped with the editing of manuscripts amidst a myriad of other auxiliary activities (346, 347). Hurston obviously respected Benedict's abilities and benefited from her editorial assistance. She solicited Benedict's help in editing *Mules and Men* (Hemenway 163). Correspondence between Hurston and Benedict about the publication of Hurston's work dates between 1932 and 1945, indicating their ongoing professional relationship.[13]

Benedict's influence on Hurston is rarely recognized, but seems telling in the light of Hurston's emphasis on individualism and her embrace of Nietzschean ideals. For both Boas and Benedict, the relationship between the individual and society was of primary importance. As Boas shifted his perspective from cultural diffusion to cultural integration, the problem of the individual in relation to society became a focus of attention.[14] Though this was a problem for anthropology in general, it was a particular problem for Benedict. Margaret Mead states in the preface that Benedict's *"Patterns of Culture* is concerned with a problem that was central to Ruth Benedict's own life— the relationship between each human being, with a specific hereditary endowment and particular life history, and the culture in which he or she lived" (ix). In this work, particularly chapters 7 and 8, Benedict discusses the rapport between the individual and society. She concludes that there is no fundamental antagonism between society and the individual: Individuals make their lives from the raw materials that culture provides. "If it is meagre, the individual suffers; if it is rich, the individual has the chance to rise to his opportunity" (251–52). Benedict stresses the mutual reinforcement between culture and the individual, but also addresses the problem of individuals who do not ascribe to the values and virtues of a society or whose response to the dominant cultural traits of a society is not congenial. Benedict as well problematizes the notions of values, virtue, and morality, seeing them as social constructions dictated by the ruling motivation or intent of a society, not as absolutes.[15] These ideas and concerns are also significant in Franz Boas's writings, but their conceptualization in Nietzschean terms is peculiar to Ruth Benedict. And it is in Nietzschean terms that they surface in Hurston.

Parallels between Hurston's intellectual stance and Nietzsche's are many. As did Hurston, Nietzsche condemned Christian morality as a system of belief predicated on guilt and fear, which undermined individual self-esteem and rendered its adherents passive, timorous, self-deluded seekers of power. His conclusions on the teleological nature of religious doctrines also show a similarity to Hurston's: "To view nature as if it were a proof of the goodness and providence of a God; to interpret history to the glory of a divine reason, as the perpetual witness to a moral world order and moral intentions; to interpret one's own experiences, as pious men long interpreted them, as if everything were preordained, everything a sign, everything sent for the salvation of the soul—that now belongs to the *past*" (*Genealogy,* Essay III, Sect. 27, pp. 160–61). Given Spinoza's influence on Nietzsche, these perspectives repeat, and Hurston's work necessarily reflected the discourses of both philosophers. Distinctly Nietzschean features of thought paralleled in Hurston's writings include the inversion of Christian values, individualism and the will-to-power, condemnation of "the herd instinct," aversion to slave morality, and the Dionysian *amor fati.*

Nietzsche questioned the ascetic and altruistic values that emanate from Christian morality: self-denial, selflessness, submission, suffering, sympathy, pity. He saw these values, imposed on humankind as *the* truth and *the* morality by which all should live, as contradictory to human instincts, the foundation of decadence, and symptomatic of weakness. According to Nietzsche, Christianity was a religion of "Thou shalt not" that suppressed the "I will" of the human ego, the *sine qua non* of the healthy, creative individual. Nietzsche's deconstruction of (Christian) morality, thus of value and truth, culminated in the proclamation "God is dead" (*Gay Science,* Book III, Sect. 125, p. 181).

Though Hurston believed in and identified with a first cause, she denounced the idea of a supreme being who was omnipotent and extrinsic to humanity. She prefaced references to such a god with the conditional "if." For Hurston, God, as conceived by Christianity, was not central to human life, and power was not vested in God but in human will—an idea central to Nietzschean thought. Nietzsche and Hurston both mocked Christianity and saw the values of Christian morality as instruments of manipulation and control for those too weak to openly assert their individual will. Both believed that the altruism of Christian morality masked what was at bottom a cravenly will-to-power. Hurston's *Seraph on the Suwanee* dramatically conveys these notions. Arvay Henson, the would-be missionary, is at the foot of the mulberry tree where, as a youngster, she contemplated heaven and the angels. It is there that Jim Meserve rapes her and ends her spurious evangelical aspirations. As Christ is purported to have died for the sins of humankind upon the cross, Arvay, having been raped, pays for her own "secret sin," of coveting her sister's husband, under the mulberry tree. Jim's talk of love and marriage afterward is the salvation for which she had desperately hoped. " 'Missionary work is for old maids and preachers,' " Jim tells her. " 'Youse a married woman now' " (56). " 'No more missionarying around for you. You done caught your heathen, baby. . . . He been hanging around the mourner's bench for quite some time, but you done brought him through religion, and saved him from a burning shell. You are a wonderful woman, Arvay' " (57). Arvay recalls her faith only when she feels powerless and finds matters out of her control. "In her fear and desperation, Arvay fled back to her old time religion. . . . She began again to take great stock in miracles. Arvay crept into the Bible and pulled down the lid" (98–99). Hurston had previously concluded that "organized creeds [were] collections of words around a wish" (*Dust Tracks* 278–79). And that wish was for power.

Hurston believed in the autonomous individual unencumbered by social institutions. Nietzsche recognized this desire of the individual to be "free from an overpowering domination by society (whether that of the state or of the church)" as a "form of the 'will to power' " (*Will to Power,* Book III, Sect. 784, p. 411). Hurston struggled against the domineering forces of both church and state. She felt the Christian doctrine she imbibed as a child to be repressive and debilitating and the social doctrines of race, gender, and class to be stultifying and dehumanizing. She refused to be dictated to by either and declared her freedom from the tyranny of both.

Hurston also viewed the mindset of the African American masses as an impediment to her self-determination. Her perception of the

masses and her ideas apropos of society and the individual are comparable to those of Friedrich Nietzsche. She despised what Nietzsche
described as "the herd instinct," a phenomenon resulting from the
deprivation of individual will and self-esteem imposed by church or
state. The "instinct to freedom," however, compelled the oppressed to
ban together to gain or regain some form of power. The modus
operandi was to impugn the strong. "All the sick and sickly instinctively
strive after a herd organization as a means of shaking off their dull
displeasure and feeling of weakness," wrote Nietzsche. "Wherever there
are herds, it is the instinct of weakness that has willed the herd. . . . For
one should not overlook this fact: the strong are as naturally inclined
to *separate* as the weak are to *congregate*" (*Genealogy,* Essay III, Sect. 18,
pp. 135–36).

Hurston decried the crowd, and she repudiated weakness in any
form. Using virtually the same metaphors and expression as Nietzsche
did in the above passages, Hurston voiced her reasons for not joining
protest organizations, particularly the Communist party, whose doctrine she described as "up-to-date slavery":[16] "Many people have pointed
out to me that I am a Negro, and that I am poor. Why then have I not
joined a party of protest? I will tell you why. I see many good points
in, let us say, the Communist Party. . . . But I am so put together that I
do not have much of a herd instinct. Or if I must be connected with
the flock, let *me* be the shepherd my ownself. That is just the way I am
made" (*Dust Tracks* 344–45). But knowing how the masses try their
leaders, or "bellwethers" in Nietzschean terminology, Hurston refused
to take responsibility for thirteen million people and solemnly declared that not only didn't she follow well, but she also didn't lead
well either, a declaration that further detached her from the masses.

Hurston perceived in the masses a character flaw that figures in
Nietzsche's concept of "slave morality." Nietzsche viewed "slave morality," the antithesis of the "master morality," as "essentially a morality
of utility" wherein the oppressed, downtrodden, and enslaved create a
system of values designed "to make easier the existence of the suffering":
"Here it is that pity, the kind and helping hand, the warm heart,
patience, industriousness, humility, friendliness come into honour"
(*Beyond Good and Evil,* Sect. 260, p. 178). Nietzsche maintained, however, that such qualities and values were disingenuous, that they were
the creation of individuals filled with *ressentiment*[17] and bent on revenge
and will-to-power. Since he recognized empowerment as a biological
imperative, Nietzsche did not condemn the struggle for empowerment
but rather the deception and artifice and its design to destroy the
"well-constituted":

They monopolize virtue, these weak, hopelessly sick people, there is no doubt of it: "we alone are good and just," they say, "we alone are *homines bonae voluntatis.*" They walk among us as embodied reproaches as warnings to us—as if health, well-constitutedness, strength, pride, and the sense of power were in themselves necessarily vicious things for which one must pay some day, and pay bitterly.... There is among them an abundance of the vengeful disguised as judges, who constantly bear the word "justice" in their mouths like poisonous spittle.... The will of the weak to represent *some* form of superiority, their instinct for devious paths to tyranny over the healthy—where can it not be discovered, this will to power of the weakest! (*Genealogy,* Essay III, Sect. 14, p. 123)

Hurston as well rejected the virtues of slave morality. To exact a debt for past wrongs, to place blame for present trials would undermine *her* strength, autonomy, and power. To view external forces, whether historical or immediate, as *the* explanation for one's situation and condition, "to direct one's view outward instead of back to oneself" would be, for Nietzsche and Hurston, "the essence of *ressentiment:* in order to exist, slave morality always first needs a hostile external world; it needs, physiologically speaking, external stimuli in order to act at all—its action is fundamentally reaction" (*Genealogy,* Essay I, Sect. 10, pp. 36–37). Paradoxically, Hurston's determination to be proactive, to act according to her own "inner urge" as opposed to external dictates, sometimes drove her to reactionary acts. For instance, in her refusal to bow to the dictates of the Black intelligentsia and what she perceived as their pathological ideology of "the Negro," Hurston castigated and ridiculed members of the intelligentsia and denied knowing anything about "the Negro," though she studied, validated, and affirmed African American folk culture. And though she fully realized the impact of historical events on the contemporary lives of African Americans, she at times dismissed it. Nonetheless, Hurston refused to bow to a slave morality, and she would not be a part of the pitiable members of the "sobbing school of Negrohood" who felt life handed them "a low-down dirty deal and whose feelings are all hurt about it" ("How It Feels to Be Colored Me" 153). She would not wear "that veiled glance ... which is a sigh! 'If only I were someone else'" (*Genealogy,* Essay III, Sect. 14, p. 122). She was determined not to become remorseful about the slice of life served her and to take no refuge in bitterness.

Hurston, too, perceived pity as nihilistic. As a rule, she did not indulge in self-pity. She rejoiced when she saw others striving to overcome it. In her article "Negroes without Self-Pity" she applauded speeches made at "a Negro meeting in Florida." The speeches advocated active (as opposed to reactive) involvement in local and national affairs and called for closer ties with "uneducated Negroes" in an effort to " 'do what we can for peace and good-will between the races.' " At this "new and strange kind of Negro meeting," she reported, there were no "tears of self-pity." "Tradition was tossed overboard without a sigh. . . . Nobody mentioned slavery, Reconstruction, nor any such matter." She found this a unique and refreshing point of view, seeing that there had been "at least a hundred years of indoctrination of the Negro" as "an object of pity" (603). Hurston's willingness to jettison her historical past in order to redefine herself as a proud and autonomous individual coincides with Nietzsche's idea that "only that which has no history is definable" (*Genealogy,* Essay II, Sect. 13, p. 80). To "forget" about slavery and Reconstruction and "settle for from now on" was part of the process of resistance and "self-overcoming" for Hurston. If she could define herself, develop her own system of valuation and morality, she would not only succeed in resisting dominating societal forces but she would also succeed in her will to self-empowerment, and, moreover, would aspire to a higher level of human existence: the Dionysian.

Nietzsche's nihilistic vision allowed only for the dualism of the slave-master morality. This vision determined that the will-to-power must necessarily culminate in the will-to-overpower and "if one cannot do that (if one is still too weak to do so), one desires *'justice,'* i.e., *equal power*" (*Will to Power,* Book III, Sect. 784, p. 412). Nothing in Hurston's writings testify to a will-to-overpower. And neither did she maintain a desire for justice or equality. She saw justice as unattainable, on the one hand, and believed herself superior to most, on the other. Thus, equality was not a goal. Hurston desired, if anything, opportunity. But aware of cardpalmers who dealt from the bottom of the deck, she relied on herself, her talent, her will. With her desire to forget the past and her continuous denial of bitterness and prejudice—even to the extent of being reactionary—Hurston showed herself beyond the *ressentiment* of Christian or slave morality, beyond, even, the master morality and more in the process of developing the spirit and virtues characteristic of Dionysus, Nietzsche's "ideal human type."

Unwilling to leave humanity in the vortex of the abyss, Nietzsche took a "new path to a 'Yes' ":

Such an experimental philosophy as I live anticipates experimentally even the possibilities of the most fundamental nihilism; but this does not mean that it must halt at a negation, a No, a will to negation. It wants rather to cross over to the opposite of this—to a Dionysian affirmation of the world as it is, without subtraction, exception, or selection —it wants the eternal circulation:—the same things, the same logic and illogic of entanglements. The highest state a philosopher can attain: to stand in a Dionysian relationship to existence—my formula for this is *amor fati.* (*Will to Power,* Book IV, Sect. 1041, p. 536)

Hurston adopted this formula for herself. "Even in the helter-skelter skirmish" that was her life, Hurston never opined that circumstances and conditions were not more propitious. She was steadfast in the face of the "logic and illogic" of human relationships: "I do not brood, however, over the wide gaps between ideals and practices. The world is too full of inconsistencies for that" (*Dust Tracks* 344). Though she professed a belief in divine order and in the power of reason, Hurston did not swallow Spinozan philosophical optimism whole. Nature, though divine, could be at once beautiful and terrible and was indifferent to humankind. Hurston leaned more toward Nietzsche's theory of a biological imperative than toward Spinoza's spiritual imperative, in which the individual will to perfection is necessarily a modality of divine substance. In Nietzsche's theory, all life is subject to chance and force or will, which is neither good nor evil, and is compelled not only to preserve itself but also to increase and accumulate force. "The stronger will directs the weaker. There is absolutely no other kind of causality than that of will upon will." Nietzsche argues further, "Spinoza's law of 'self-preservation' ought really to put a stop to change: but this law is false, the opposite is true. It can be shown most clearly that every living thing does everything it can not to preserve itself but to become *more*" (*Will to Power,* Book III, Sect. 658, p. 347; Sect. 688, p. 367).

Hurston's standpoint in relation to others and to existence itself amounts to a "Dionysian affirmation":

> Like all mortals, I have been shaped by the chisel in the hand of Chance, bulged out here by a sense of victory, shrunken there by the press of failure and the knowledge of unworthiness. But it has been given to me to strive with life, and to conquer the fear of death. I have been correlated to the world so that I know the indifference of the sun to human emotions. I know that destruction and construction are but two faces of Dame Nature, and that it is nothing to her if I choose to make personal tragedy out of her unbreakable laws.[18] (*Dust Tracks* 347–48)

In Nietzsche's philosophy, the Dionysian personality, symbolized by the child, represents the third and ideal level of human development.[19]

> The child is innocence and forgetfulness, a new beginning, a sport, a self-propelling wheel, a first motion, a sacred Yes.

> Yes, a sacred Yes is needed, my brothers, for the sport of creation: the
> spirit now wills *its own* will, the spirit sundered from the world now
> wins *its own* world. (*Zarathustra* 55)

The Dionysian, like Spinoza's "first cause," is autogenetic, a creator, a mythmaker. In *The Birth of Tragedy,* Nietzsche concludes that humanity is predicated upon culture and culture is founded on myth. In spite of his pronouncement that God was dead, he saw that creativity, "the religious impulse," remains and humankind continues to stand in need of myths and mythmakers: "Without myth every culture loses the healthy natural power of its creativity: only a horizon defined by myths completes and unifies a whole cultural movement. Myth alone saves all the powers of the imagination and of the Apollinian dream from their aimless wanderings" (135). In her writing and her life, Hurston exhibited the Dionysian spirit. From *Jonah's Gourd Vine* to *Seraph on the Suwanee,* there is a continuum of the development of the Dionysian personality, represented in its most excellent form in *Moses.* Just as Hurston created the mythologies that fashioned her ideal male characters, she also created a mythology from which she fashions herself. Out of that mythology, she created a world and invested it with values that made it possible for her to live and create. The outside world she encountered was a Naysayer. She relied upon her singular, creative will to voice "a sacred Yes"—to herself and her culture. For, as did Nietzsche, Hurston perceived that a people's humanity was expressed in its culture. She also discerned that unless African Americans valued and embraced their culture, they would lose the source of their creative power and their means of empowerment. Thus she endeavored to preserve Black cultural texts—myths, stories, legends, songs—and profess the value of the African American folk ethos.

# 3

## African American Folklore
## as Style, Theme, and Strategy

Negro folklore is not a thing of the past. It is still in the making.
Its great variety shows the adaptability of the black man.

—"Characteristics of Negro Expression"

Lessons Hurston learned in the environs of family, community,
and the academy empowered her to say "Yes" to herself and her culture.
The disciplines of history and philosophy and her anthropological studies and fieldwork gave her penetrating insights into the value and power
of culture and cultural production. Her initial fear that Black folklore
was disappearing compelled her to collect, document, and preserve as
much of it as she could. It also propelled her in her determination to
bring about a recognition of Black folk culture and a respect for Black
cultural texts. Hurston early on equated creativity with vitality, survival,
and individual and collective empowerment. She perceived that it was
within their own African-centered traditions that Black people were
to find the alternative images, self-definitions, and strategies for continued resistance to European cultural hegemony. In his literary and
political campaign against cultural repression in Kenya, Ngugi wa
Thiong'o emphasizes the role of cultural production in combatting
cultural domination—a key element in the subjugation of a people.
Ngugi clearly and strongly states in his writings that in a people's culture are "the seeds of revolt." A contemporary artist-activist, Ngugi
articulates the same profound point of view at which Hurston, and to
some extent her contemporaries, had arrived decades earlier. The idea
of cultural affirmation and production as both a means of survival and
a means of resistance to negative images that inspired in Black people
a sense of dependency, inferiority, and indebtedness were the seeds
that flowered into the Harlem Renaissance, the African American cul-

tural movement of the 1920s. As a major participant in this movement, Zora Neale Hurston figures significantly in African America's legacy of struggle against European cultural hegemony. Nietzsche had concluded that "only a horizon defined by myths completes and unifies a whole cultural movement." Hurston's efforts at preserving Black cultural texts and her advocation of the value of Black folklore can be seen as her attempt to provide the Harlem cultural movement with the mythology and folklore essential in defining its horizon.

The dawn of the twentieth century brought what Alain Locke described as the renaissance of a "New Negro." In "The New Negro," contained in his signature work *The New Negro* anthology, Locke pronounced the Black community's "spiritual coming of age," a rite of passage marked by a change in self-perception and a temperament of defiance. No longer willing to be viewed and treated as a "social bogey or a social burden," the New Negro, according to Locke, had rejected the status of a beneficiary and a ward and had become a conscious collaborator in and contributor to American and world civilization (3–4, 15). This renascent self-respect and self-reliance was quickened by the growing social sophistication of thousands of rural Blacks who migrated North, transformed by participation in an industrial economy and the experience of urban life and by the martial spirit of Black heroes returning from war. The zeitgeist that characterized the period, more than anything else, Locke maintained, "is to be explained primarily in terms of a new vision of opportunity, of social and economic freedom, of a spirit to seize, even in the face of an extortionate and heavy toll, a chance for the improvement of conditions" (6).

Though Locke's general figuration of the New Negro included the masses of Blacks infused with this renewed spirit, it described, more specifically, a group of intellectuals whom Locked considered the vanguard of "the race." They were members of the "enlightened minority" who would, through cultural and political channels, combat the discrepancies between the American social creed and the American social practice that rendered Blacks second-class citizens (13–14). This enclave would consciously act as "the advance-guard of the African peoples in their contact with Twentieth Century civilization" and would assume the "mission of rehabilitating the race in world esteem from that loss of prestige for which the fate and conditions of slavery have so largely been responsible" (14).

Locke claimed for the New Negro a liberating modernity. The New Negro would prove that claim warrantable by engaging in artistic production that reflected the cultural legacy of the African American folk and of Africa and that expressed a Black nationalist and pan-Africanist vision. In the *Harlem Renaissance,* Nathan Huggins points out that Harlem intellectuals, consistent with the prevailing attitude of their day, equated human worth with cultural worth and measured civilization in terms of artistic production. "Thus they promoted poetry, prose, painting, and music as if their lives depended on it" (9). A stated goal of the Renaissance and an undertaking central to its development and progress, states Larry Neal, was "the reevaluation of African-American history and folk culture" and the development of "a truly original literature" that, in form and sensibility, would document "the cultural ramifications of the African presence in America" (162). The New Negro's task, then, was to discover and define "distinctive racial cultural contributions" "to what had been thought a white civilization" (Huggins 59, 78–79). The Harlem intellectuals argued that Blacks provided American culture with "its only genuine folk tradition. From the Afro-Americans had come a rich and complex folklore and music which was the most distinctively American contribution to world culture" (Huggins 72). However, "with the possible exception of Sterling Brown," Zora Neale Hurston was "the only important writer of the Harlem literary movement to undertake a systematic study of African-American folklore" (Neal 162). As Alain Locke conveyed in "The Legacy of the Ancestral Arts," "the American Negro brought over as an emotional inheritance a deep-seated aesthetic endowment. And with a versatility of a very high order, this off-shoot of the African spirit blended itself in with entirely different culture elements and blossomed in strange new forms" (254). In literature, these "strange new forms" evidenced the vibrant and dynamic expressive modes of African American folk culture. However, Locke pointed out, "with the rude transplanting of slavery, that uprooted the technical elements of [Blacks'] . . . former culture," much of this aesthetic legacy was lost. But, "the legacy is there at least, with prospects of a rich yield" (254, 256). With "a closer knowledge and proper appreciation of the African arts," as Locke suggested, and with proper study of African American folk culture, the repository of residual African culture, the New Negro could produce an original literature.

Creating an African American literature, reverberant with the spirituality of "African arts" and infused with the ethos of African American experience, would be one phase of the overall movement toward self-definition and self-determination. This ethos or sensibility, as Neal describes it, "pertains to the cluster of psychological, emotional and psychic states that have their basis in mythology and folklore" (162). But few writers gave themselves to the task of exploring African American mythology and folklore and projecting it in their literature. "In terms of the consummate uses of the folk sensibility," Neal comments, "the Harlem movement leaves much to be desired. There was really no encounter and subsequent grappling with the visceral elements of the black experience but rather a tendency on the part of many of the movement's writers to pander to the voguish concerns of the white social circles in which they found themselves" (162). Langston Hughes and Sterling Brown were notable exceptions. Both were "aware of the literary possibilities of black folk culture," but Zora Neale Hurston's "interest in folklore gave her a slight edge on some of her contemporaries " (162).

Hurston's interest in folklore, and her keen intellect, helped her understand the immense value of African American folk culture and the full import of her work in uncovering it. She realized in folk life the origin of an authentically *African* American ethos. Her excitement over her find can be described as typical Hurstonian exuberance. She proclaimed African American folklore to be "the greatest cultural wealth of the continent." She worked to display its riches and garner recognition of its worth. In "The Race Cannot Become Great until It Recognizes Its Talent," she predicted that "this sunburst of Negro art . . . [was] going to do so much for America and the world in general." Hurston's exuberance was not unfounded. She perceptively fathomed the depths of her discovery. Hurston saw folk culture—her own culture—as the source of renewed Black national dignity and pride. She saw in it the foundations of African American self-affirmation and independence and the foundation of resistance to European cultural domination. And she saw herself as the herald and harbinger of this new consciousness.

From "How It Feels to Be Colored Me," in 1928, to "The Race Cannot Become Great until It Recognizes Its Talent," in 1934, one sees Hurston's evolution and maturation from a naive, callow individual to a self-assured, brilliant woman-scholar; from one who could write that slavery was the price she paid for civilization to one who redefined civilization and could conceive of an emancipatory spiritual renaissance for African American peoples. In "The Race Cannot Become Great," Hurston compares the plight of African Americans with that of the erstwhile oppressed English:

Along in 1066 William, the Conqueror, fell upon England and conquered it. He was a thorough man. He enslaved the British and put iron collars around their necks—the beginning of a serfdom that lasted many centuries. It wasn't that the iron collars were so enduring, but the effect of the mastery that the collars represented. The English mind got the habit of looking up to the Norman conquerors. People slaved and starved in English, but dined and took all pleasures strickly in French. It required nearly five hundred years for an Englishman to regain enough self-respect to consider beauty of any kind except in Norman form and Norman terms. (3)

Subdued in body and spirit, worshipping at the shrines of other cultures, it was difficult to believe in self. "And, of course, nobody dreamed of writing a line of literature in the dialect of the licked and lowly Englishman" (3). Chaucer and Shakespeare, writers who recognized the value of their cultural inheritance, found little acceptance and appreciation in their day.

As Hurston compares the situation of African Americans with that of the English, she implicitly compares herself and her task with Chaucer and Shakespeare and their tasks. She writes that "the memory of the iron collar" about the necks of the English prevented their preference for the genius of the natural and universal Shakespeare, who shed "so great a radiance upon English history and folklore." "Yes, folklore," she states emphatically: "Sprites, fairies, Puck, Caliban, Twelfth Night celebrations, Mid-Summers' Night observances are just as much a part of English folk-lore and folk ways as hoodoo practices and Brer Rabbit are a part of Aframerican folk ways." Assessing the situation of African Americans, she continues: "Now we stand in America where the English stood in the days of Chaucer, physically but not spiritually free, unable as yet to turn our eyes from the distorted looking glass that goes with the iron collar" (3). Hurston observes that the slavish aping of whites and a problematic myopia induced African Americans to effectively silence the voices of their geniuses. Decrying what she perceived as intellectual lynching, she asserts, "The world's most powerful force is intellect. The only reality is thought" (3). And until African Americans nourish the love of self and pride in culture necessary to recognize and esteem its talent, she warns, "we are right back where we were when they filed our iron collar off" (3).

Hurston ofttimes felt herself the victim of the "rope and faggot." She was consistently censured or condemned for embodying in her work the very goals propounded by the Renaissance leadership. She created literary works that had their basis in African American folklore and mythology. Whereas today her work is considered by most critics to be authentic, profound, and seminal, a positive celebration of African American life, earlier critics considered her work to be nonserious, "folksy," outdated caricature. In his review of *Their Eyes Were Watching God,* for example, Richard Wright could find no "basic idea or theme that lends itself to significant interpretation." Instead of moving "in the direction of serious fiction . . . Miss Hurston *voluntarily* continues in her novel the tradition which was *forced* upon the Negro in the theatre, that is, the minstrel technique that makes the 'white folks' laugh" ("Between Laughter and Tears" 22–23). Alain Locke concurred: "As always thus far with this talented writer, setting and surprising flashes of contemporary folk lore are the main point." Her "cradle-gift" for poetic phrases, dialect, and folk humor "keep her flashing on the surface of her community and her characters and from diving down deep either to the inner psychology of characterization or to sharp analysis of the social background." Though he described the book as "folklore fiction at its best," he questioned if the author would ever "come to grips with motive fiction and social document fiction" (" 'Jingo, Counter-Jingo' " 10). Locke praised *Mules and Men* as a real contribution to local color and characterization but decried its "lack of social perspective and philosophy" (" 'Deep River' " 8–9). He judged the work to be oversimplified and too "Arcadian." "The depression has broken this peasant Arcady," Locke declared, "and while it is humanly interesting and refreshing enough, it is a critical duty to point out that it is so extinct that our only possible approach to it is the idyllic and retrospective" (9). Sterling Brown leveled similar charges. Hurston's characters were "socially unconscious" and made to appear "easy-going and carefree." He concluded that *Mules and Men* "should be more bitter; it would be nearer the total truth" (Hemenway 219).

Evaluation of the style and content of Hurston's work was a complicated matter due to the popularity of the degrading and dehumanizing Black minstrelsy tradition popular in the latter nineteenth century. Influenced by this tradition, racist white writers tended to present in their literary works negative, stereotypic, and distorted representations of African American folk life. Images of the childish, backward, indolent, sensual, carefree, and happy "darky" prevailed.[1] And since the New Negro was to assert to white America *his* self-reliance and dignity, his manhood, he condemned all that would in any manner raise the specter of the "Old Negro," a construct of racist white America's imagination, which he sought to lay to rest.[2] Any discourse that, in the evaluation of the established literary powers, contradicted the ideology of the New Negro was excoriated, silenced, or otherwise dismissed. Ironically, many Black intellectuals constructed an elite profile of the New Negro that contradicted ideals fundamental to the Renaissance: namely the affirmation of "the folk" and expression of the Black folk ethos. Alain Locke, prim Howard University professor, "press agent" for the Renaissance, and a means through which artists found financial support, was a devotee of culture. "By 'culture' he meant all that was not common, vulgar, or racially distasteful" (Lewis 149). His New Negro must also be an aesthete. For W. E. B. Du Bois, a director of the National Association for the Advancement of Colored People and editor of its journal, the *Crisis,* the New Negro was, like himself, an intellectual elite. Du Bois's *Souls of Black Folk* sketched the New Negro's portrait. Drawn from the ranks of the "Talented Tenth," a cadre of "bolder and brighter minds," the New Negro must be, in actual life and in any artistic representation, an individual of "culture and character." In his "Criteria of Negro Art," set forth in the *Crisis,* Du Bois outlined the aesthetics to which the New Negro was bound. Art was to be viewed as "part of the great fight we are carrying on" (290). Beauty and Truth, he unabashedly proclaimed, were "unseparated and inseparable" (292). "Thus all Art is propaganda and ever must be, despite the wailing of the purists. . . . Whatever art I have for writing has been used always for propaganda for gaining the right of black folk to love and enjoy. I do not care a damn for any art that is not used for propaganda" (296). James Weldon Johnson's New Negro was a class-conscious cosmopolitan. Convinced that "people in the same sphere" would accept one another as social equals, race was less of an issue for James Weldon Johnson than class (*Autobiography* 95). In his article "A Negro Looks at Race Prejudice," Johnson wrote that he had "long ago reached the conclusion that the so-called race problem is not based upon innate racial antipathies." At the root of the problem was "a feeling of class, of caste." From his perspective, Johnson contended, "it is plain that the crisis in this whole national malady will not be passed until culture on the part of Negroes begins to have the effect of lessening prejudice" (54, 55). The sociologist Charles S. Johnson, director of research for the National Urban League and editor of its journal, *Opportunity,* also had an agenda for the New Negro. Anticipating the full assimilation of African Americans into American society (Lewis 46), Johnson focused on interracial as opposed to intraracial relations. Art and letters would be the medium. In an *Opportunity* editorial, Johnson challenged New Negro writers to replace their "out-worn representations," "triumphantly articulate" an "inter-racial good-will," and "make themselves better understood" (258). And based on his socialist vision, Richard Wright's "Blueprint for Negro Writers" had drawn the New Negro as a nationalist infused with "the highest possible pitch of social consciousness." Accordingly, the Black writer must depict the lives of the proletariat and the middle class in context of a nationalism that "knows its ultimate aims are unrealizable

within the framework of capitalist America" (42–43). Wright emphasized that the consciousness and creative expression of the Black writer
should be grounded in "the folklore of the Negro people" (39).[3]

Zora Neale Hurston, like several other "younger Negro artists"
offended the sensibilities of the established literati with their persistent depiction of the vicissitudes of "the Negro farthest down" and
their refusal to depict "the Negro" in the context of the predominant
ideologies of the literati. These younger artists complained of the pressure to produce "party-line art." And they mocked the elitism, snobbery,
and hypocrisy of the Harlem literati, which Hurston and Wallace
Thurman dubbed "the Niggerati" (Lewis 193). Thurman, Hurston,
Hughes, and other Harlem figures rebelled against the genteel morality and social and political propaganda of "the older Negroes" in *Fire!!*
a "Negro quarterly of the arts." The idea was, Hughes explained, "that
it would burn up a lot of the old, dead conventional Negro-white
ideas of the past, *épater le bourgeois* into a realization of the existence of
the younger Negro writers and artists, and provide us with an outlet
for publication not available in the limited pages of the small Negro
magazines then existing, the *Crisis, Opportunity,* and the *Messenger*—the
first two being house organs of inter-racial organizations and the latter
being God knows what" (*Big Sea* 235–36).

In a *New Republic* article, "Negro Artists and the Negro," Thurman
articulated the aesthetics of the magazine: *Fire!!* "was not interested in sociological problems or propaganda. It was purely artistic
in intent and conception. Its contributors went to the proletariat
rather than to the bourgeoisie for characters and material. They
were interested in people who still retained some individual race
qualities and who were not totally white American in every respect
save color of skin" (37). Thurman conceded that African Americans
had been misinterpreted and caricatured by insincere artists, but
did not agree that all who had "the ear of the public" should "ex-
pend [their] spiritual energy feeding the public honeyed manna on
a silver spoon," exhibiting always "specimens from the college rather than from the kindergarten, specimens from the parlor rather
than from the pantry." The editors of *Fire!!* would not sprout "sociological jeremiads" or build "rosy castles around Negro society."
Rather, they represented in their magazine "those elements within
the race which are still too potent for easy assimilation" (38). Within the pages of *Fire!!* were stories of a "potential prostitute," a confused
bisexual, and a boxer-turned-jazz-band-member; poems featuring an
elevator boy and a "street woman"; and drawings of "Negro types"
with kinky hair. Hurston's contributions were a short story, "Sweat,"

about a washer-woman in a desperate and abusive marriage, and a play, *Color Struck,* about a woman who has a preference for "light-skinned" individuals. In the play Hurston dramatized the woman's tragic loss of love and loved ones because of her jealousy and emotional insecurity about her own dark skin. This sad drama unfolded in the midst of a gala folk event, a cakewalk contest. The editors also included an essay titled "Intelligentsia," which discounted the intelligentsia's contributions to society "as negligible as gin at a Methodist picnic" (45). Its author, Arthur Huff Fauset, declared it was "high time that a halt is called on these snobbish sychophantish highbrow hero-worshippers who . . . deign to damn with their sneers and jibes any activity, institution, or mortal it strikes their fancy to treat in such a manner" (46).

This "folk-centered masterpiece," as David L. Lewis called it, was the only issue published. The artists, nevertheless, used a variety of other means to voice their frustration with and their resistance to the established literati. In "The Negro Artist and the Racial Mountain," notably, Langston Hughes spoke eloquently and forcefully for the collective. The mountain standing in the way of "true Negro art," Hughes wrote, was "this urge within the race toward whiteness, the desire to pour racial individuality into the mold of American standardization, and to be as little Negro and as much American as possible" (692). This tendency among the Harlem leaders became more and more apparent. But Hughes believed it the younger artists' duty to help change, through the force of their art, "that old whispering 'I want to be white,' hidden in the aspirations of his people, to 'Why should I want to be white? I am a Negro—and beautiful!' " (694). He and his comrades were duty bound to defy establishment ideology and practice. "We younger Negro artists who create now intend to express our individual dark-skinned selves without fear or shame. If white people are pleased we are glad. If they are not, it doesn't matter. We know we are beautiful. And ugly too. The tom-tom cries and the tom-tom laughs. If colored people are pleased we are glad. If they are not, their displeasure doesn't matter either. We build our temples for tomorrow, strong as we know how, and we stand on top of the mountain, free within ourselves" (694).

In a number of journal essays and articles, Hurston also manifested the discontent, struggle, and defiance that characterized the "younger Negro artists." In "The Hue and Cry about Howard University" (1925), for example, Hurston expressed outrage that Howard students decried the spirituals as "low and degrading, being the product of slaves and slavery." Hurston recalled her own halcyon days at Howard when she took part in the "sings," having felt no shame nor fear of being dragged "back into slavery" (315). As she exhorted in "The Race Cannot Become Great" (1934), African Americans had to, in spite of the pained experience of enslavement and in spite of the truly degrading minstrel tradition, learn to appreciate their folk arts in order to embrace their essential selves. Changing that "old whispering" from a lamentation to an exalted praisesong was an ongoing battle. Hurston questioned the superior attitude of northern Blacks in "The 'Pet' Negro System" (1943), challenged the stereotypical images of Blacks held by Whites in "What White Publishers Won't Print" (1950), and denounced communist doctrine in "Why the Negro Won't Buy Communism" (1951). The style and content of Hurston's creative expression and ethnographic writings were as much protest against establishment dictates, both white and Black, as they were affirmations of Black folk culture. Hurston steadfastly refused to write sociological treatises just as she insisted on interesting herself "in the problems of *individuals,* white ones and black ones" as opposed to "the *race* problem" (Ford 96).

•  •  •

The pronounced coming of age of Black Americans, Locke said, would be successful to the extent that they could construct an "Americanism on race values" ("The New Negro" 12). Locke, along with the civil rights leadership of the NAACP and the Urban League, envisioned a mass movement of Blacks toward "the larger and more democratic chance" in American life. Racial solidarity among Blacks and mutual respect between "the rank and file" and the leaders were key elements in realizing this vision. However, the movement would be balked as much by the elitism of the Renaissance leadership as by entrenched racist policies and practices. The intelligentsia celebrated the democratic spirit of the masses and applauded their renewed determination for self-direction. Yet, they believed only themselves capable of speaking for "the Negro." And though they advocated "race consciousness" and racial solidarity, they strived for assimilation and agreed that the fate of Blacks must needs rest in the hands of an integrated intellectual elite. Locke firmly believed that "the only safeguard for mass relations in the future must be provided in the carefully maintained contacts of the enlightened minorities of both race groups" ("The New Negro" 9). He observed from the outset that "the Negro [was] rapidly in process of class differentiation, if it ever was warrantable to regard and treat the Negro *en masse* it is becoming with every day less possible, more unjust and more ridiculous" (5–6). In "The New Frontage on Ameri-

can Life," Charles Johnson also remarked, "There are as great differences, with reference to culture, education, sophistication, among Negroes as between the races" (297). Nevertheless the "more advanced
and representative classes" would presume to speak for the collective.
"Race-pride" was the watchword, but the self-styled "thinking Negro"
spoke disparagingly of the populace. In *Souls of Black Folk,* Du Bois
likewise romanticized a "loving, reverent comradeship between the
black lowly and the black men emancipated by training and culture"
(138). "Progress in human affairs," he reasoned, "is more often a pull
than a push, a surging forward of the exceptional man, and the lifting
of his duller brethren slowly and painfully to his vantage-ground" (127).
He, too, summoned "broad-minded, upright men, both white and
black" to spearhead the struggle (135).

Pundits of the Renaissance were convinced that current racial en-
mity was in large part due to "the fact that the more intelligent and
representative elements of the two race groups have at so many points
got quite out of vital touch with one another" (Locke, "The New
Negro" 9). They bemoaned lost contact with their "Nordic" compeers,
while overlooking the distance between themselves and the Black
populace. As Nathan Huggins recounts, "Sometimes the Negro masses
were a source of real embarrassment" for the established leadership,
"something to be explained, to be understood" (49–50). All they perceived as vulgar and reprehensible in the masses seemed embodied in
the personage and politics of Marcus Mosiah Garvey. A Jamaican-
born "Bookerite," a charismatic pan-Africanist, Marcus Garvey preached
Black was beautiful. His vision of Africa for Africans inspired him to
launch a Back-to-Africa movement that captured the imagination,
allegiance, and economic support of Blacks the world over. Garvey
founded the Universal Negro Improvement Association in 1914 and
established its weekly newspaper, *Negro World,* in 1918. Tony Martin
asserts in *Literary Garveyism* that Garvey's organization had "over eleven
hundred branches in over forty countries" (2). And the *Negro World,*
published in French, English, and Spanish, was distributed worldwide
with a peak circulation of 200,000 (5, 156). Marcus Garvey headed
one of the largest mass movements of Blacks in United States history.
William Pickens, a field secretary for the NAACP, suggested that
"Garvey built up the largest single organization of Negroes in the world,
with a membership of several million in the United States, the West
Indies, Central America, and Africa (Cronon 206).[4] The civil rights
leadership and its Talented Tenth following openly despised and opposed Garvey. They vehemently and categorically disagreed with his
separatist politics and were repulsed by his predilection for the flam-

boyant and the spectacular. Deprecatingly described as "a Jamaican Negro of unmixed stock," squat, and black, Garvey was not considered representative of "the race." He was not Harvard-, Yale-, or Fisk-educated, and rather than laud and aspire to bourgeois ideals, he thoroughly castigated "upper-class Negroes." Impelled by their total rejection of his populist leadership, the establishment vilified Garvey as a disgrace, a traitor, and a nuisance, and conspired with the federal government to depose him.[5] A representative number of the opposition expedited an open letter "to the United States attorney-general asking that Washington use 'full influence completely to disband and extirpate this vicious movement' " (Lewis 44).

This internecine conflict effectively undermined whatever possibilities there were for the realization of Black social, economic, and political freedom through Black nationalism. The promise of a mass movement was eclipsed by the Harlem intelligentsia's class movement. Though the intelligentsia spoke in terms of Black solidarity, Black nationalism, and pan-Africanism, uppermost in their aspirations was to become "full-fledged Americans, with all the rights of other American citizens." Assimilation into mainstream upper-class American culture was their goal, whereas repatriation of Blacks to Africa was Garvey's goal. Interestingly, Garvey's political campaign also had a literary component. Like the intelligentsia, Garvey saw the production of art and letters as strategic in the struggle of "racial uplift." Tony Martin argues that Garvey "had an important direct impact on the purely literary aspects of the Renaissance" (5–6). Though defamed as an ignorant, uncouth, boorish philistine, Garvey was a journalist and poet as well as a philosopher and statesman. His organization, the UNIA, reflected the intellectual interests of its founder. The UNIA spawned literary clubs in its branches across the globe. "They arranged concerts and poetical readings, staged plays and held debates" (31). With an eye toward stimulating artistic production amongst the masses of Blacks, the *Negro World* sponsored literary contests as early as 1921, predating those of the *Crisis* and *Opportunity* magazines in 1925 (39).

Like those of the genteel school of literature, Garvey was a propagandist. He could be as Victorian and dogmatic as his adversaries. In a front-page article in *Negro World* titled "Marcus Garvey, Foremost Negro Leader, Condemns Harmful Trend of Books of a New Group of Race Writers," Garvey railed against Claude McKay and his *Home to Harlem* as well as other writers, including James Weldon Johnson, Eric Walrond, W. E. B. Du Bois, and Walter White, whose works he charged "earned wholesale condemnation of Negroes." He branded them "literary prostitutes" whose writings exhibited those unseemly aspects of Black life that white publishers would circulate amongst "the white peoples of the world, to further hold us up to ridicule and contempt and universal prejudice." As were his contemporaries, Garvey was engaged in an image war. The general summoned support for "writers who will fight the Negro's cause": "We must encourage our own black authors who have character, who are loyal to their race, who feel proud to be black, and in every way let them feel that we appreciate their efforts to advance our race through healthy and decent literature." The Black intelligentsia made the same appeal, but only to the Talented Tenth. Garvey appealed to the folk. In the *Negro World*, Martin writes, "the emphasis was clearly on fostering a mass interest in literature and the arts" (26). "It is here, in the pages of the *Negro World*," he pointed out, "that anyone must look who would discover the real artistic voice of the rank and file New Negro" (45). The Garvey paper regularly featured the "Poetry for the People" section, which provided a forum for the "would-be writers" of the Black masses.

Contradictions inherent in the idea of a Black nationalistic, mass movement headed by an interracial social elite did not give the intelligentsia cause to question their convictions and praxis. They thoroughly believed in the superiority of their position and perspective and in the possibility of overcoming systemic inequities based on race through a demonstration of intellectual and social parity with whites. Thus they "aspired to *high* culture as opposed to that of the common man, which they hoped to mine for novels, poems, plays, and symphonies" (Huggins 5). The Harlem Renaissance leaders looked to the folk for inspiration and artistic material, but they deracinated and "refined" these materials, purifying them of their "barbarisms," presenting them in a manner that would reflect the "cultured" sensibilities of the Black intelligentsia, that is, in a manner they considered acceptable and palatable to whites, while safeguarding their elitist image of the New Negro. By contrast, authentic folk life is what Hurston sought to preserve and celebrate. Though Hurston did not ascribe to Garvey's separatist politics, she believed, as did he, in the dignity of the masses. Neither dumb nor dull, the folk could articulate their own experiences. She did not feel compelled to speak for them or to explain them. Hurston's cultural relativist bent made it highly unlikely that she would embrace the elitist claims of the establishment or evaluate Black folk life in the context of a Black bourgeois morality. One of the folk herself and self-proclaimed native bard of her people, Hurston had her own esteem bound up with her struggle to achieve recognition of and respect for an authentically African American folk ethos. Folklore was not "a thing of the past," "extinct," as Locke eulogized it. It was alive and well and "still in the making." Pointing this out, Hurston felt, was her critical duty.

The New Negro's presentation of Black spirituals is one example of how authentic African American folk culture was deracinated for white audiences. The expression was restrained and harmony was regular and consistent. The songs were often sung in "standard" English and solo. The singer or singers usually remained motionless. Depth of feeling, rhythm, and spontaneity of expression and movement were spurned. Hurston notes that, prior to her concerted efforts to present authentic Black spirituals to the world, others shied away from doing so, preferring to present what she describes as "neo-spirituals":

> There never has been a presentation of genuine Negro spirituals to any audience anywhere. What is sung by the concert artists and glee clubs are the works of Negro composers or adaptors *based* on the spirituals. Under this head come the works of Harry T. Burleigh, Rosamond Johnson, Lawrence Brown, Nathaniel Dett, Hall Johnson and Work. All good works and beautiful, but *not* the spirituals. These neo-spirituals are the outgrowth of the glee clubs. Fisk University boasts perhaps the oldest and certainly the most famous of these. They have spread their interpretation over America and Europe. Hampton and Tuskegee have not been unheard. But with all the glee clubs and soloists, there has not been one genuine spiritual presented. ("Spirituals and Neo-Spirituals" 80)

Hurston's intimate knowledge of the folk and her anthropological spyglass allowed her to discern between the spurious and the genuine:

> To begin with, Negro spirituals are not solo or quartette material. The jagged harmony is what makes it, and it ceases to be what it was when this is absent. . . . The harmony of the true spiritual is not regular. The dissonances are important and not to be ironed out by the trained musician. The various parts break in at any old time. Falsetto often takes the place of regular voices for short periods. Keys change. More-over, each singing of the piece is a new creation. The congregation is bound by no rules. . . .
>
> *Negro songs to be heard truly must be sung by a group, and a group bent on expression of feelings and not on sound effects.* (80)

David L. Lewis points out that the refined performances of Black spirituals by singers such as Roland Hayes and directors such as Hall Johnson held great appeal for the Black elite. These artists, bringing to the stage an art form drawn from the African American tradition but translated into European-American forms, were admired and acclaimed by white audiences and critics. Thus, the Black elite felt at once pride in their heritage and acceptance into mainstream American society. Paradoxically, the artistry the audiences admired and acclaimed was not authentically African American. Lewis writes, "Now that Roland Hayes had taken spirituals into the concert hall, cultured Afro-Americans were suddenly as pleased as southern planters to hear them again. In 1925, Harlem violinist Hall Johnson organized his choir to 'preserve the integrity of the Negro spiritual.' Like Hayes, Johnson's idea of 'integrity' was so refined that his white radio listeners generally believed the Hall Johnson Choir was white" (163).

Removed from their folk origins, the songs became more European-American than African American. Like the English, these African Americans maintained a preference for the culture of the "the conquerors"; they maintained a "colonized mind." Hurston worked to counter this phenomena:

> I had collected a mass of work-songs, blues and spirituals in the course of my years of research. After offering them to two Negro composers and having them refused on the ground that white audiences would not listen to anything but highly arranged spirituals, I decided to see if that was true. . . .
>
> So on money I had borrowed, I put on a show [*The Great Day*] at the John Golden Theater on January 10, 1932, and tried out my theory. The performance was well received by both the audience and the critics. (*Dust Tracks* 207–8)

Hurston tested her theory on a New York audience and was excited and inspired by the results. The play dramatized events of a day in a railroad camp. It featured work songs, children's games, sermons, spirituals, storytelling, and blues. Arthur Ruhl, in the *New York Herald Tribune,* proclaimed *The Great Day* a complete success:

> The difference between these various "turns" and the thing usually seen in Negro plays and musical comedies was that this was the real thing; unadulterated, and not fixed and fussed up for purposes of commerce. The evening was altogether successful, and carried off with a verve, a lack of self-consciousness, an obviously spontaneous enjoyment, as eloquent as it was refreshing. . . . If there is such a thing as natural and unpremeditated art, here it seemed exemplified, by every one concerned.
>
> The experimental entertainment was so warmly received that doubtless it will be offered later to the general public. (11)

Hurston was triumphant: "The world wanted to hear the glorious voice of my people" (Hemenway 181). *The Great Day*'s success fueled Hurston's ambition to establish a *real* Black theater. It also corroborated her earlier conclusion that a sense of drama and a "will to adorn" were the genius of the African American people. In her productions, she allowed performers to express themselves in accordance with authentic African American folk tradition. The "individualistic flights," the "harmony and disharmony, the shifting keys and broken time," and the physical movement expressive of deep feeling were encouraged: "I know that music without motion is not natural with my people, I did not have the singers stand in a stiff group and reach for the high note. I told them to just imagine that they were in Macedonia and go ahead." "LET THE PEOPLE SING," she says, "was and is my motto" (*Dust Tracks* 207–8).

At the urging of the president and faculty members at Rollins College, in Winter Park, Hurston produced three folk concerts (*Dust Tracks* 209). On January 20, 1933, Hurston, with Bob Wunsch of Rollins, produced *From Sun to Sun,* a work in the same vein as *The Great Day.* The play was performed before a segregated, white-only audience at the community theater, the Museum. Hurston's play was the first production of the experimental theater, and it was met with high acclaim. In "The Listening Place" column of the *Winter Park Herald, From Sun to Sun* was described as "perhaps the most dramatic entertainment . . . given in Winter Park." "It gripped the audience with a sense of native rhythm and harmony which is hard to fully comprehend unless seen and felt and this column advises all who can to go and "listen." . . . We feel that Winter park is the birthplace for this native folk-lore that, once known, will sweep the country" (5). The directors inaugurated the experimental theater with Hurston's work "because they want[ed] to make themselves and others more familiar with the richness of the material at their own doorstep" (5). Like Hurston, they perceived African American folk culture to be a treasure-trove: "What the negro has brought America is too vital to be allowed to vanish from the earth. His barbaric color adds pattern to the Nordic restraint about him. America needs this because its civilization, like Minerva, sprung full grown from the head of Europe, and so there is not the wealth of native folk-lore as in Europe, Asia, Africa and other continents where civilization had to grow through long ages" (5). The enthusiastic response led to a second performance, which was held at Recreation Hall, the major theater on Rollins's campus (O'Sullivan and Lane 134). Hurston was a phenomenal success and was in demand. In March of the same year, the cast gave a command performance before one of the school's visitors, the dancer Ruth St. Denis. On January 5, 1934, at the request of Hamilton Holt, Rollins's president, Hurston produced another play, *All De Live Long Day* (136). Hurston's successes contradicted Hall Johnson's assumptions. There was no expedience for "white-washing" Black tradition. One could produce art based on Black folk materials while maintaining the cultural integrity of the Black folk experience.[6]

In her zeal to establish the authenticity of an *African* American folk ethos, Hurston emphasized in her work the "African presence" in African American culture, one of the main mandates of the Harlem Renaissance literati. In "Characteristics of Negro Expression," she traced Black people's inclination toward dramatic oral expression to African oral tradition and communal life. The tendency toward angular and asymmetrical expression she traced to an African aesthetic evidenced in African sculpture, carving, and shield paintings. In "Conversions and Vision," "Shouting," and "The Sanctified Church," essays collected in *Sanctified Church,* she asserted that Black spirituality, religious practices, and dance were continuations of African religious expressions and African " 'Possession' by the gods." The rhythm of Black song and dance recalled the African drum, which, for Hurston, symbolized the "deep-seated aesthetic endowment" Blacks brought over from Africa. She expressed it this way in *Jonah's Gourd Vine:* "It was said, 'He will serve us better if we bring him from Africa naked and thing-less.' So the buckra reasoned. They tore away his clothes that Cuffy might bring nothing away, but Cuffy seized his drum and hid it in his skin under the skull bones. The shin-bones he bore openly, for he thought, 'Who shall rob me of shin-bones when they see no drum?' So he laughed with cunning and said, 'I, who am borne away to become an orphan, carry my parents with me. For Rhythm is she not my mother and Drama is her man?' So he groaned aloud in the ships and hid his drum and laughed" (29–30).

Hurston battled with the Black intelligentsia in her attempt to promote and present an authentic picture of African American folk life. All her literary works evidence her efforts. Hurston's study of English history and literature allowed her to see the empowering possibilities of embracing self and culture. In her heritage, she could see hope, a means of survival, strategies for becoming and overcoming, and a way of being in the world that could mitigate conflict and create harmony. She could see in it the strength and creativity essential to an uprooted and oppressed people. In spite of continual condemnation of her efforts, Hurston struggled to give voice to the folk, and in effect, to give voice to herself. She chose to infuse her writings with authentic African American folk expression, thus creating a "truly original literature" that served not only to reflect African American culture but also to suggest a sociopolitical direction for (African) America. Hurston argued, sometimes implicitly, sometimes explicitly, that individual and group liberation and empowerment could be achieved and an effective battle against "negative-isms" could be waged if the cultural values of the African American folk would be recognized and drawn upon.

· · ·

Perhaps the most significant concept that Hurston drew from African American folk culture is that of the primacy of the spoken word to order reality as it empowers the self. Geneva Smitherman argues in *Talkin and Testifyin* that "the oral tradition has served as a fundamental vehicle for gittin ovuh" in Black America. "That tradition," she writes, "preserves the Afro-American heritage and reflects the collective spirit of the race. Through song, story, folk sayings, and rich verbal interplay among everyday people, lessons and precepts about life and survival are handed down from generation to generation.... Indeed the core strength of this tradition lies in its capacity to accommodate new situations and changing realities" (73). Hurston recognized the adaptive qualities of the oral tradition and its role in her own survival and that of African Americans, collectively. She realized the transforming power of words and that through words, the individual could assume autonomy, naming and unnaming self and world. Hurston's use of sermonic language, which will be the focus of chapter 4, established the primacy of the word as it is expressed in the Black vernacular tradition and as it is privileged in African American oral culture. As the *Dust Tracks* narrative illustrates, the word is a vital, pro-creative force. It is with words that the narrator creates a world wherein she can survive and become a self-determined individual. Hurston's sense of the word reflects her discovery in African American folk life of the remnants of an African cosmology that supports her view of the self as an autonomous, self-sufficient force that can exert control over the external world. This African cosmology, preserved through the sermon form, is embodied in the African concept of *Nommo*. Janheinz Jahn, in *Muntu,* writes that "Nommo, the life force, is the fluid as such, a unity of spiritual-physical fluidity" (124). It is the driving, transforming force "that gives life and efficacy to all things" (101). Based on his interpretation of Bantu ideology, Jahn outlines an African philosophy, delineating four basic categories representative of the four universal forces: *Muntu,* any force endowed with *ubwenge* (intelligence) "which has control over *Nommo*"; *Kintu* (plural of *Bintu* ), things; *Hantu,* place and time; and *Kuntu,* modality. Human beings—living and dead, also orishas, loas, and Bon Dieu—are among the first category (100, 102). They are created by and create through

*Nommo.* "Through nommo, the word, man establishes his mastery over things"—*Bintu* (132). *Hantu* and *Kuntu,* likewise, are forces subject to the command of *Muntu* (136). "Thus all the activities of men, and all the movement in nature, rest on the productive power of the word" (126).

This principal of *Nommo* is pervasive in Hurston's work. In the autobiography, it is the source of the narrator's identity. With words she creates a strong, positive, confident self-image. Jahn writes that "image is created through Nommo—that is, it is *designated.*" The designation of an image or its naming is what gives it its meaning. Without designation, an image is *kintu,* meaningless (157). He points out that even *muntu* is but *kintu* until it is designated: *"a complete human being, a personality, a muntu"* is created "only when the father or the 'sorcerer' gives him a *name* and *pronounces* it" (125). The designation of a human being corresponds with the designation of images. When images are confused, they are again meaningless things. It is necessary then, that "the onlooker . . . renew the designation" (157). Likewise, and importantly, when human identity is confused or when controlling images oppress and delimit an individual, it is necessary that the individual is named again. As *muntu,* possessor of *Nommo,* Hurston assumes power by naming herself. Like the God of the Old Testament who declares "I am that I am," Hurston, as *muntu,* speaks herself into being. She becomes autonomous and powerful. She becomes a complete, self-determined human being. Of all the self-designations set forth in her autobiography, these are most notable: "I am of the word-changing kind" (27); and, "I am one with the infinite" (274). It may be significant that the former statement is made early in the narrative and the latter toward the end. The sequence suggests that as Hurston *changes* words throughout her narrative, as she names, unnames, transforms, and creates through words, she simultaneously shapes her self and her world. As she conjures image after image, she recognizes her word force, which compels her to recognize and acknowledge her intrinsic and inseparable union with *"NTU,"* "the cosmic universal force," which is an integral part of all that is (Jahn 101).[7]

Hurston's recognition and understanding of "word force" is evident in her decision to integrate oral tradition into the style and content of her work. As style and theme are one, the oral quality that characterizes Hurston's work sets forth an ideology, reflective of an African cosmology, which says that the self is powerful and the word is law.

• • •

Hurston's sense of the power of the word is evident, also, in her use of the African American verbal ritual of *signifying* as a rhetorical strategy to protect her world and to caution those who would shatter her images to maintain a certain distance. Scholars such as Donald C. Simmons and Philip Mayer indicate that *signifying,* specifically the "dozens" variety, may be of African origin. In *Mother Wit from the Laughing Barrel,* Alan Dundes discusses Mayer's fieldwork among the Gusii, a Bantu people. In "The Joking of 'Pals' in Gusii Age-Sets" Mayer describes a "game or play which involves insult exchange," wherein the "addressee is not supposed to get angry but he is rather expected to return in kind." Mayer observes that "a frequent kind of verbal insult consists of the 'use of expressions normally considered indecent, obscene or unutterable'" (296). This play of language among the Bantu parallels the act of *signifying* in African American folk culture and Hurston's use of it in her work. Claudia Mitchell-Kernan describes *signifying* in African American culture as a tactic used in the verbal dueling game, "which is engaged in as an end in itself." She explains that *signifying* can also refer to the art of verbal play in a general sense (311). In *Deep Down in the Jungle* Roger Abrahams describes *signifying* in this instance as a verbal art that "can mean any number of things; in the case of the toast about the signifying monkey, it certainly refers to the trickster's ability to talk with great innuendo, to carp, cajole, needle, and lie. It can mean in other instances the propensity to talk around a subject, never quite coming to the point" (51–52).[8] It also includes the tactics of "broadcasting," or what Hurston also describes as "loud-talking," among other tactical variations such as sounding and specifying. When used in the general sense Mitchell-Kernan explains that *signifying* "refers to a way of encoding messages or meanings which involves, in most cases, an element of indirection. This kind of *signifying* might be best viewed as an alternative message form, selected for its artistic merit, and may occur embedded in a variety of discourse" (311). A fundamental criterion of *signifying* is its indirect mode of presentation. According to Mitchell-Kernan,

> *signifying* involves the recognition and attribution of some implicit content or function, which is potentially obscured by the surface content or function. The obscurity may lie in the relative difficulty it poses for interpreting (1) the meaning or message the speaker is adjudged as intending to convey; (2) the addressee—the person or persons to whom the message is directed; (3) the goal orientation or intent of the speaker. A precondition for the application of the term *signifying* to some speech

act is the assumption that the meaning decoded was consciously and purposely formulated at the encoding stage. In reference to function the same condition must hold.[9] (314)

Hurston uses the act of *signifying* as a stylistic technique and as a rhetorical device in her work. She also treats Signifying as a major thematic element of African American folklore. Whether as style, theme, or strategy, characteristics of Signifying permeate Hurston's oeuvre. In *Mules and Men,* Hurston cleverly foregrounds the game of *signifying.* Her characters-informants at once *signify* upon one another and analyze their activity. Abrahams's and Mitchell-Kernan's definitions are somehow explicitly or implicitly illustrated. As Hurston and her company sat around the lake, fished, and told "lies," Big Sweet found an opening through which she would speak her mind on more personal issues:

> "And speakin' 'bout hams," cut in Big Sweet meaningly, "if Joe Willard don't stay out of dat bunk he was in last night, Ah'm gointer sprinkle some salt down his back and sugar-cure *his* hams."
> Joe snatched his pole out of the water with a jerk and glared at Big Sweet, who stood sidewise looking at him most pointedly.
> "Aw, woman, quit tryin' to signify."
> "Ah kin signify all Ah please, Mr. Nappy-chin, so long as Ah know what Ah'm talkin' about." . . .
> "Lawd, ain't she specifyin'!" sniggered Wiley. . . .
> "Lawd," Willard said bitterly. "My people, my people," as de monkey said. "You fool wid Aunt Hagar's chillun and they'll sho distriminate you and put yo' name in de streets."
> Jim Allen commented: "Well, you know what they say—a man can cackerlate his life till he git mixed up wid a woman or git straddle of a cow."
> Big Sweet turned viciously upon the old man. "Who you callin' a cow, fool? Ah know you ain't namin' *my* mama's daughter no cow."
> "Now all y'all heard what Ah said. Ah ain't called nobody no cow," Jim defended himself. "Dat's just an old time by-word 'bout no man kin tell what's gointer happen when he gits mixed up wid a woman or set straddle of a cow."
> "I done heard my gran'paw say dem very words many and many a time," chimed in Larkins. "There's a whole heap of them kinda by-words. Like for instance:
> " 'Ole coon for cunnin', young coon for runnin',' and 'Ah can't dance, but Ah know good moves.' They all got a hidden meanin', jus' like de Bible. Everybody can't understand what they mean. Most people is thin-brained. They's born wid they feet under de moon. Some folks is born wid they feet on de sun and they kin seek out de inside meanin' of words." (133–35)

Big Sweet demands clarification of message and addressee. As Jim Allen defends his intentions, Larkins comes to Jim's rescue with an explanation of Jim's statement while Larkins, undetected, Signifies upon Big Sweet. Larkins covertly refers to Big Sweet as one of those "thin-brained" people since she could not decipher Jim's "by-word."

In "Story in Harlem Slang," there is a plethora of Signifying activity as Hurston's characters sound, *signify,* boast, exaggerate, check each other, and play the dozens. Jelly, hoping to "confidence Sweet Back out of a thousand on a plate," regrettably tells him the truth of his desperate situation: " 'Oh, just like the bear—I ain't nowhere. Like de bear's brother, I ain't no further. Like de bear's daughter—ain't got a quarter' " (84). Sweet Back reads Jelly's response as an opportunity to bring him down a peg or two: " 'Cold in hand, hunh? . . . A red hot pimp like you say you is, ain't got no business in the barrel. Last night when I left you, you was beating up your gums and broadcasting about how hot you was. Just as hot as July jam, you told me. What you doing cold in hand?' " (84). The two argue and bluff each other. Jelly attempts to save face with, " 'How can I be broke when I got de best woman in Harlem? If I ask her for a dime, she'll give me a ten dollar bill; ask her for a drink of likker, and she'll buy me a whiskey still. If I'm lying, I'm flying!' " (84). Sweet Back checks Jelly's "boogerbooing":

> "Buy you a whiskey still! Dat broad couldn't make the down payment on a pair of sox."
> "Sweet Back, you fixing to talk out of place." Jelly stiffened.
> "If you trying to jump salty, Jelly, that's your mammy."
> "Don't play in de family, Sweet Back. I don't play de dozens. I done told you." (85)

Signifying as "the propensity to talk around a subject, never quite coming to the point" is best illustrated in Hurston's short story "Cock Robin on Beale Street." Having spent his pay without the help or advice of his wife, Uncle July attempts to fend off any argument about it by a pretense of anger that launches a story about Cock Robin: " 'Hit's a sin before de living jestice!' July exploded. 'Dese white folks ought to talk whut dey know, and testify to whut dey see. . . . Going 'round letting on dat Cock Robin was a bird!' " (69–70).

Uncle July's multivalent story Signifies on several themes of the Renaissance period—racial purity, racial superiority, intraracial conflict, classism, human nature. Embedded in the story's many layers as well is, perhaps, the explanation of just what became of Uncle July's pay. Uncle July narrates the what, why, and where of the killing of Cock

Robin, the confusion over who'll bury him, and the decision to leave his burial to the white folks since "dey always loves to take charge" anyway. The would-be mourners agree to form "one big amalgamated, contaminated parade" and head down to "Sister Speckled-Hen's place and enjoy de consequences" of "a big fish fry and barbecue" (73). Aunt Dooby, however, is not amused and not taken in by Uncle July's circumlocutionary Signifying: " 'Humph!' Aunt Dooby snorted. 'Old coon for cunning; young coon for running. Now tell me whut you done wid your wages. I know you been up to something. Tell me! You and your Mucty-Ducty Beetle-Bugs!' " (74).

Hurston recognized *signifying* as a defensive as well as an offensive rhetorical strategy. Henry Louis Gates, Jr., points out in "The Blackness of Blackness: A Critique of the Sign and the Signifying Monkey" that she is "the first author of the tradition to represent signifying itself as a vehicle of liberation for an oppressed woman, and as a rhetorical strategy in the narration of fiction" (290). "*Their Eyes* represents the black trope of signifying both as thematic matter and as a rhetorical strategy of the novel itself. Janie, the protagonist, gains her voice, as it were, in her husband's store not only by engaging with the assembled men in the ritual of signifying (which her husband had expressly forbidden her to do) but also by openly *signifying upon* her husband's impotency" (290). Jody, anxious to keep Janie in "her place" and too willing to put her down, hurled this chastising invective at her: " 'Don't stand dere rollin' yo' pop eyes at me wid yo' rump hangin' nearly to yo' knees!' " (*Their Eyes* 121). Janie defends herself from Jody's stinging insult with payment in kind: " 'Talkin' 'bout *me* lookin' old! When you pull down yo' britches, you look lak de change uh life' " (123).

The art of Signifying functions as style and rhetorical strategy in Hurston's autobiography as well. The text's meaning defies definitive interpretation; identifying the intended audience is problematic; and the author's intentions are obscured. On the surface level, the author purposely creates a confusing narrative to cloak her intentions and avoid self-disclosure. On the deep structure level, her intention is to attain power. The confused content functions to bring about the intent. These aspects of Signifying are utilized as rhetorical strategies in *Dust Tracks,* especially in chapters that deal with the author's political and private life and particularly when political and private life seem most adversely influenced or affected by external concepts of race, class, or gender. Hurston's inclination is to "talk around" these subjects. On the surface, she is noncommittal, ambiguous, inconsistent, or silent. The narrative reflects a studied avoidance of racial issues and an ardent determination to resist being defined, that is, named, by imposed ideologies of "Race" and the "Race Problem." She manages to "talk around" the problem of race by suggesting that there is no problem—for there isn't even a race. In one instance, she describes African Americans in accordance with the folk myth that explains how "the hosts" got their color. As she tells it, God arbitrarily designated a color for each of the multitudes. There was nothing significant about the designations. However, one late group, rushing to the throne to get their color, was accidentally designated as black. Having mistaken God's command for them to "Get back! Get back!! . . . they got black and just kept the thing agoing." "So According to that, we are no race" but merely mistakenly designated images, "a collection of people who overslept our time and got caught in the draft" (306). In this manner, Hurston both levels distinctions based on color and avoids committing herself to the ideologies of the intelligentsia.

The issue of skin color was a paradoxical one, especially during the Renaissance. Though some declared pride in skin color and race, others took pride in the lightness of their pigmentation. David L. Lewis reveals that Renaissance figures such as Walter White and James Weldon Johnson believed that one of the major handicaps African Americans faced was that white America would not permit them to forget they were Black (192–93). "The American Negro is not innately ashamed of his color," Johnson wrote in the *American Mercury*. "Such efforts as he makes to approach the American color standard are due fundamentally to strong economic and social urges." Since "the United States puts a higher premium upon color, or, better, lack of color than upon anything else," and because "a shade or two of complexion" can determine one's socioeconomic status, Johnson reasoned that the desire to approach the national color standard and the color prejudice Blacks practiced was "quite natural" and an understandable expedient, particularly for Black men who wanted to give their families the advantages to which they were entitled (52). Johnson therefore was pleased to remark upon the change in pigmentation among Blacks: "Now, in the little over three hundred years that the Negro has been in America his complexion has undergone considerable lightening" (52). Hurston recognized the hypocrisy, and, no doubt, resented the superior attitude that stemmed from such prejudiced and elitist notions. Her tale, then, not only allows her to remain noncommittal but it also becomes a strategy that allows her to subtly expose what she perceives as the hypocrisy of "Race Pride" and the pretension of elitists.

Hurston also treats *signifying* as thematic matter in *Dust Tracks*. In "Research," for example, she describes and explicates the actions of Big Sweet, who was " 'specifying' up this line of houses from where I lived." She had "her foot up on somebody" and was giving them "a reading," which the narrator explains "is another way of saying play the dozens, which is also a way of saying low-rate your enemy's ancestors and him, down to the present moment for reference, and then go into his future as far as your imagination leads you" (186, 187).

*Signifying* is used in the *Dust Tracks* narrative, as it is in *Their Eyes,* as rhetorical strategy. More importantly, Hurston's use of this strategy in her autobiography emphasizes its practical applicability beyond its use as a narrative device and illuminates one aspect of her attempt to free herself from race and, particularly in the case of "smart talking" and "playing the dozens," sex and class domination. For the author sees herself in the midst of an assembly of elite "Race Men and Women" who, by censuring and otherwise condemning her, attempt to silence her as Joe Starks tries to silence Janie. And as Janie *signifies* upon her husband's impotence as a means of asserting her own voice, the narrator in *Dust Tracks signifies* upon the pride of the Race Leaders. Through various tales in the autobiography, Hurston denounces the high-brow attitudes of the intelligentsia or the "dicty Negro." She portrays them as poor imitators of whites who cannot direct their own paths, let alone lead the masses of African Americans.

Signifying acts in Hurston's texts often serve to vent her anger against and frustration with authoritarians and elitists who represent patriarchal and classist repression. Instead of confronting her antagonists on issues specifically related to gender and class, she attacks them on issues related to race—their rallying point. Thus, Hurston's statements appear to be directed against African Americans generally—"the Race" —as opposed to those individuals with whom she disagreed. To a certain extent, Hurston's aggression was displaced. Given that the New Negro was characterized as male and the Black intelligentsia was concerned first and foremost with whether or not Blacks as a people would achieve "manhood," it is wholly logical that Hurston would conflate issues of race and sexism and race and classism. Her jibes at "the Race" and "the Race Problem" seem more an attack against the men who represented both.

Filomina Chioma Steady's insights put Hurston's *signifying* tendencies into perspective. Steady points out that the "art" or "game" of ridicule was originally developed to allow African women to assert themselves and express their discontents: "Tensions have always existed between the sexes, and African societies traditionally have developed mechanisms to regulate these tensions. Apart from the more publicized protests and boycotts by women, institutionalized mechanisms for releasing tensions between the sexes exist in most societies and provide opportunities for striking back" (33). In her examination of secret societies among Mende and Temne peoples, she finds that both "provide institutionalized means of diffusing tensions that might arise in the domestic sphere and between men and women." And further, that "ridicule and scapegoating are also used as effective mechanisms for neutralizing tensions between the sexes. These can take the form of direct taunts, group pressure or ritual satire" (33).

Indirection, as a fundamental feature of Signifying, is characteristic of African oral tradition. In "Proverbs—Exploration of an African Philosophy of Social Communication," Oyekan Owomoyela suggests that the oral tradition favors circuitousness and opacity. Further, he explains that as opposed to the explicit communication characteristic of written culture, the Yoruba, who are representative of many African cultures, prefer proverbial communication (7–8). Enslaved Africans maintained this predilection for indirect expression, which manifests itself in African American traditions such as masking. As "Dat Lie 'Bout Big Talk" illustrates, the enslaved could not articulate themselves explicitly without penalty. It was necessary to cloak one's express point of view. Hurston's identification with "the bookless" and her use of the implicit, indirect communication of folk expression in her writings emphasize as well her preference for oral tradition.

Indirect communication, in the form of Signifying, folktales, folk sayings, jokes, proverbs, songs, and parables, is also a stylistic and thematic feature of Hurston's texts. In *Jonah's Gourd Vine,* for instance, John Pearson's courting of Lucy Potts results in a veiled marriage proposal, replete with a variety of indirect discourse:

> "Lucy, you pay much 'tention tuh birds?"
>
> "Unhunh. De jay bird say 'Laz'ness will kill you . . .' and den de doves say, 'Where you *been* so long?' "
>
> John cut her short. "Ah don't mean dat way, Lucy. Whut Ah wants tuh know is, which would you ruther be, if you had yo' ruthers—uh lark uh flyin', uh uh dove uh settin'?"
>
> "Ah don't know whut you talkin' 'bout, John. It mus' be uh new riddle."
>
> "Naw 'tain't, Lucy. Po' me, Lucy. Ahm uh one wingded bird. Don't leave me lak dat, Lucy." (75)

Having tied a love knot in a handkerchief she nervously pulled at, Lucy shouts, " 'Look, John, de knot is tied right, ain't it pretty?' 'Yeah, Lucy iss sho pretty. We done took and tied dis knot, Miss Lucy, less tie uh 'nother one' " (75).

In *Moses,* the sagacious Mentu teaches young Moses through storytelling. Mentu "had answers in the form of stories for nearly every question that Moses asked" (54). Upon his death, Mentu admonishes Moses to remember his stories:

> "Oh, I won't forget anything that you have ever taught me, the sayings, and the proverbs and all. They have helped me a lot."
> "You are right to listen to proverbs. They are short sayings made out of long experience." (80)

Storytelling, as a form of Signifying, implies an attention to issues that are controversial and are usually allowed to remain unarticulated. Indirect communication, as Owomoyela's article suggests, is utilized in "broaching delicate, sensitive matters" (9). Race and racial issues were such matters. Typically, Hurston used storytelling, joking, and *signifying* to broach these subjects. In *Dust Tracks,* she makes a subtle but pointed statement that, in this instance, is directed toward racists and America's racist power structure. She acknowledges their unjust and oppressive practices and implies her resentment of these practices. To these forces, she subtly articulates her demands:

> What do I want, then? I will tell you in a parable. A Negro deacon was down on his knees praying at a wake held for a sister who had died that day. He had his eyes closed and was going great guns, when he noticed that he was not getting any more "amens" from the rest. He opened his eyes and saw that everybody else was gone except himself and the dead woman. Then he saw the reason. The supposedly dead woman was trying to sit up. He bolted for the door himself, but it slammed shut so quickly that it caught his flying coat-tails and held him sort of static. "Oh, no Gabriel!" the deacon shouted, "dat aint no way for you to do. I can do my own running, but you got to 'low me the same chance as the rest." (284)

Although Hurston claimed that there were no racial problems in the United States—one aspect of Signifying is lying—this passage contradicts that claim. Through a parable, she can express her discontent and expose white oppression without incurring a penalty. The parable also reemphasizes Hurston's philosophy of individualism as she suggests that African Americans should be allowed the same individual opportunity as whites. Thus, she indirectly criticizes whites and Blacks who would treat any individual prejudicially.

· · ·

Hemenway remarks in his literary biography of Hurston that her public approach to racial issues is characterized by "indirection, subtlety, and humor" (290). She uses parables as rhetorical strategies and as strategies of self-preservation and liberation. Indirect presentation mitigates the poignancy of statements made, and humor is intended to mollify the response of those to whom the statements are directed. Humor is another aspect of African American folk life that Hurston emphasizes. It is also an intrinsic part of the concept of *Nommo*. Quoting the Dogon sage Ogotommêli, Janheinz Jahn writes, " 'The Nommo ... is water and heat. The vital force that carries the word issues from the mouth in a water vapour which is both water and word.... The vital force of the earth ... is water. God has solidified the earth with water. Again, he makes blood with water. Even in stone there is that force, for dampness is everywhere' " (124). The etymology of "humor" shows it to be an element of the "spiritual-physical fluidity" which is *Nommo*. Although "humor" is an English word, its relation to the African *nommo* is significant and warrants examination in context of Hurston's rhetorical and practical use of it. Webster's *Third International Dictionary* defines "humor" as "a normal functioning bodily semifluid or fluid," "a secretion ... that is an excitant of activity." It is derived from the Latin *humor* or *umor,* meaning "moisture," "fluid." It is akin to Middle Dutch *wac,* "damp," "wet"; Old Norse *vökr,* "damp"; and the Greek *hygros,* "wet." Humor, then, is a vital spiritual-physical, procreative force.

Ruth Finnegan's discussion in *Oral Literature in Africa* shows humor to be a prominent feature in African oral narratives. Some proverbs of the Ila of Zambia, for instance, are characterized by ridicule and mockery. Paraphrasing ideas of E. W. Smith, Finnegan writes, "of Ila proverbs, wit has a utilitarian aim; laughter is never far away" (410). African stories and tales, especially animal tales and those of the trickster variety, are also distinguished by their humor. Arna Bontemps writes that many of these humorous folktales, like those featuring the hare and the monkey, survived the middle passage and were "safely transported" across the Atlantic (*Negro Folklore* viii-ix). Hurston collected such tales in *Mules and Men,* analyzed them in her writings in *Sanctified Church,* and utilized them in her fiction and nonfiction. The chapter "My People! My People!" in *Dust Tracks* is a prime example of the narrator's infectious sense of humor and her inveterate appreciation of the storytelling art. In this chapter, the narrator relates numerous tales about the wiles and the ridiculous antics of the monkey (as they provide commentary on the African American experience). Though consistently censured and condemned by critics who felt her folk humor and storytelling tendencies perpetuated the "darky" tradition, Hurston persisted in making them both an integral part of her work and life.

The function of folktales in African American folk culture parallels their function in African society: they educate, socialize, moralize, and admonish individuals in an effort to achieve social integration and maintain social stability. They also entertain as well as provide an opportunity for the display of a storyteller's verbal skills. But as Finnegan points out, the specific function or purpose of a story is determined by the particular culture or society whence they are derived (326–28). The discrimination, exploitation, and racially motivated violence African Americans suffer and the sexism African American women suffer can destroy the human spirit. Humorous tales, anecdotes, and jokes help to counter these malevolent forces and nullify their effects. They help to transform pain, frustration, and despair into relief, perseverance, and hope. The vital, life-giving, and life-sustaining forces of wit and humor quicken the spirit and restore life.

Hurston saw humor as the balm of an oppressed people. It revitalized the soul while it calmed tension and anxiety. In *Dust Tracks* the narrator writes that humor and laughter relieved the anxiety of her father and other men in the community who feared that a fellow neighbor might be the victim of Klan violence. Their fears unrealized, they returned, heralded by "a bubble of laughing voices": "The men all laughed. Somebody marked Bronner's cries and moans a time or two and the crowd laughed immoderately. They had gone to rescue a neighbor or die in the attempt, and they were back with their families. So they let loose their insides and laughed. They resurrected a joke or two and worried it like a bone and laughed some more. Then they just laughed. . . . They shoved each other around and laughed" (231).

In *Muntu,* Jahn expressly identifies laughter as a *kuntu* force. He demonstrates its independent, modal force by citing a passage from *Palm Wine Drinkard,* a novel by Amos Tutuola: "We knew 'Laugh' personally that night, because as every one of them stopped laughing at us, 'Laugh' did not stop for two hours. As 'Laugh' was laughing at us on that night, my wife and myself forgot our pains and laughed with him" (103). One senses that, as the narrator in *Dust Tracks* describes the continuous and persistent laughter among the community's men, who just laughed then laughed some more, "Laugh," as Tutuola portrays it, is an independent force whose contagious presence acts as a curative and a restorative. Hurston considered humor and laughter the wellspring of life and the outward indication of an inner spirituality. As discussed in chapter 2, Hurston considered this wellspring of life a gift from Africa transmitted by High John de Conquer, the "hope-bringer." This gift High John gave to the enslaved. It allowed them to endure the worst conditions and maintain hope in the face of despair, life in the face of death.

The functions ascribed to folktales give insight into the ethos of the people from whom they sprang. They also comment on the emotional and psychological state of the teller; for they are "projections of personal experience and hopes and defeats" (Hughes and Bontemps, *Negro Folklore* viii). A comparison of Hurston's rendition of the High John tale with Julius Lester's points up the personal aspect of tales. In Hurston's version of the tale collected in *Sanctified Church,* High John is amicable and even moves "Ole Massa" to laughter. In her revised version in *Negro Folklore* (93–102), she even proffers High John's gifts to whites. In Lester's version, High John is a vexation to Old Massa, whom he always outsmarts. High John *accidentally* breaks Massa's hoes, plows, and the mule's leg and burns down the barn. At the end of the story, High John dupes him and throws him in the river in a gunny sack. The reconciling sentiment in Hurston's versions is nowhere to be found in Lester's. There are several ways to read Hurston's conciliatory tone. Perhaps Hurston suggests that a little humor could work wonders on the human soul—no matter whose it is. Perhaps the laughter coming from someone as indurate as a slaveholder creates a dramatic irony that releases tension. Perhaps, also, Hurston suggests that revenge isn't necessary, as in the case of Lester's version, and that whites, symbolized by "Ole Massa," really aren't the threat they are believed to be; that time might be better spent building one's own barn than burning down another's; and that by not being consumed with "Ole Massa," Blacks become the center of their own lives.

Hurston's consistent use of humorous tales in *Dust Tracks* suggests to what extent she was sensitive to racism, sexism, and classism and to what extent she struggled to control their impact. While it may be that Hurston related tales to entertain or educate the reader or to display her talents, it seems obvious, too, that the wit and jest mask feelings of humiliation, anger, and frustration—a few of the possible "hundred meanings" of African American laughter. Langston Hughes's discussion of racial jokes and riddles in his essay "Jokes Negroes Tell on Themselves" comments on the dynamics of reconciliation behind them. He writes, "Their humor is the humor of frustration and the laughter with which . . . sallies are greeted . . . is a desperate laughter" (639). But it is one that amuses and allows individuals to forget their troubles—for a time—and keep anger in check. Paulette Cross's essay "Jokes and Black Consciousness: A Collection with Interviews" also reveals these dynamics. One of her two informants allowed, "These [racial] jokes represent a true feeling, a human feeling. But it's the kind of thing that's self-defeating" (661). The predominant attitude amongst her informants was that the purpose of jokes was to evoke laughter as a way of relieving tension and pent-up frustrations.

Hurston's desperate struggle to escape her frustrating circumstances is also covered under patterns of verbal play that function to reconcile internal and external reality. In this sense, she uses humor as a means to bring about harmony in her public relations with African Americans and whites and in her private relationship with her self. Even as Hurston *signifies* upon sexist and elitist Race Leaders and the idea of race, she expects that the jesting quality of the *signifying* act will pacify the confusion and disturbance created. She laughs off the notions of race in order to create racial and social harmony and to free herself from racial and social constraints. Whatever function humor might play in Hurston's works, whether purgative or palliative, entertainment or rhetorical strategy, Hurston sees it as essential to psycho-spiritual balance and well-being. Arvay Meserve, in *Seraph,* is the personification of humorlessness. She takes herself and her family quite seriously. Because she cannot control every circumstance of their lives, she becomes embittered and, paradoxically, alienates her family. During Arvay and Jim's courtship, Arvay was never appreciative of or receptive to Jim's sense of humor. " 'I don't favor so many jokes, Mister Meserve. I don't like to be took for a fool' " (28). But humorlessness drove her to desperate and foolish acts

Hurston defiantly pronounces in *Dust Tracks,* "My sense of humor will always stand in the way of my seeing myself, my family, my race or my nation as the whole intent of the universe" (281). She suggests that a sense of humor inspires a more tolerant and accommodating attitude that obviates race pride and race consciousness—barriers to social harmony in the United States. The verbal games she plays to bring about harmonious relations are understood by those African Americans who also understand the multifaceted function of humor. Perhaps, then, another reason Hurston's works drew severe criticism was that she and her critics were not speaking the same language. Hurston's atypical experience of growing up in an all-Black folk community meant she was deeply rooted in the expressive traditions of the folk. In addition to this fundamental difference, many of her colleagues and contemporaries were of the "upper class" and did not understand or did not appreciate her *signifying* acts. They are like the lion in the "Signifying Monkey" toast who is duped by the monkey because the style of discourse between them differs.

In *Mules and Men,* the author recounts how the folk combat racism and intrusive paternalism through wit, laughter, and indirection, while simultaneously maintaining harmony and personal integrity:

> The Negro, in spite of his open-faced laughter, his seeming acquiescence, is particularly evasive. You see we are a polite people and we do not say to our questioner, "Get out of here!" We smile and tell him or her something that satisfies the white person because, knowing so little about us, he doesn't know what he is missing. The Indian resists curiosity by a stony silence. The Negro offers a feather-bed resistance. That is, we let the probe enter, but it never comes out. It gets smothered under a lot of laughter and pleasantries.
>
> The theory behind our tactics: "The white man is always trying to know into somebody else's business. All right, I'll set something outside the door of my mind for him to play with and handle. He can read my writing but he sho' can't read my mind. I'll put this play toy in his hand, and he will seize it and go away. Then I'll say my say and sing my song." (4–5)

Hurston's use of African American linguistic patterns in her fiction and, particularly, in her nonfiction indicate her belief in African American folklore as a source of individual and collective power. Hurston valued and embraced the African American cultural traditions from which she derived her self-love and self-respect. As she states: " 'My kinfolks,' and my 'skin-folks' are dearly loved. My own circumference of everyday life is there" (*Dust Tracks* 285). It is from within that circumference that the author drew the stuff of her writing, her personal strength, courage, and power. And it is there, in the reclamation of cultural traditions, that the author believed African Americans would find the strength and courage to file off the iron collar.

# 4

## The Folk Preacher and the Folk Sermon Form

---

I had been pitched head-foremost into the Baptist Church when I was born. I had heard the singing, the preaching and prayers. They were a part of me.

—*Dust Tracks on a Road*

In her reclamation and celebration of African American folklore, Hurston often expressed her ideas in sermonic form and through the voice of the folk preacher—the very embodiment of African American oral tradition. That Hurston appropriated the folk preacher's voice as a vehicle to inspire spiritual rebirth as well as to incite resistance to European cultural hegemony is telling. The sermon of the African American folk preacher has historically expressed the collective liberatory voice of African Americans since enslavement. Through the antiphonal dynamics of the folk sermon, preacher and congregation merged in a ritual of spiritual renewal and empowerment. Like the spirituals, sermons were mediums of psychic and spiritual regeneration, transforming silenced objects into speaking subjects. Through the visionary words of the folk preacher and the response of the congregation, African Americans created a world wherein they were at the center, where they found comfort and consolation. With the Word, they armored themselves to cope with and survive daily indignities, to continue their struggle for emancipation, and to resist systemic exploitation. In *Talking Back* bell hooks argues that the struggle to end domination is expressed in the establishment of "the liberatory voice—that way of speaking that is no longer determined by one's status as object—as oppressed being. That way of speaking is characterized by opposition, by resistance" (15). The folk preacher and the folk sermon are prime examples of Black folks' efforts to establish a liberatory voice, to cast themselves as speaking subjects, and to resist oppression.

The liberatory voice of the folk preacher and the rhetoric and form of the folk sermon are often consciously and unconsciously utilized by African Americans who continue to struggle against domination in all forms. Zora Neale Hurston appropriated this traditional evangelical style as she evoked the voice of the folk preacher and the rhythm and rhetoric of the folk sermon form to articulate her own struggles and individual standpoints. No matter how much she rubbed her head against college walls or how cosmopolitan her perceptions became, Hurston remained a part of the religious folk tradition into which she was born. Through her father, a traveling Baptist minister, her mother, the superintendent of the Sunday school, and her community, faithful churchgoers, Hurston was indelibly impressed with the beliefs and practices of the Black Southern Baptist religious tradition. She was captivated by the poetic, vivid, dramatic language of the church as it was preached and performed. She was no less awed by the entrancing and uplifting power of the preacher, who could make congregations respond with "a ready acceptance" of all that was said.

Hurston greatly admired the verbal virtuosity of the Baptist minister. Of her father, she wrote, "He had a poetry about him that I admired. That had made him a successful preacher" (*Dust Tracks* 91). Hurston "had always maintained that the black preacher was essentially a poet," Larry Neal points out, and "the only true poet to which the race could lay claim." She considered "the black preacher as the principal dramatic figure in the socioreligious lives of black people" (162). The preacher, with the congregation "bearing him up," created what Hurston described as "high drama." Having "tumbled into the Missionary Baptist Church," she too took part in that drama. Many of the characteristics of the Southern Baptist tradition, those of the folk preacher and the folk sermon in particular, mark the rhetoric, style, and force of her work. Hurston's essays, short stories, novels, and autobiography are demonstrative not only of her belief in the primacy and power of the spoken word but also of her intimate knowledge and understanding of the sermonic tradition as well. It is the preacher "as the principal dramatic figure" who is most prominent in her works. Her fascination with the preacher and the sermon is most apparent in *Jonah's Gourd Vine, Moses, Man of the Mountain*, "Book of Harm," "The 'Pet' Negro System," "The Sanctified Church," and *Dust Tracks on a Road*. It is also apparent, though less conspicuously so, in *Their Eyes Were Watching God, Seraph on the Suwanee*, and *Mules and Men*.

Hurston recounts in *Jonah's Gourd Vine* a representative transformation of an "ordinary" man into a folk preacher—a man of the people and a man of God. As a boy, John Pearson attends church and imbibes its rituals. He learns the traditional prayers, prayers in which he finds comfort and the strength to fight and resist his personal vices. Embattled by the conflict between his love for Lucy Potts and his lust for other women, he finds "uh prayin' ground" where, kneeling in prayer, he eases his emotional distress: " 'O Lawd, heah 'tis once mo' and again yo' weak and humble servant is knee-bent and body bowed—Mah heart beneath mah knees and mah knees in some lonesome valley cryin' fuh mercy whilst mercy kinst be found. O Lawd! you know mah heart, and all de ranges uh mah deceitful mind—and if you find any sin lurkin' in and about mah heart please pluck it out and cast it intuh de sea uh fuhgitfullness whar it'll never rise tuh condemn me in de judgment' " (25). John becomes a member of Macedony Baptist Church and joins the choir to be near Lucy Potts, whom he later marries. His first prayer in church is enthusiastically received: " 'Uh prayer went up tuhday,' Deacon Moss exalted to Deacon Turl. 'Dat boy got plenty fire in 'im and he got uh good strainin' voice. Les' make 'im pray uh lot. . . . Dat boy is called tuh preach and don't know it' " (89). John had the voice, the language, and the spirit, and he could sing. He had the power of words " 'dat sets de church on fire.' " He could bring his hearers to a frenzy that made them forget all else. So one Sunday, "he arose in Covenant Meeting and raised the song 'He's a Battle-Axe in de Time uh Trouble,' " and when it was done he said, " 'Brothers and Sisters, Ah rise befo' yuh tuhday tuh tell yuh, God done called me tuh preach' " (111). The song John raised to announce his call to preach is one that characterizes the act of preaching as a discourse of resistance. God and God's servant, the preacher, are warrior-leaders who battle and inspire their followers to battle against "trouble"—whether personal or collective, whether spiritual, physical, economic, or social. Helping and inspiring the congregation to cope with the adversity of daily life is a fundamental part of the preacher's role.

Hurston's appreciation of the folk preacher and the sensibilities of the congregation are also evidenced in *Moses, Man of the Mountain*. An allegory on one level, *Moses* represents the struggles of African Americans through those of the ancient Hebrews. On another level, *Moses* is a work of protest. Imperialism, colonization, and oppression are condemned. The Hebrews' struggle against Egyptian domination is led by Moses, the quintessential preacher-leader and deliverer of the Hebrew host. Like John Pearson, Moses is called but does not initially heed the call. When he does, he is well prepared. A conjure man who knows nature's secrets, Moses is powerful, like a god himself, and without the faults of John Pearson. His only flaw—if it be one—is his introverted nature, which is also a source of his strength. His propensity for deep reflection leads him to the knowledge that empowers him as he combats Pharaoh and guides the Hebrews to Canaan. As leader of the Hebrews, Moses speaks with a liberatory voice and stands in opposition to all Egypt. With sword and staff, he helps the Hebrews resist oppression in Egypt and domination by other nations after the exodus. Moreover, his sermons help the Israelites to resist their own diffidence and trepidation and their inclination to be enthralled by the memory of Pharaoh's iron collar.

In *Jonah's Gourd Vine* and *Moses,* Hurston focuses her attention on the preacher. In "Book of Harlem" and "The 'Pet' Negro System" the preacher's poetry, the sermon, is emphasized. Both works are deliberate representations of the sermonic form as a popular expressive mode. "The Book of Harlem" is a story in fifty biblical verses told by the implied persona of a prophet. The opening commentary is an overview of the story set forth in the verses. Also written in biblical language, the opening parallels the text of a sermon. With allusions to the biblical stories of Babylon, the prodigal son, and Sodom and Gomorrah, among others, the introduction is an allegory of the Harlem social scene of the 1920s. The prophet describes the experiences of Mandolin, a youth of Standard Bottom, Georgia, who becomes a slick Harlemite and is sought after by all women. To "make him wise," a "damsel of scarlet lips" instructs Mandolin thus: " 'Go thou and buy the books and writings of certain scribes and Pharisees which I shall name unto you, and thou shalt learn everything of good and of evil. Yea, thou shalt know as much as the Chief of the Niggerati, who is called Carl Van Vechten' " (80). Following Mandolin's experiences, the reader is taken on an excursion through Harlem life and witnesses Mandolin's transformation from an uncouth seeker of " 'swell Shebas in mail-order britches' " to a wise and eminent figure in the Book of Harlem whose name becomes Panic: "for they asked one of the other, 'Is he not a riot in all that he doeth?' " (80).

"The 'Pet' Negro System" is a homily on the complex social dynamics among southern Blacks and whites. Hurston assumes the voice of a "lowly" but wise scribe whose insider's experience affords her the "inside truth" of things. She expresses this "truth" in typical sermonic form. In *The Art of the American Folk Preacher,* Bruce Rosenberg analyzes the structure and various nuances of the folk sermon form: The biblical text of the sermon is read first and is followed by the context, a prosaic explanation of the text. Then the message the preacher derives from that text is preached or chanted. Rosenberg distinguishes the chanted sermon from the nonchanted one: In the former, the preacher abandons the text and is taken over by the spirit. The sermon at this point is chanted and becomes poetic. In the latter, the sermon is basically "orally presented prose" and is characterized by its conversational oratory and conversational, non-chanted, speech (9–10). In part 1 of "The 'Pet' Negro System," the text and context are given:

> Brothers and Sisters, I take my text this morning from the Book of Dixie. I take my text and I take my time.
> Now it says here, "And every white man shall be allowed to pet himself a Negro. Yea, he shall take a black man unto himself to pet and to cherish, and this same Negro shall be perfect in his sight. Nor shall hatred among the races of men, nor conditions of strife in the walled cities, cause his pride and pleasure in his own Negro to wane." (156)

In the context created, the "pet Negro" system is described as an irreducible fact of southern life that defies and balks northern "Race Champions," who are viewed as "well-meaning outsiders" who know not whereof they speak. Accordingly, their vested interest in the "race-adjustment business" and their skewed angle of vision, obtained from the vantage point of "some New York office," is rebuked as a simplistic "race-agin-race" dogma, which is characterized as naive and counterproductive.

Part 2 of the essay shows the application of the text to daily southern life. Specific examples of "the web of feelings and mutual dependencies" that structure the pet system are enumerated. In part 3, the results and usefulness of the system are given, and part 4 is the winding down, the peroration. Main points are succinctly reiterated. The retribution of "trouble" is threatened should the holy writ of "The 'Pet' Negro System" be sinned against. And the ritual allusion to a possible utopian condition—of racial harmony—is evoked.

Scribe Hurston declares that her purpose is only to explain the pet system. "Who am I to pass judgment?" she asks. She assumes the posture of a disinterested prophet of God, speaking whys and wherefores. However, Hurston also uses the issue of the pet Negro system to stage an offensive against elitist "Race men" who are thinly disguised in the essay as "dwellers in the bleak North." She attacks, as well, white "Southern lawmakers" who foolishly attempt to legislate racial purity in their campaigns to promulgate racist ideologies. As scribe-prophet-preacher, Hurston seeks to establish an objective, authoritative voice, one justified in its resistance to class domination and race prejudice and in its pointed aggression against external dictates from Blacks and whites alike. She also uses the liberatory voice and expressive mode of the folk preacher to advance her campaign against racial categorization and to further her personal philosophy of individualism: "The orators at both extremes may glint and glitter in generalities, but the South lives and thinks in individuals. The North has no interest in the particular Negro, but talks of justice for the whole. The South has no interest, and pretends none, in the mass of Negroes but is very much concerned about the individual" (157).

That Hurston's use of sermonic rhetoric and form was not restricted to her fiction or limited to academic discussions of the preacher is significant. Hurston considered the folk preacher a forceful wielder of words, a speaking subject, and an empowered individual. In assuming the voice of the folk preacher and in appropriating the sermonic form as primary modes of expressing and structuring her own social and political standpoints, Hurston gives testimony to her own militancy and her resistance to coercive forces and racist politics.

• • •

Hurston's use of the evangelical style illustrates the juncture of sacred and secular in African American culture, wherein the use of religious expression often signifies a militant posture. In *Black Religion,* Joseph Washington, Jr., explains that "Negro religious institutions . . . developed out of the folk religion" and folk religion was created out of the "common suffering of segregation and discrimination" (30):

> The folk religion is not an institutional one. It is a spirit which binds Negroes in a way they are not bound to other Americans because of their different histories. . . . The root of this folk religion . . . is racial unity for freedom and equality. Every ecclesiastical expression of Negro congregations and institutions is but a variation or frustration of this theme. . . . Born in slavery, weaned in segregation and reared in discrimination, the religion of the Negro folk was chosen to bear roles of both protest and relief. Thus, the uniqueness of black religion is the racial bond which seeks to risk its life for the elusive but ultimate goal of freedom and equality by means of protest and action. It does so through the only avenues to which its members have always been permitted a measure of access, religious convocations in the fields or in houses of worship. (30–33)

(In spite of Hurston's resistance to the racial agenda of the intelligentsia, she maintained a very strong sense of racial identity. Hurston frequently spoke in a collective voice about what "the Negro" did or did not mean, want, or need, particularly "the Negro farthest down." Even her ardent belief in individual liberty evolved into a ministry, so to speak, that addressed the welfare of the collective folk. It characteristically opposed any social or political practice that would circumscribe an individual or deny an individual, not equality, but equal opportunity for achievement and advancement.)

Washington compares folk religion to secularism, both having in common "a non-ecclesiastical affirmation." Given Hurston's general disparagement of institutionalized religion, it might be argued that she is more an adherent of African American folk religion than of the African American religious tradition or the Black church. Nevertheless, the voice she adopts to express her views in "The 'Pet' Negro System" and "Book of Harlem" is that of a prophet, and in *Dust Tracks* it is that of the folk preacher. Though the author does not look to the church for affirmation, she nonetheless proclaims, in *Dust Tracks,* the one attribute tantamount to an ecclesiastical affirmation: "the call."

Receiving the call, the divine summons, is an indispensable formality within the African American religious tradition. Like the characters John Pearson and Moses, and like most folk preachers, the author-narrator in *Dust Tracks* also receives the divine call. This phenomenon entails visions and conversions, confusion, resistance, suffering, and, finally, conviction and acceptance. We can better see Hurston's use of these conventions by comparing experiences of visions and conversions related in *Dust Tracks* with those of actual preachers in Bruce Rosenberg's *The Art of the American Folk Preacher* and in Hughes's and Bontemps's *The Book of Negro Folklore.* Rosenberg interviewed several Baptist preachers and noted their responses to "the call":

> According to the clergymen I interviewed, the calling to the church comes from God. There is no other way. In nearly all instances, as with [the Reverends] Lacy, Brown, and McDowell the calling comes against the will of the preacher. On one occasion Lacy said that he did not want to preach when he first felt the spirit of God come to him, and he resisted for many years. . . . He says a voice came to him then and said, "The next time it will be death. . . ."
>
> Lacy tells another story about a friend who was deathly ill and who called out, "God if you spare me I'll do what you want, and become a preacher." God did and the man kept his promise. (22–23)

In *The Book of Negro Folklore,* one preacher testified that in seeking God he spent "seasons at fasting and praying." But it was only when God called him that he began to change. "God started on me when I was a little boy"; then God "began to show me things":

> Once while I was sick I saw in a vision three people and one was a woman. They looked at me and said, "He is sick." The woman said, "I can cure him." So speaking she took out a little silver vial, held it before me and vanished.
>
> At another time I saw myself travelling down a big road. I came to three marks . . . [that] represented the number of times I had started to find God and turned back.

> After this, one day, I was putting a top on our little log house. . . . It was broad open day and I was as wide awake as ever I was in this world . . . when a voice called my name three distinct times. . . . I never have been able to find out what it meant. (258–59)

After his visions, God directed the man to "Go preach my Gospel."

Hurston attested to similar experiences. After running out of her yard to avoid punishment for a childish prank, she came to a vacant house, where she experienced her visions.

> I had not thought of stopping there when I set out, but I saw a big raisin lying on the porch and stopped to eat it. . . . I sat down, and soon I was asleep in a strange way. Like clear stereopticon slides, I saw twelve scenes flash before me, each one held until I had seen it well in every detail, and then be replaced by another. There was no continuity as in an average dream. . . . I knew that they were all true, a preview of things to come, and my soul writhed in agony and shrunk away. . . . I did not wake up when the last one flickered and vanished, I merely sat up and saw the Methodist Church, the line of moss-draped oaks, and our strawberry patch stretching off to the left. (57)

Many of the motifs in the vision parallel those found in religious traditions: The eating of "strange" fruit, falling asleep, panoramic viewing of events, religiously symbolic numbers. The assertion of the truth of the vision, the shrinking from it, and the return from extraordinary to ordinary scenes are all part of the religious tradition. As in the traditions of mystical literature, the call and the visions that accompany it come when the individual is alone, usually in some isolated place. And these experiences usually begin in childhood. Hurston wrote, "I do not know when the visions began. Certainly I was not more than seven years old, but I remember the first coming very distinctly" (56). The Reverend Lacy also "recalled that when he was very young he was considered 'peculiar' and given to religious thought" (Rosenberg 22). Hurston also felt herself "different" from other children, especially after the visions came: "I consider that my real childhood ended with the coming of the pronouncements. True, I played and fought with other children, but always I stood apart within" (*Dust Tracks* 60).

The visions occurred for an extended period of time, and like the preachers, Hurston resisted the call implicit in them: "These visions would return at irregular intervals. Sometimes two or three nights running. Sometimes weeks and months apart. I had no warning. I went to bed and they came" (58). Sometimes she would wake up shivering, feeling alone, in an "arctic wasteland with no one under the sound of my voice" (115). Her visions caused her to suffer, and like others who were called, she resisted and shrank from what she saw and heard: "Oh, how I cried to be just as everybody else! But the voice said No. I must go where I was sent. The weight of the Commandment laid heavy and made me moody at times. . . . I would hope that the call would never come again. But even as I hoped I knew that the cup meant for my lips would not pass. I must drink the bitter drink" (59).[1] In spite of her suffering, she did not submit to the call until threatened with death. And like Reverend Lacy's friend, she made a bet with God. Hurston suddenly had to undergo an appendectomy:

> When I was taken up to the amphitheatre for the operation I went up there placing a bet with God. I did not fear death. . . . But I bet God that if I lived, I would try to find out the vague directions whispered in my ears and find the road it seemed that I must follow. How? When? Why? What? All those answers were hidden from me. . . .
>     I scared the doctor and the nurses by not waking up until nine o'clock that night, but otherwise I was all right. I was alive, so I had to win my bet with God. (145–46)

The author's impending death served as a catalyst to recall her earlier experiences, renew her commitment to the call, and reconsider its portents. Her bet with God and her earlier determination to go where she was sent indicate her belief that God had some specific task for her. She was to suffer but not in vain. Her suffering would not only lead her to a new life of peace and love but it would also strengthen her and lead her in directions that were not yet clear.

It is notable that the author did not seek her visions through fasting and praying. They came to her unsought. In her essay titled "Conversions and Visions" in *Sanctified Church,* Hurston writes,

> The vision is a very definite part of Negro religion. It almost always accompanies conversion. It almost always accompanies the call to preach.
>     In the conversion the vision is sought. The individual goes forth into waste places and by fasting and prayer induces the vision. . . .
>     The call to preach is altogether external. The vision seeks the man. Punishment follows if he does not heed the call, or until he answers.
>     In conversion, then, we have the cultural pattern of the person seeking the vision and inducing it by isolation and fasting. In the call to preach we have the involuntary vision—the call seeking the man. (85–87)

Hurston insinuates, then, that since the involuntary vision is not derived from the cultural pattern, it is a more authentic call to preach, and the individual who receives it is chosen. Nevertheless, because involuntary visions are common among folk preachers, they are also, to some extent, culturally derivative. In any case, the author's choice to present her visions as involuntary is a definite indication of her call into the special fold of the folk preacher.

In his literary biography of Hurston, Robert Hemenway proposes that the visions were probably meant to structure the autobiography and explain Hurston's success in a way that would allow her to ignore the "race problem":

> Although meant to explain Hurston's life, the visions do not success-fully structure the autobiography. They fade into insignificance as the story unfolds. . . .
> . . . What the prophetic visions really do is direct us toward Zora Neale Hurston's contradictory understanding of her own success and her uneasy interpretation of it. Whether they occurred or not, they are inadequately integrated into the literary structure. While they may con-firm the uniqueness of their recipient, they also are a key to Hurston's literary dilemma in her autobiography. She is searching for an appropri-ate voice for the post-Eatonville Zora Neale Hurston. The visions are a way to avoid confronting the reality of her own success, a fame wrested from a society that she admitted elsewhere confronted her with humili-ating Jim Crow experiences. (282–83)

The visions in *Dust Tracks* have more than a structural function. They do identify the narrator as someone special, but they also mark a point of departure for the author—a rite of passage into a less restricting and oppressive existence, a transition into the mythic dimension, where, as folk preacher, she can assume the power of divine agency and create the world she envisions. Hemenway states that the visions are "inade-quately integrated into the literary structure" of the autobiography. I read this "flaw" in the narrative as an authenticating feature that further illustrates the narrative's resemblance to the sermon. Bruce Rosenberg's work shows that the folk preacher's delivery is basically spontaneous and sometimes extemporaneous. But even with the varied rhetorical strategies utilized to organize the sermon, the folk preacher generally moves from point to point in more of an associational pattern as opposed to a strict linear progression. This movement accounts for the discursive nature of the sermon. Rosenberg writes that in the orally presented prose sermon, "logical development from sentence to sen-tence occurs more frequently than in chanted sermons" (10). He writes that "it is in the nature of sermons to use examples, proverbs, parables, etc.," and that the "welding together [of] such illustrative materials with set passages and phrases" often defies a consistent "principle of organization" (33).

Hurston does search for an appropriate voice in telling her story. The one that emerges is that of the folk preacher. The evangelical voice in her narrative suggests that, her success notwithstanding, she identified with and considered herself still "one of the folk." It also suggests that she was still in a "warrior mode," resisting that very society from which she wrested her fame. "The term *warrior mode*," explains Kesho Scott, "designates an attitude, a style of approaching life, in which one perceives existence as a continuous battle" (11). Further evidence of Hurston's militant stance is apparent in her tendency to associate visions with powerful individuals, thereby suggesting her own power. She writes of Constantine's "famous vision of the cross with the injunction: *'In Hoc Signo Vinces'* ... [which inspired Constantine to arise] next day ... to win a great battle" (275). She mentions "the Apostle Paul, who had ... arisen with a vision when he fell off of his horse," a vision that inspired his dedication to the propagation of Christianity (277). And in *Moses,* the narrator says of Moses: "All night he traveled and thought. He found his unformed wishes taking shape. ... He was seeing visions of a nation he had never heard of where there would be more equality of opportunity and less difference between top and bottom" (100). What the prophetic visions really do is direct us to the narrator's daimon of empowerment. Hurston, therefore, does not avoid confronting a hostile reality so much as she continues to battle it.

•  •  •

Hurston professed a divine inspiration that recalls those biblical writers said to have been inspired by God. "You take up the pen when you are told, and write what is commanded" (*Dust Tracks* 213). Her works, then, are sacred texts—sermons. As with all oral performances that are written down, the sermon loses some of its distinguishing features, which depend upon the dynamic between speaker and audience, folk preacher and congregation. However, some aspects of those dynamics are noted or otherwise implied in the written texts. In "The Sanctified Church" and "The Sermon," Hurston demonstrated the format of the chanted sermon. In the latter essay, she transcribed a sermon (*Sanctified Church* 95–102). The spoken part (text and context) is designated "spoken," and the chanted part is noted by poetic delineation. The rhythm of the preacher's delivery is suggested by the metrical arrangement of lines, and the written "ha!" of the preacher is indicative of the audible breathing that is an integral part of the oral performance.

Linguistic features suggestive of sermonic influences in Hurston's work are legion. Ecclesiastical and biblical diction, for instance, abound. In syntax, grammar, and diction, Hurston's writing imitates the characteristically uncomplicated language of sermonic discourse. Rosenberg describes the Reverends D. J. McDowell and C. L. Franklin as "well-educated," erudite men who "for the most part keep their language simple on the pulpit"; and since the preacher "has to speak the language of his flock," they believe communication is facilitated by their use of everyday language (102). Whether or not Hurston viewed her audience as a "flock," the *Dust Tracks* narrative is written in the language of the folk. The metaphors, similes, aphorisms, and proverbs that render folk expressions poetic are an integral and significant part of her narrative. They allow for the creation of such poetic passages as this one: "The Master-Maker in His making had made Old Death. Made him with big feet, soft and square toes. Made him with a face that reflects the face of all things, but neither changes itself, nor is mirrored anywhere. Made the body of Death out of infinite hunger. Made a weapon for his hand to satisfy his needs. This was the morning of the day of the beginning of things" (87).

This passage, cast in biblical expression, imagery, allusion, and rhetoric, conjures up a picture of God, the creator, ironically creating death, as opposed to life, on the first day. The passage is also representative of narrative and dramatic exempla, which are important sermonic features (Rosenberg 47). The two working together serve to intensify the passage's poetic quality. The narrative exempla tell a story about the creation of death. The dramatic exempla enumerate death's descriptions and duties, thereby heightening the narrative and dramatic effect. In "The Characteristics of Negro Expression," Hurston distinguished between characteristics of everyday storytelling and those of religious expression, suggesting a stylistic difference between narrative and dramatic exempla: "In story telling 'so' is universally the connective. It is used even as an introductory word, at the very beginning of a story. In religious expression 'and' is used. The trend in stories is to state conclusions; in religion, to enumerate" (68). Although the *Dust Tracks* passage quoted above has features of both exempla, it tends to be more characteristic of the dramatic exempla of religious expression. The omission of the connective "ands" is perhaps a consequence of conforming to the stylistics of written composition. The *Dust Tracks* passage is comparable to the following excerpt from the Reverend C. C. Lovelace's sermon "The Wounds of Jesus," which is transcribed in "The Sermon." Narrative and dramatic exempla blend. The metrical delineation, as Hurston devised it, suggests how the *Dust Tracks* passage might also be chanted.

And he arose
And de storm was in its pitch
And de lightnin played on His raiments as He stood on the prow of the
  boat
And placed His foot upon the neck of the storm
And spoke to the howlin winds
And de sea fell at His feet like a marble floor.

(100)

Both narrative and dramatic exempla create a rhetorical schema, which, on the one hand, allows the preacher flexibility in creating a story and buys her or him time in considering the next lines. On the other hand, it allows the preacher to set up poetic structures, establishing a basic rhythm that leads to the chanted part of the sermon.

Narrative and dramatic exempla of the folk sermon are derived from both the storytelling dynamics of African American oral culture and from biblical rhetoric. The storytelling and the "picture-making" Hurston wove into her narratives are also rooted in and typical of the communal activities on Joe Clarke's porch. So are the tales, anecdotes, and jokes that are interspersed in traditional folk sermons. The church was imbued with the utterances of the folk who "sat around the store on boxes and benches" and the folk imbibed the biblical expression of the church. Karla Holloway writes in *The Character of the Word,* "It is significant that the most poetic dialect in the folk stories is found within the stories that have a religious theme. This form of story and the language within it are similar to the sermon form . . . that also relies on abundantly poetic/adorned language. It is as if the spiritual topic demands a language that can accommodate it" (94). The fusion of folk and sermonic expressions is nicely rendered in *Their Eyes.* Mayor Starks officiates at a lamplighting ceremony that has the overtones of a religious service. His speech, dedicating the lamp, sounds very much like the opening remarks of a sermon—complete with snatches of gospel lyrics and an invitation to prayer:

"Folkses, de sun is goin' down. De Sun-maker brings it up in de mornin', and de Sun-maker sends it tuh bed at night. Us poor weak humans can't do nothin' tuh hurry it up nor to slow it down. All we can do, if we want any light after de settin' or befo' de risin', is tuh make some light ourselves. So dat's how come lamps was made. Dis evenin' we'se all assembled heah tuh light uh lamp. Dis occasion is something for us all tuh remember tuh our dyin' day. De first street lamp in uh colored town. Lift yo' eyes and gaze on it. And when Ah touch de match tuh dat lamp-wick let de light penetrate inside of yuh, and let it

shine, let it shine, let it shine. Brother Davis, lead us in a word uh
prayer. Ask uh blessin' on dis town in uh most particular manner."
(72–73)

Davis "chanted a traditional prayer-poem" and those gathered sang
"We'll walk in de light, de beautiful light."

Spiritual or religious themes inspire a heightening of poetic expression peculiar to the sermon. An emphasis on the Old Testament as
subject matter also adds to its poetry and drama. The Old Testament
is rich in metaphor and action—elements essential to a successful folk
sermon. Moreover, the Old Testament stories offer an oppressed people
hope and inspire them to continue to struggle. Someday they, too,
like the ancient Hebrews, will be delivered from enslavement and
exploitation. Joseph Washington asserts that Christianity is "a faith
among Negroes of endurance and of suffering" (101). But it is also
one that inspires a spirit of active, combative struggle. This Old Testament–inspired resistance to degradation and exploitation has its roots
among the Black folk preachers of the antebellum United States.
Gayraud S. Wilmore writes in *Black Religion and Black Radicalism,* "the
Black Christian, under the influence of educated Black clergy and gifted
laymen like [Robert A.] Young and David Walker, felt a particular
affinity to the people of the Old Testament. The God of Israel was the
Lord of Hosts, the God of battle who swept the enemies of his people
before him" (51). The sermons of the early preachers were often fused
with this militant spirit. The Old Testament God condemned injustice,
promised succor for the oppressed, and threatened retribution. Instruments of God's divine will, Black preachers and prophets could do no
less. Abolitionist, lecturer, and religious layman David Walker, for
example, wrote "Appeal, in Four Articles; Together with a Preamble,
to the Colored Citizens of the World, But in Particular, and Very
Expressly, to Those of the United States of America" in 1829, knowing that having done so, his incarceration or death was imminent. In
the liberatory voice of the Old Testament prophet, Walker appealed
to Blacks to rebel against the "wretched condition" of enslavement.
Convinced that Black freedom was the "cause of God," Walker urged
Blacks to engage in "divinely justified armed struggle" against anyone
who would attempt to keep them bound (Harding 88).

Inspired by Walker's publication of an 1828 speech and by a prophetic vision of a Black Messiah, Robert Young published "The Ethiopian Manifesto, Issued in Defense of the Blackman's Rights, in the
Scale of Universal Freedom" in 1829. In the same biblical language
and prophetic voice, Young called for Blacks to form "a body politic"

to promote the "welfare of our order." For "the time is at hand, when, with but the power of words, and the divine will of our God, the vile shackles of slavery shall be broken asunder" (Harding 85). Many preachers and laypersons such as Walker and Young "found in the Bible—especially in the apocalyptic writings—a power for resistance that required no human justification and gave them license to become oracles of retribution. Young's words were "an unmistakable call to militancy, if not Black revolution," Wilmore writes. Most significantly, "Young placed the responsibility for freedom squarely on the shoulders of Black people themselves. . . . God by his powers had decreed to man 'that either in himself he stands, or by himself he falls' " (50–51). Wilmore notes that in like manner, David Walker's "Appeal" was "a summons to Black manhood. It [was] a call to rebellion, to throw off the chains of slavery and fight in self-defense for freedom and dignity in the name of the Lord of Hosts" (58).

Maria Stewart, the first American-born Black woman to speak publicly and "America's first Black woman political writer," was also a firebrand prophet of God. Marilyn Richardson relates that Stewart "underwent a conversion or 'born-again' experience" that renewed and strengthened her religious conviction and sense of duty to God and humanity. Stewart made a public declaration of her faith in Christ in 1831 and expressed her willingness to "sacrifice my life for the cause of God and my brethren" (8–9). Stewart's vision and commitment was heavily influenced by David Walker, whom Stewart extolled as "the most noble, fearless, and undaunted" soldier in the battle for human rights for Africa's sons and daughters (12). Richardson observes that Stewart exhibited the same evangelical fervor in her life and writings as did Walker and, like him, dedicated her life to a social activism inspired by the inextricable cause of God and social justice: "An opponent not only of slavery, but also of political and economic exploitation, she invoked both the Bible and the Constitution of the United States as documents proclaiming the universal birthright to justice and freedom. Resistance to oppression was, for Stewart, the highest form of obedience to God" (9). As Walker's "Appeal" may be interpreted as a "summons to Black manhood," Stewart's lectures and writings, which pled "the cause of oppressed Africa," also appealed directly to Black women: "How long," she queried in an 1831 religious tract, "shall the fair daughters of Africa be compelled to bury their minds and talents beneath a load of iron pots and kettles?" Reprehending Africa's "fair daughters" for possessing "too mean and cowardly a disposition," she made her standpoint clear: "Do you ask the disposition I would have you possess? Possess the spirit of independence. The Americans do, and why should not you? Possess the spirit of men, bold and enterprising, fearless and undaunted. Sue for your rights and privileges. Know the reason that you cannot attain them. Weary them with your importunities. You can but die if you make the attempt; and we shall certainly die if you do not" (38). Like Young and Walker, Stewart emphasized self-reliance as fundamental to the cause of emancipation: "We need never to think that anybody is going to feel interested for us, if we do not feel interested for ourselves" (38). Also like her predecessors, Stewart spoke as an oracle of retribution. She believed too that although Africans were responsible for their own liberation and advancement, God would bring vengeance to bear on white America: "Oh, America, America, foul and indelible is thy stain! Dark and dismal is the cloud that hangs over thee, for thy cruel wrongs and injuries to the fallen sons of Africa. The blood of her murdered ones cries to heaven for vengeance against thee" (39).

The militancy and action of the Old Testament that infused the writings of these early African American preachers and laypersons prevail in the sermons of traditional folk preachers. As the Reverend John J. Jasper said in his sermon "De Sun do Move," "de God of peace is also de man of war" (Hughes and Bontemps, *Negro Folklore* 228). Themes of resistance and empowerment are characteristic features of sermons based on the Old Testament. Stock phrases symbolic of stock themes of power and empowerment figure significantly in Hurston's work as well. Stock phrases and themes function as mnemonic devices preachers draw on to facilitate delivery as well as to illuminate and explicate the subject and create, by association, new clusters or formulas (Rosenberg 108–9). These formulas subtly underscore and reinforce the notion of empowerment, a theme central to African American folk religion. "Zig-zag lightning and grumbling thunder," "with sword in hand," and "I stood on the mountain" are some of the more prominent and recurrent thematic stock phrases in Hurston's texts. Each is a metonym of strength and power. "Zig-zag lightning-thunder" phrases occur most frequently in *Dust Tracks,* and they invariably occur in contexts wherein power or force is an issue. Significantly, the narrator writes that during her initiation as hoodoo priestess, she had "strange exalted dreams": "In one, I strode across the heavens with lightning flashing from under my feet, and grumbling thunder following in my wake" (191). In this ceremony, "the symbol of lightning was painted on my back. This was to be mine forever" (192). In the detailed account of her initiation ceremony in *Mules and Men,* Luke Turner, under whom Hurston studied, envisions Hurston's future as he ritualistically (re)names her: "I see her conquering and accomplishing with the lightning and making her road with thunder. She shall be called the Rain-Bringer" (209).

Hurston's induction into the Voodoo priesthood in Haiti is not only an indication and actualization of her anthropological skill and genius but it is also suggestive of her capacity for spiritual leadership. Historically, the induction ceremony is conceived of as a process of transubstantiation from which the inductee emerges as a spiritual leader. Wilmore explains that the African American folk preacher evolved from African priests who practiced conjure. "Actually, not a few of them were among the shipments of slaves from Dahomey and Togo, and it is they who must have formed the original cadres out of which the earliest Black preachers . . . began to emerge as the leaders of the slave society" (23). These Black preachers, as "conjurers" or "Voodoo doctors," used their powers to inspire the enslaved to resistance and revolt. "Whenever we find [Voodoo] converging with pneumatascopic elements in Black religion in America, as in the earliest days, we can expect to find a militant, religiously inspired rejection of white values and white control" (29). Wilmore's tenets are evidenced in several of Hurston's texts. In *Dust Tracks,* the author's spirit of defiance is explained in terms of her need to follow the commandments of a "force from somewhere in Space." Emboldened by her conversions and visions and the security of having the "inside truth" of things, she is determined to perform her duties as she sees fit, in spite of external forces. *Dust Tracks* proves to be a transforming, mythic narrative, a discourse of resistance to stereotypical, controlling images of Black womanhood. Hurston's introduction to *Mules and Men,* which details her findings and experiences with hoodoo in the southeastern United States, suggests how white control is undermined as the work itself opposes white values on many levels. Hurston's decision to use a participant-observer stance in collecting her material demonstrates her refusal to operate within the confines of Western scientific methodology and its attendant notion of "objectivity." Both *Mules and Men* and *Tell My Horse,* Hurston's account of Voodoo in Haiti and Jamaica, question the notion of the supremacy of Anglo-European culture. The works privilege African-centered oral traditions and respect the epistemologies, the systems of thought and ways of knowing, reflected in those traditions. And in *Moses, Man of the Mountain,* Hurston casts Moses in the role of the greatest conjure man who ever lived. Compelled by his promise to God and empowered by his knowledge of hoodoo, Moses inspires the oppressed Hebrews to revolt against Egyptian powers and leads them out of bondage.

The image of the snake also figures as a symbol of power in Hurston's work. During her initiation ceremony, she "became blood brother to the rattlesnake. We were to aid each other forever" (*Dust Tracks* 192). "The snake is the symbol of the life force in all mythologies since it is capable of self-renewal in sloughing off its skin," writes Jacqueline de Weever. It also symbolizes self-recovery, healing, self-knowledge, enlightenment, and wisdom and signifies transformation and rebirth (72–88). This symbology is suggested in *Seraph on the Suwanee,* in which Jim Meserve battles with but is defeated by a six-foot rattler whom Jim describes as a gentleman and a general. It is seen even more clearly in *Moses,* as Moses' rod of power is transformed into a serpent, a sign to Pharaoh and his magicians of Moses' superiority.

Phrases featuring the sword also occur in contexts dealing with power, strength, and force. In *Dust Tracks* an allusion is made to Constantine, who started "out on his missionary journey with his sword" (275). More importantly, Hurston uses this symbolic phrase in reference to herself: "I am in the struggle with the sword in my hands"; and "I am still in there tussling with my sword in my hand" (280). The sword is a metonym designating battle and the spirit of struggle. The mountain is a metonym designating strength and endurance. They both combine in this statement to signify the author's sense of empowerment: "I have stood on the peaky mountain wrappen in rainbows, with a harp and a sword in my hands" (280). In *Moses,* the mountain symbolizes Moses' strength, power, and endurance. These images along with the attendant symbolic images of lightning and thunder imply a likeness to the Old Testament God. In Exodus 19:16, God descends upon Mount Sinai to greet the Israelites. Lightning, thunder, and fire signal his power and force: "And it came to pass on the third day in the morning, that there were thunder and lightnings, and a thick cloud upon the mount, and the voice of the trumpet exceeding loud; so that all the people that *was* in the camp trembled."

• • •

Though a few women do preach and pastor congregations, women were not and, for the most part, are not welcome in the pulpit or at the podium. Jacquelyn Grant's essay "Black Women and the Church" states that women were kept in the background and relegated to the position of "support workers." Women who were called usually were not ordained; and the ministry of those who were ordained was always controversial. In her discussion of Maria Stewart's evangelism, Marilyn Richardson writes, "The authoritative word, written or spoken, was a longstanding male prerogative, not easily relinquished" (25). So even after Stewart experienced a religious conversion and was convinced of her calling, not only as an instrument of God, but also as a prophet, she was still held suspect by the Black church (26). Stewart met with much opposition from those who considered her vocation as public speaker and published writer to be incompatible with her gender. Her career was therefore short-lived, lasting only from 1831 to 1833. Even in "Mrs. Stewart's Farewell Address to Her Friends in the City of Boston" in 1833, she still felt compelled to explain her activism and to justify her answer to God's call. Her frustration is evident in the caveat she issued against those who might continue to belittle women's efforts:

> What if I am a woman; is not the God of ancient times the God of these modern days? Did he not raise up Deborah, to be a mother, and a judge in Israel? Did not queen Esther save the lives of the Jews? And Mary Magdalene first declare the resurrection of Christ from the dead? . . .
>
> If such women as are here described have once existed, be no longer astonished then, my brethren and friends, that God at this eventful period should raise up your own females to strive, by their example both in public and private, to assist those who are endeavoring to stop the strong current of prejudice that flows so profusely against us at present. No longer ridicule their efforts, it will be counted for sin. For God makes use of feeble means sometimes, to bring about his most exalted purposes. (68–69)

Stewart's authoritative and militant voice never sat well with her audience, "a number of whom were no doubt still struggling with the propriety of encouraging a woman who had appropriated the patriarchal voice of the language of the King James Bible to publicly express her views from a speaker's platform" (Richardson 15–16). According to Jacquelyn Grant, the "status of Black women in the community parallels that of Black women in the church" (145). A look at Hurston's work and the responses to it from this angle of vision puts in relief Hurston's isolation as an outspoken woman in a male-dominated career and cultural movement. I do not suggest that Hurston was a frustrated preacher. But she, like Maria Stewart, had her own social gospel, and the efforts of both to "stop the strong current of prejudice" against African Americans was met with contempt and derision.

We do see portrayed in *Their Eyes Were Watching God*, however, a frustrated woman preacher. The sermon as a vehicle of the liberatory voice is most profoundly illustrated in a sermon that was never delivered. Nanny was a preacher who received the call but was never able to realize it. Born enslaved and feeling her complete objectification as

" 'nothin' but uh nigger and uh slave,' " Nanny says, " 'It wasn't for me to fulfill my dreams of whut a woman oughta be and to do' " (34, 31). After emancipation, however, she had hopes for her daughter Leafy. But the schoolteacher raped Leafy, who was only seventeen. She " 'took to drinkin' likker and stayin' out nights' " (37). With Janie, Leafy's daughter, Nanny feels she has another chance to vicariously fulfill her dreams: " 'Ah wanted to preach a great sermon about colored women sittin' on high, but they wasn't no pulpit for me. Freedom found me wid a baby daughter in mah arms, so Ah said Ah'd take a broom and a cook-pot and throw up a highway through de wilderness for her. She would expound what Ah felt. But somehow she got lost offa de highway and next thing Ah knowed here you was in de world. So whilst Ah was tendin' you of nights Ah said Ah'd save de text for you' " (31–32). For Nanny, the folk preacher's voice is the voice of liberation, of freedom. Thus, it is her will to preach. The sermon would embody her liberatory message. The freedom she wishes for herself, daughter, and granddaughter would not only remove the shackles that objectified her as nothing but "uh nigger and uh slave" but it would also remove those shackles that objectified her as female "other." For the express purpose of the sermon Nanny wanted to preach was to save her daughter and granddaughter from the " 'menfolks white or black,' " who would make " 'a spit cup outa' " them (37).

That there was no pulpit for Nanny, no congregation to hear her sermon on "colored women sittin' on high," speaks to the silence and repression of women in the African American community and in the church. Nanny's sense of frustration is evinced in her reconciling herself to the fact that "there wasn't no pulpit for me." But her "habit of survival"[2] gave her the courage and strength to "take a broom and a cook-pot," symbols of women's sphere, tombstones of women's minds and talents says Stewart, and make a way anyway. That she felt her text was worth saving, worth passing to a third generation, and worth preaching still speaks to her ardent belief in African American religious traditions as intrinsically defiant and emancipatory. It speaks as well to her belief in the necessary empowerment of Black women as speaking subjects, a conclusion Maria Stewart came to as early as 1831.

· · ·

Hurston's "gospel" is that achievement, resistance, and individualism are the avenues to self-empowerment. Her "message" requires the individual to look to self, follow the "inner urge," and work untiringly to achieve one's goals. The "inner urge" is also a thematic stock phrase that reinforces the themes of industry, achievement, and empowerment. "Inside urge," "individual urge," and "internal drive" are variations on the same themes in Hurston's texts. The idea of self-reliance is a fundamental one among African American folk preachers. The Reverend C. L. Franklin draws on it in his sermon "Moses at the Red Sea":

> The instrument of deliverance
> Is within your hands
> It's within your possession
> . . . . . . . . . . . . . . . . . . . . .
> The powers that need to be brought into exertion
> Is within you
> Good God.
> What are ya cryin' about Moses
> What are ya lookin' for
> What do ya think that ya want
> Why the rod of your deliverance is in your own hand
> Stretch out the rod that's in your hands
> I don't have a new rod to give ya
> I don't have a new instrument to give ya
> I don't have a new suggestion for ya
> I do not have a new plan
> Your course has already been charted by destiny.
>                                    (Rosenberg 107–8)

In like manner Hurston also remonstrates against African Americans for "crying" about their conditions and praying about them when the "powers that need to be brought into exertion is within" them.[3] She argues that the power for change is individual and internal. This idea is foregrounded in *Moses* and becomes a pivotal one for Moses as he struggles to understand the Hebrews and his role as their leader. Further, she argues that in order to achieve individual power, it is necessary for African Americans to renounce the past just as "sinners" have to renounce their worldly ways and be reborn to a new life. Unencumbered by history, they, like she, can work, struggle, and direct their own destiny.

Hurston ends her autobiography with a testimonial to the faith of individualism and an extension of fellowship to friend and foe. As the humble prophet-scribe, Hurston closes "The 'Pet' Negro System" in the same manner. In *In Search of Our Mother's Gardens,* Alice Walker bemoans the "unctuousness" that closes Hurston's autobiography:

> For me, the most unfortunate thing Zora ever wrote is her autobiography. After the first several chapters, it rings false. One begins to hear the voice of someone whose life required the assistance of too many transi-

tory "friends." A Taoist proverb states that *to act sincerely with the insincere is dangerous.* . . . And so we have Zora sincerely offering gratitude and kind words to people one knows she could not have respected. But this unctuousness, so out of character for Zora, is also a result of dependency, a sign of powerlessness, her inability to pay back her debts with anything but words. (91)

Given Hurston's self-description of "sham and tinsel, honest metal and sincerity," one might question Hurston's sincerity. More to the point, Hurston's footnote describing the "love feast" puts in perspective the tradition that occasions her ritualistically magnanimous benediction: "The 'Love Feast' or 'Experience Meeting' is a meeting held either the Friday night or the Sunday morning before Communion. Since no one is supposed to take Communion unless he or she is in harmony with all other members, there are great protestations of love and friendship. It is an opportunity to reaffirm faith plus anything the imagination might dictate" (266–67). Hurston is not so much "out of character" as she is faithful to the cultural script of African American religious folk ritual.

The same argument can be made for Maria Stewart, whom Richardson also characterizes as out of character in her farewell address at Boston:

The uncharacteristic serenity of tone in much of her Farewell Address suggests that Stewart had embraced a decision to, in effect, annihilate her public persona. She addressed her audience in the language of one dying into a new life, with such remarks as, "Farewell. In a few short years from now, we shall meet in those upper regions where parting will be no more." She proclaimed a spiritual testament advocating the pursuit of godliness and peace, the cultivation of intellect and morality, and finally, thinking herself to be a prophet distinctly without honor in that land, bade farewell to Boston. (27)

The closing peroration of the traditional folk sermon marks Stewart's farewell address as it does the closing of Hurston's autobiographical narrative. One can hear the voice of reckoning and the striving for peace of mind in Stewart's words below. They are the same ritual words and sentiment resonant in Hurston's narratives and in the traditional prayers and sermons of the contemporary Black church: "The bitterness of my soul has departed from those who endeavored to discourage and hinder me in my Christian progress; and I can now forgive my enemies, bless those who have hated me, and cheerfully pray for those who have despitefully used and persecuted me" (74). This ritual is typical of early African American folk preachers who disguised their radical ideologies and revolutionary tendencies with the cloak of peaceful religious contentment. Though their masked rage sometimes gave way to open rebellion, Wilmore writes that it also found recourse in "the same subtle use of suggestion and innuendo as we find in . . . spirituals" (69). He explains further: "Subterfuge, sabotage, fraud, trickery, foot-dragging and other behavior patterns of resistance were insinuated into the daily intercourse with white people in the guise of stupidity and obsequiousness, as a tactic of simple survival" (73).

The liberatory voice of the African American folk preacher resounds throughout Hurston's writings. Because the folk sermon has historically functioned as a means through which psychic and spiritual transformation is experienced and by which opposition to oppression is inspired, its trace in Hurston's texts is a further indication of Zora Neale Hurston's daimon of empowerment. To speak in the voice of the folk, to urge autonomy and empowerment through self-reliance and industry was an act of defiance, a radical act in the tradition of the African American folk preacher. As the words of the early preachers, laymen, and laywomen inspired in the folk a faith in a just and avenging God, they also challenged the daughters and sons of Africa to actively struggle for the freedom and equality denied them. The instrument of deliverance was in their hands. Hurston also demonstrated an active faith. Her gospel of individualism expressed itself in a multifaceted political activism. Central in her political ideology is the recurrent theme of generations of liberatory voices: Blacks must "possess the spirit of independence."

# 5

## Politics, Parody, Power, and
## *Moses, Man of the Mountain*

———

Power loves to meet power and strength loves strength.

—*Moses, Man of the Mountain*

"Conditional integrationist," separatist, accommodationist, and sellout are but a few of the shibboleths describing Zora Neale Hurston's political thought. Because of her anticommunist stand, her support of Republican politicians, and her stand against the Supreme Court's 1954 ruling on desegregation, she is labeled a conservative, a right-winger, and a reactionary. Her association with *Fire!!* "the literary magazine of the younger Negro Renaissance artists," makes her a radical. Her Black cultural nationalist agenda casts her as a militant.[1] And her portrayal of women in certain of her texts heralds her a feminist and a womanist. As Robert Hemenway states, Hurston's "politics were never simple" (329). Her varied and shifting political stances were castigated in her day and were not looked on favorably in the decades of the seventies and the eighties either. Charges of opportunism, naivete, and shallowness yet obtain.

Whereas the shortcomings, flaws, or wrongheadedness of other Renaissance figures are examined and explained in the context of the conflicting, often paradoxical sociopolitical milieu of the period, Hurston's are not. Contradictions or progressions in her thought are characterized as fickle-minded wishy-washiness. In other members of the intelligentsia, contradiction is viewed as the natural outcome of the "torture of paradox" that haunted every effort of African American leadership to effect social and economic change in a hostile, resisting, and inveterately racist country. Opportunism in Hurston is described as pragmatism in other artists and political pundits. What is naive, shallow, and compromising in her work is ascribed to her naturally

naive and shallow self. For others, these traits are justifiable consequences of negotiating within "the American context."

Nathan Huggins, for instance, writes of "the naïveté of men like
[James Weldon] Johnson" and "most Harlem intellectuals [who] aspired to *high* culture." He determines, however, that "most Negroes
were apt to agree that it was a good thing" (5). He extols Johnson's
"conciliatory temperament" as a political asset. Alain Locke's dissem-
bling is glossed over, and his enthusiasm to nurture "every suspicion
of talent" no matter how artificial is explained, absolving Locke of any
responsibility in decisions he made: "If the American context forced it
to be artificial and contrived, it should not be thought Alain Locke's
fault" (65). And "while DuBois shifted his ground under the torture of
paradox" on issues such as Black participation in World War I and
segregation, "his argument, wherever he stood, was always literate and
forceful" (29). His political pragmatism—supporting whatever candi-
date or party that served African American interests as Du Bois conceived them to be—is described as the "American way out" (34). "Consistent leadership was impossible," Huggins concludes (47). Though
David L. Lewis describes Du Bois as "maddeningly inconsistent," he
similarly explains and praises him. Ambiguity and ambivalence plagued
artists and politicians alike. Huggins describes these qualities, as manifested in the life and works of artists such as Countee Cullen, Claude
McKay, Jean Toomer, and Wallace Thurman, as "authentic." Yet he
categorically dismisses Hurston as a mere opportunist (74). Lewis's
assessment of the politics of the period and its practitioners is a bit
more even-handed. Nevertheless, he continues the conventional characterization of Hurston as a con artist and dubs her a "problem child"
of the Harlem Renaissance (96, 179).

Though the labels used to describe Hurston have been apt at times,
they in no way characterize the totality of Hurston's political thought.
The gradual and remarkable maturation that attended Hurston's artistic growth also characterizes her increasing political awareness and her
growing mastery of the discursive strategies Houston Baker applauded
as modernist features of African American intellectual history. With
few exceptions, however, Hurston has been dismissed as a pseudo-
intellectual with little or no political acumen. Arna Bontemps claimed
that Hurston ignored the serious aspects of Black life. Darwin Turner
countered, "Miss Hurston did not always ignore the serious aspects of
the life of Afro-Americans; inexplicably, she denounced some of their
efforts to secure equal opportunities in America" (95). This latter charge
is far more injurious. Though Turner reasoned that, perhaps, "excessive
pride in her race" or "her experiences in the all-black settlement of

Eatonville" were at the bottom of Hurston's "inexplicable" political actions and pronouncements, he denounced Hurston as an "irritatingly naive" disappointment (97–98, 118). On at least one issue—Hurston's response to the 1954 Supreme Court desegregation decision—Turner saw some noteworthy perceptivity on her part. He finds it "understandable that a black person would be insulted by the too common assumption that black teachers are incompetent and that black education in a black school is inevitably inferior" (97). He found some validity in her stance against the Fair Employment Practices Commission as well. Hurston feared its policies would allow whites to penetrate and control Black businesses and allow whites to usurp the jobs of Black educators (96). Turner noted: "Perhaps history will prove Zora Neale Hurston wiser than she once seemed to Afro-Americans who optimistically looked only at the advantages of integration. Certainly her fears of the deleterious effects of the influx of white teachers in black schools seem justified in light of recent allegations of the mass firings of black teachers and the demotions of black principals as integration creeps across the South" (135).[2]

Turner's discussion marks the first extended examination of Hurston's politics. Most critical appraisals of Hurston's work thereafter tend toward a pattern of assessment that echoes Turner's: Hurston's political thought is recognized but is ultimately rejected as naive. Lillie P. Howard in her biographical *Zora Neale Hurston,* for instance, observes in one brief paragraph that Hurston's analysis of the political and social climate in Haiti, depicted in *Tell My Horse,* "is the first indication of Hurston's profound interest in politics which would consume her life during the years between . . . 1948 and her death in 1960." Howard points out, however, that Hurston was "barely a novice" at this point. "Her opinions on the causes of the social upheavals are to be taken as simply that—her opinions which may or may not have had any basis in fact" (158).[3]

Some apologists of Hurston's views continue a conspiracy of silence since many find it difficult to appropriate Hurston's contentious mixture of political standpoints without damaging particularly favorable constructions of the author and her work. This has resulted in a bifurcation of Hurston's essential self that encourages an assessment of the artist in contrast to that of the politician. "I think we are better off if we think of Zora Neale Hurston as an artist, period—rather than as the artist/politician most black writers have been required to be," suggests Alice Walker. "This frees us to appreciate the complexity and richness of her work in the same way we can appreciate Billie Holiday's glorious phrasing or Bessie Smith's perfect and raunchy lyrics, without the necessity of ridiculing the former's addiction to heroin or the latter's excessive love of gin" ("Dedication" 3). Implicit in this statement is an indictment. A political philosophy is compared to drug addiction and alcohol abuse, two insidious social diseases potentially destructive to the individual and everyone around her. The implication is that Hurston's politics were harmful to herself and potentially destructive for the African American masses. Ironically, it is not Hurston whom Walker wishes to protect but "us" and "our appreciation" of her. So "*we* are better off" to separate the artist from her politics.[4] But, this, of course, is impossible. Nathan Huggins rightly points out that "the problems of Afro-American artists then and now" revolve around the issues of "the Negro as artist or advocate, the writer as individual or race man, art as self-expression or exposition of ethnic culture" (193). Because members of the Black intelligentsia believed proof of culture and civilization among African Americans to be the key to social acceptance, economic opportunity, and political viability, they became cultural politicians, and any African American whose work offered evidence of cultural achievement was pressed into service. Willy nilly, art and artists were sociopolitical entities.

Artist versus politician is a false and problematic dichotomy that perpetuates a fragmented understanding of human personality. Whether or not Black writers are *required* to be politicians, they are. Whether or not critics find value in the political views writers directly or indirectly express, whether they agree or disagree with them or find them complementary or contrary to their own ideological constructions, the various political assumptions of these artists remain. To take a part, without considering the whole, can only result in a distorted view. This is one reason Hurston remains "a woman half in shadow" (M. H. Washington 7).

The various political labels used to characterize Zora Neale Hurston do little to explain her politics. Superficial descriptions leave unsounded the philosophical underpinnings from which her politics are derived. Robert Hemenway's analysis of Hurston's politics continues the critical examination initiated by Darwin Turner and sounds further Hurston's philosophical worldview. Hemenway discerns that Hurston's politics "must be understood both within the context of the times and within the development of an intricate, sometimes willful political philosophy": "Hurston's conservatism grew primarily from three sources: an obsessive individualism that began with the self-confidence of Eatonville and expanded to generate great self-pride, almost a kind of egotism; a long suspicion of the Communist party and collectivist government . . . ; and the social science philosophy that informed her folklore collecting" (329). Hemenway emphasizes and explores more closely the last source, which he considers "by far the most complex." But because one source informs and reinforces the others, the three cannot be separated. Hemenway determines that Hurston's celebration of Blacks as psychologically and spiritually healthy and whole and her representation of them as "cultural creators," as opposed to pathological case studies, was a gutsy and radical position to hold during the period of the New Negro. He surmises that the political ramifications of such a position could have been far-reaching in terms of social legislation: "White politicians want to believe in the notion of cultural deprivation . . . because it suggests that the racial tensions in the society are caused solely by poverty; they can attack material want among black people without having to confront the capitalism that created it, or the racism that helps perpetuate it. Hurston rejected the pathological stereotype because she knew that material poverty and ideological poverty were distinct entities" (331). Hemenway saw Hurston's views as prophetic. Yet, in a manner characteristic of the all but overly romanticized scholarship on Hurston, Hemenway praises her achievement only, in the end, to tout her failures:

> Zora's problems came when she attempted in the late forties and early fifties to transfer her cultural perceptions to the political arena. If she could have found a political outlet for her cultural theories, she might have altered the premises of the American racial dialogue. But she made two mistakes. First, she interpreted all personal criticism in the context of her social science theories, refusing to admit that one could both celebrate Afro-American culture and deplore many of the conditions that helped to shape it; and second, she fixed her vision so narrowly on Eatonville that eventually she came to ignore the multiplicity of the southern black experience. (333)

The political expression of Hurston's social science theories, no matter how wrongheaded it is perceived to be, could not have been otherwise. Her political thought and action, as informed by the sources Hemenway outlines, is also wholly logical. The ardent individualism that fueled Hurston's will-to-power was radical and uncompromising. Hemenway grants Hurston a political *philosophy,* but devalues that philosophy by dubbing it "willful"—a term much used in reference to a recalcitrant child. But it is the *will* that is at the very core of Hurston's worldview. In every political essay written, one finds Hurston's fundamental value orientations manifested. The self-reliant, self-willed disposition that spurred her achievements could, she assumed, lead to achievement and empowerment of African Americans as a whole. In her writings, Hurston either praises individual or group achievement, pride, and autonomy or she is incensed and indignant at anyone who expresses anything to the contrary. "Pessimists, and grouches, and sycophants I do despise," she fumes (Nathiri, "Reunion" 74).

Her review of Lance Jones's *The Jeanes Teacher in the United States* is replete with copious praise. "We could make it the Second Book of Revelation," she suggests. The review applauds the development of rural schools for Blacks. Booker T. Washington was one of a number of "great administrators" named in connection with the schools. The review also gives an optimistic view of the South and praises the book's rendering of social relations and its positive depiction of Blacks:

> When one finishes the book, it is impossible to believe anything other than that the New South will work out all its problems. It is just a matter of effort and time. There is an honesty about the book that should be appreciated in this day and time. There is no patronizing attitude toward a minority group, nor glossing over the unfortunate facts of the Negro being in part responsible for lack of progress by his own indifference to consequences. No attempt to make anything else out of the reconstruction period but what it was, a second forceful conquest of the South by the carpetbaggers, by the setting up of Negro governments inadequate to their fate, the inevitable result being immediate chaos and violence and bitterness that is just now beginning to wane.[5] ("Rural Schools" 24)

In "Why the Negro Won't Buy Communism" (1951), Hurston berates "the commies," who, from her vantage point, perceive African Americans as a downtrodden people whose case was to be deeply pitied, a perception personally repulsive to her. Everything to do with "the Negro" Hurston felt deeply and took personally; for it had everything to do with her. She interpreted everything according to her individual, personal experience and philosophy. She steadfastly believed fairness, justice, and equanimity could be achieved only if people were considered individually, "duck by duck," rather than as one undifferentiated mass. The individual should be seen in light of that individual's merit, not in light of some stereotyped conception extrapolated from an entire group of people.[6] Because she equated her own potential for self-realization with the potential of the folk to achieve status as individuals, Hurston, necessarily, assumed the "willful" posture she did.

Any implication that Blacks were some monolith was met with an extreme response. Hurston expressed outrage that "an organization from the North was going to come into Florida to organize and deliver the Negro vote in a lump." In "I Saw Negro Votes Peddled"

(1950), she was infuriated at the assumption that "the Negro vote could be handled as a dark, amorphous lump. Then and there I made up my mind to be in Florida for this struggle at all costs" (13). Hurston, therefore, supported Congressman George Smathers's senatorial campaign against Senator Claude Pepper, who was supported by the CIO, the northern union organization to which Hurston alluded. This "struggle," fought in Hurston's birthplace, was, for Hurston, personal. It was there, in Florida, that she imbibed her ideals of individualism. To campaign against Pepper, then, was to protect herself and resist deformation of her personally constructed individualist mythos and ideology. For Hurston, it *was* "a struggle at all costs." Her actions might be described as reactionary, but how else might a staunch individualist with a very strong ego react? "She took things personally and defined herself in relation to those who opposed her" (Hemenway 333). But so did every other artist, activist, and politician of the period. Alliances of all kinds—by class, color, gender, sex, politics—were formed based on personal agendas, and enemies were made and attacked accordingly. The men, however, were generally not charged with emotionalism or with taking things too personally. Their sanguine antagonisms against one another are explained as a consequence of their impassioned convictions. Du Bois's deeds, for instance, are painstakingly analyzed and enthusiastically appraised. His battles with Booker T. Washington and Marcus Garvey are duly and respectfully recounted. The politics involved in racial uplift, as practiced by these "Race Leaders," was certainly personal and often self-serving. For example, Alain Locke's misogyny precluded effective support and promotion of women. And though he "functioned within a homosexual coterie of friendship and patronage," he was not vilified for his "bedroom politics" or for allowing his personal life to influence his professional life (Hull 8). As a general rule, male figures of the period were discussed and evaluated in the broad context of their vision and life's work.[7]

Hurston's egotism might well be considered problematic, and it might well have manifested itself in wrongheaded stances and actions. But to divorce the author from individualistic political standpoints and pronouncements that evolved from her egotistical self *is* to make of her the shallow, naive, irresponsible woman she was not. Darwin Turner writes that Hurston's racial pride "caused her to defend it against attack without understanding what issues were involved" (97). Hemenway writes that Hurston "was an instinctive black nationalist—or at least a cultural nationalist—without quite realizing the implications of her position" and that she "was not a systematic political thinker"

(334, 333). However sympathetic and well-intentioned these statements may be, they are nonetheless condescending and undermining.
They rob Hurston of any political awareness and astuteness and render
her an overly emotional, irrational nonintellectual. They deny her
agency. A careful and studied sounding of Hurston's writings, from a
holistic point of view that seeks to understand her particular standpoint, contests such claims. Hurston well understood the implications
of her cultural nationalism, as her article "The Race Cannot Be Great"
attests. She well understood the liberating and empowering possibilities of cultural pride and the self-worth that emanates therefrom. The
political actions she took are a direct result of that realization.

The critic David Headon continues the needed exploration of the underpinnings of Hurston's philosophical and political thought. Astutely
remarking that Hurston had "discovered ways to combine her literary
aspirations and highly individual sense of social commitment" (35),
Headon takes a both-and approach to Hurston's work that begins to
realize the unity of the artist and the politician. In his article " 'Beginning to See Things Really': The Politics of Zora Neale Hurston,"
Headon undertakes "to revise the conventional wisdom regarding the
broad range of her writings, both fiction and non-fiction from 1924
to about 1950, in order to demonstrate her evolving political consciousness—individual and eccentric on occasion, yes, but perceptive
and lucid, ahead of its time also. I want to show that the cutting edges
of Hurston's thought have more in common with the directions of
radical African-American literature of this century than has previously
been recognized" (30). He argues that the evolution of Hurston's political consciousness eventually led to "the adoption of a stance as potentially revolutionary in its way as that of the most militant black
activist" (30). In his examination of her work, Headon discusses Hurston's emphasis on self-worth, self-image, and self-empowerment,
insightfully concluding that "Zora Hurston confronted, ultimately,
the complex politics of self" (36). Further, Headon pronounces "the
revolutionary message of Hurston's writing: Liberate the self, and all
else follows. Never succumb" (36). Headon sees the significance of *self*
in Hurston's revolutionary message, but he, ironically, finds *self,* as
(Black, female) ego, problematic and out of place. Though his critique
helps to revise the "conventional wisdom" regarding Hurston's politics,
it reinforces some conventional perspectives that are pivotal in the
appraisal of Hurston as an intellectual and the intellectual significance
of her work. Headon denounces her commentary on enslavement and
Reconstruction in *Dust Tracks,* finding it devoid of a sense of history
and contemporary affairs. He describes her response to these issues as

insensitive, naive, and callous—perspectives typical of the conventional
wisdom. The "cockiness of her position," he judges, "is at best mis-
placed; at worst, it is a gross misreading of the priorities and aspirations of the black community at the time" (29). The charge of "cockiness" is also characteristic of the critical judgment leveled against
Hurston when her politics are considered unpalatable or "individual
and eccentric." The accusation of "cockiness" intimates that Hurston
assumed the attributes of a man. "Cock," a vulgar term for "penis,"
also refers to "a chief person," "a leader." And in patriarchal society,
"penis" is generally mixed up with male ego. Since Hurston is not a
man, her egotistical self-assertion is out of place. She cannot be a figure of authority, a pundit, since she misreads the needs and priorities
of her community. In a woman, even a sassy one, too much ego is
unseemly. Hurston's "cockiness," however, is less a symptom of occa-
sional eccentricity than it is an extension of the *self* Headon earlier
recognizes, a fundamental component of Hurston's philosophy of individualism and her "complex politics of self."

• • •

Hurston's individualist philosophy and politics are promulgated in
her novel *Moses, Man of the Mountain.* Though this narrative of Moses
and the children of Israel has been proclaimed a masterpiece, it is one
of the most unexamined masterpieces extant. One explanation may be
that most critics who praise it in one stroke, condemn it a failure in
the next.[8] And Hurston also questioned her achievement in *Moses:* " 'I
have the feeling of disappointment about it. I don't think that I
achieved all that I set out to do. I thought that in this book I would
achieve my ideal, but it seems that I have not yet reached it. . . . It still
doesn't say all that I want it to say' " (Hemenway 273). Hurston's
doubt of her accomplishment is felt precisely because of the monu-
mental task she set for herself. It is indeed difficult to articulate the
whole of several contending cosmologies in one book. But this, in the
end, is what Hurston has done.

Perceiving *Moses* as a major accomplishment, Ruthe Sheffey observes,
"From our angle of vision, it seems that what she did achieve was a
tour de force which ambitiously and successfully merged Afro-American folklore—its wit and its humor . . . —with the universal folk hero,
popularized in the Judeo-Christian tradition. Moreover, the work
makes a definitive statement about the role of leadership, its sacrifice . . . its loneliness . . . , and its imperative to make former slaves feel
free and noble" (220).

Blyden Jackson remarks also on Hurston's analysis of African American leadership and on the "regrettably wide and deep division in loyalties among its upper class, its black bourgeoisie, and the Negro masses from whom her folklore came" (xvii-xviii). Jackson asserts, as does Hemenway, that *Moses* can be interpreted as racial protest since "in the context of black culture Moses himself is inseparable from protest . . . so that merely to write a novel about Moses is to initiate a double train of thought and emotion associated with the Negro's struggles in America to be free" (xviii).

As allegory, *Moses* expresses a multiplicity of meanings. With the various legends of Moses functioning as a centrifugal force, the novel comments on the mythohistorical evolution and transformation of the ancient Hebrews; the enslavement and manumission of African Americans; the colonization of Africans and those of the African diaspora; and oppressors and the oppressed in every spatial and temporal dimension. It comments on the politics of leadership and the dynamics between (Race) leaders and those led and between the individual and the group. *Moses* is nothing less than a critique of power that examines the concept of individual human power in the context of and as an elemental component of natural, universal forces. The novel dramatizes the Spinozan theory that self-knowledge and self-empowerment are contingent upon an understanding of the natural world and the individual as an integral part of that world.

*Moses* is, indeed, *one* of Hurston's masterpieces. This novel reveals more about Hurston's personal philosophy and worldview than any other work. The character of Moses has many functions, including that of a mouthpiece. When Moses speaks, his utterances draw a configuration of Hurston's ideal self and the political philosophy that formed it. Blyden Jackson's introduction to *Moses* suggests the kind of critical eye needed to perceive and explore the novel's multivocality and multivalence. He discerns that Hurston conducts an "absorbing investigation of a theme. Hardly less than Machiavelli in *The Prince,* she discusses power—the kind of power, political in its nature, which is the prime object of concern for the Florentine in his famous treatise on statesmanship" (xvi).

But even when the political aspect of *Moses* is acknowledged, it is usually treated as a factor either separate from or irreconcilable with the book's humor. Another self-defeating dualism emerges: the serious versus the humorous. Blyden Jackson sees humor as the book's *"vade mecum,"* a "constant solvent for any of its possible hypertension" (xix). Turner sees it as "the chief art of the book," concluding, however, that the book, though Hurston's "most accomplished achievement," is a mere joke (*Minor Chord* 109, 111). Hemenway suggests that "one must be careful not to overemphasize the comic qualities of the novel; for, contrary to Turner's assertion, the final direction of the book is serious" (268). The division made between the book's comic and serious aspects is a superficial one. Mikhail Bakhtin's *The Dialogic Imagination* illustrates that the comic and the serious are not antipodal categories of discourse. In his investigation of early Greek and Roman genres, he found that the "serious, straightforward form was perceived as only a fragment, only half of a whole; the fullness of the whole was achieved only upon adding the comic *countre-partie* of this form" (58): "Parodic-travestying literature introduces the permanent corrective of laughter, of a critique on the one-sided seriousness of the lofty direct word, the corrective of reality that is always richer, more fundamental and most importantly *too contradictory and heteroglot* to be fit into a high straightforward genre" (55).

Bakhtin's parodic-travestying literature can be compared with the Signifying tradition in African and African American literature and culture. Signifying also functions as a corrective and critique on the lofty, the serious, and the "other." Parodic-travestying, Signifying literature provides more than the second, complementary element in a binary pair. It erases received myths, ideologies, and worldviews, creating a multiplicity of meanings and voices "of a given culture, people, and epoch," clearing a space for conscious reflection and for "completely new ideological heights." The "laughing word" necessarily objectifies the straightforward, direct word. In this circumstance, "any direct word and especially that of the dominant discourse is reflected as something more or less bounded, typical and characteristic of a particular era, aging, dying, ripe for change and renewal" (Bakhtin 60, 61). "Of course all these processes of shift and renewal of the national language . . . are inseparable from social and ideological struggle, from processes of evolution and of the renewal of society and the folk" (67–68).

In *The Political Unconscious: Narrative as a Socially Symbolic Act,* Fredric Jameson also emphasizes the essentially political nature of cultural texts: "There is nothing that is not social and historical. . . . Everything is 'in the last analysis' political" (20). All texts, all speech acts, all communications are hermeneutic formulations. As such, texts—all cultural artifacts—are interpretations. For Jameson, interpretation "is construed as an essential allegorical act, which consists in rewriting a given text in terms of a particular interpretive master code" (10). An analysis of this "master code" or interpretive approach reveals a text's "metaphysical and ideological underpinnings." Further, "the working theoretical framework or presuppositions of a given interpretive method are in general the ideology which that method seeks to perpetuate" (58). As allegory, *Moses, Man of the Mountain* is, on one level, an interpretation of the African American experience from days of enslavement to the Renaissance period. It is also, on another level, a formulation of Hurston's interpretation of the politics and power dynamics of the period and a documentation of her own politics and political agenda. As Signifying, parodic-travestying discourse, *Moses* is also a dialogue of contending ideologies and cosmologies. It is a corrective. It is protest. It is resistance. And it is prophesy.

The predominant interpretive master codes or approaches in *Moses* are ethical and aesthetic. Hurston's code of ethics proposes a system of values and principles predicated on the ideologies of individualism, achievement, and empowerment. That ethical system is described, analyzed, and projected through modes of African American linguistic expressions that reflect an African American folk aesthetic. Through the use of humor, dialect, sermonic rhetoric, Signifying, storytelling, lying, and proverbial expressions, Hurston privileges African American linguistic traditions and foregrounds the African American folk ethos as a valid and viable means to individual and group achievement and empowerment. Hurston's ethical and aesthetic approaches in the novel provide a running commentary and critique on the prevailing concepts, ideologies, discourses, and cultural practices of the period. They also create a matrix from which to construct new theories, ideologies, perspectives, worldviews, and modes of action.

• • •

Though *Moses* allegorizes the African American experience and speaks to the issues of collective struggle for freedom, self-determination, and self-definition, it is first and foremost an analysis of individualism and individual self-empowerment. Hurston was fascinated with Moses as another representation of the ideal individual and self-made man. His character is sketched in the 1934 story "The Fire and the Cloud," thus preceding, but in many respects also devolving from, the figuration in her works of fictional and nonfictional personages such as Joe Clarke, Booker T. Washington, Joe Starks, Haitian houngans, African American hoodoo priests, and Baptist preachers. His character and image resonate in figures such as Jim Meserve and Herod the Great. Moses is the epitome of the self-possessed man who calls other men to attention, awes women into submission, and then makes a way out of no way. Hurston portrays him as the ideal to which other men should aspire. Moses can be appreciated in the context of the Judeo-Christian, African, and African diaspora traditions as Ruthe Sheffey suggests (206). He is also to be understood in the context of his point of origin—the author. Moses is Hurston's alter ego. He is an example of Spinozan self-perfection. He is to Hurston what the likewise eponymous Zarathustra is to Nietzsche—the ideal individual.

The Judeo-Christian legend of Moses redounds with its own greatness. But Hurston gives Moses new stature. She baptizes Moses in his own Africanness and creates for him a new mythos. She recreates Moses in her own image. Blyden Jackson writes that Hurston's narration of the legend "does not deviate by one essential whit from the same story as it is told in the Bible" (xv). But Hurston radically alters the story, particularly in regards to the relationship between Moses and God. Hurston establishes for Moses an autochthonous status. First she renders his birth questionable since Moses is not figured as the son of Amram and Jochebed. The child born of them is set afloat upon the Nile and his fate is never disclosed. Jochebed stations Miriam nearby to watch him, but Miriam, in the manner of the disciples at Gethsemane, falls asleep at her post. "She woke up with a guilty start and looked for the little ark on the river which contained her baby brother. It was not there. She looked all around her to see if anyone was watching her and feeling sure on that score, she crept down to the spot where the basket had been and parted the bulrushes. The child and his basket were gone, that was all" (40). That was all, but that was enough to decenter the Judeo-Christian mythology built around Moses that identifies Moses as Hebrew. Contrary to the biblical account, Pharaoh's daughter does not rescue a child from the river. The object that her maid-servant retrieves is " 'the casket in which is kept the things for washing the Princess' " (42). And when Jochebed—believing Miriam's lie that the Princess found and kept the child—offers herself as a nurse, she is told, "There was no new baby to be nursed" (51).

The infant son in the palace is presented as the issue of the Egyptian princess and the Assyrian prince. Moses, therefore, is of a Semitic people of West Asia who are not Hebrew and of an African people who are Egyptian—that is, Black. Within Hurston's Moses are united the two peoples, African and Asian, from whom also are derived legends of Moses that differ from the biblical account. The Asian and African legends, particularly those African legends refigured in Haitian and African American cultures, allow Hurston to portray Moses as a powerful, self-created man. What Africa sees in Moses to worship, Hurston writes, is power, and "he is worshipped as a god" (*Moses* xxi). Indeed, the Hebrews in Hurston's novel fear him as much, if not more, than they fear God. The people confuse God's words with Moses' and are ever wary of Moses' raised right hand. When Moses asks Miriam, " 'Do you think that I am God,' " she responds:

"Indeed, I don't know, Moses. That's what I been trying to figure out for years. Sometimes I think you're just that Egyptian Prince that took up with us for some reason or other. Then again I would agree with some of them others that you was an Ethiopian. Once or twice I thought you was the sacred bull of Egypt with the known markings but the unknown history. Sometimes I thought God's voice in the tabernacle sounded mighty much like yours. But ever since you punished me with leprosy, I knew you had power uncommon to man." (321)

Moses is powerful long before he becomes a servant of God. He gains his power through the help of the folk, embodied in the servant Mentu, from whom Moses learns to appreciate nature—the source of empowerment. With Mentu's guidance, Moses becomes the "finest hoodoo man in the world," possessor of "the black cat bone." The tricks he learns from the Egyptian priests are just that. The knowledge and power he gains under the tutelage of Mentu, then later under that of Jethro, his down-to-earth father-in-law and another representative of the folk, are increased manifold upon his reading of the Book of Thoth. "'When you read only two pages in this book,'" Mentu tells Moses, "'you will enchant the heavens, the earth, the abyss, the mountain, and the sea. You will know what the birds of the air and the creeping things are saying. You will know the secrets of the deep because the power is there to bring them to you. And when you read the second page, you can go into the world of ghosts and come back to the shape you were on earth. You will see the sun shining in the sky, with all the gods, and the full moon'" (73). Eagerly, Moses observes, listens, and learns. Nothing is given him or divinely bestowed upon him or bequeathed him.

The power Moses acquires comes from his own efforts, his own inner urge to seek and to find. In a ritualistic sermonic chant, Hurston, like God in the book of Job, removes the hedge from around Moses. After Moses slays the Egyptian overseer and his royal birth is questioned, Moses is forced to flee Egypt. Standing at the banks of the Red Sea, he decides to cross over:

Moses had crossed over. He was not in Egypt. He had crossed over and now he was not an Egyptian. He had crossed over. The short sword at his thigh had a jewelled hilt but he had crossed over and so it was no longer the sign of high birth and power. He had crossed over, so he sat down on a rock near the seashore to rest himself. He had crossed over so he was not of the house of Pharaoh. He did not own a palace because he had crossed over. He did not have an Ethiopian Princess for a wife. He had crossed over. He did not have friends to sustain him. He had crossed over. He did not have enemies to strain against his strength and

> power. He had crossed over. He was subject to no law except the laws
> of tooth and talon. He had crossed over. The sun who was his friend
> and ancestor in Egypt was arrogant and bitter in Asia. He had crossed
> over. He felt as empty as a post hole for he was none of the things he
> once had been. He was a man sitting on a rock. He had crossed over.
> (103–4)

In other words, he is a "nobody." Behind him lies everything that is
supposed to make anybody a "somebody" and powerful: distinguished
birth and lineage, a royal name, fame, fortune, material wealth, degrees
and titles, social status. He, like the children of Israel, like enslaved
Africans, like Job, like Hurston herself, is reduced to a state of deprivation, left with little more than his natural self. Hurston, here, mocks
not only racist and chauvinistic white Americans who look to their
race and nationality as an indication of superiority, but also the snobbish,
social-climbing bourgeoisie and self-styled Black elites. Stripped of
worldly goods and position, Moses must start over. He must (re)create
himself. He must be responsible for his own welfare. He must start at
the "bottom" and work his way "up." Through Moses, Hurston shows
the possibility and the necessity of overcoming obstacles of all kinds.
Moses' positive and determined attitude is an animadversion against
pessimism and self-defeatism. Because of his firm belief in self and his
positive outlook, Moses is transformed from a man sitting on a rock
to a man standing on a mountain. His wealth lies neither in vacuous
words and phrases nor in materialism or haughty, puffed-up pride,
but in a self-confidence and assuredness founded on deed and ability.
As Moses, himself, says to the Egyptian priests, " 'Tell me, and then
again show me, so I can know' " (81). Moses concludes from his
ruminations as he sat upon the rock, " 'The man who interprets Nature
is always held in great honor. I am going to live and talk with Nature
and know her secrets. Then I will be powerful, no matter where I may
be' " (100). He acts on that decision. He was a man with a made up
mind.

Moses has what Hurston described as the internal drive, the *sine
qua non* of individual achievement. With a determined daimon, one
can challenge whatever fate metes out and whatever circumstances it
creates. As Hurston saw life as a haphazard course of events, indifferent to human wishes, so she fabricated for Moses an aleatory existence.
After Miriam petitions Moses to let her die, he contemplates Miriam's
life, his own, and the hand of chance:

> He thought how the threads of his life had gotten tangled with the
> threads of this homely slave woman. He wondered if she had not been

born if he would have been standing here in the desert of Zin. In fact, he wondered if the Exodus would have taken place at all. How? If she had not come to the palace gates to ask for him and to claim him as a brother, would he have left Egypt as he did? He doubted it. He never would have known Jethro, nor loved Zipporah, nor known the shiny mountain, nor led out a nation with a high hand, nor suffered as he had done and was doomed to keep on doing. A mighty thing had happened in the world through the stumblings of a woman who couldn't see where she was going. (323–24)

This mighty thing that happened is not attributed to the divine will of God, but the haphazard hand of chance. Whatever the circumstances, one has to deal with them and make the best of every opportunity to be and do the best one can. Moses rises from the rock on the far side of the Red Sea to a power greater than any *man's* and comparable to that of a god.

Though a leader, Moses derives his power and greatness not from ruling others or through acquiring property. Moses' decision to lead as opposed to rule illustrates Hurston's distinction between formal and effective power and her conception of effective leadership. Formal power is what Ta-Phar has and Moses refuses. Moses renounces the fame he had won by commanding armies and wielding a sword: " 'I have led many a battle and chopped down my share of men,' " he says. " 'But I doubt that any life I have ever taken benefited anybody. The property I took from conquered countries didn't make anybody rich. It just whetted their appetites for more' " (109–10). Donning robes of state and wearing a crown gives the appearance of power, but Moses understands the limitations of rulers and the confining and exacting demands of affairs of state. Ta-Phar is like the bear and the hunter and Moses envies him not. Distressed by the plagues Moses visits upon Egypt, Ta-Phar wishes he could have dismissed with the Hebrews and been done with his troubles, but he could not. He is compelled by the force of his position as Pharaoh and by his family legacy to do other than he wishes:

> If Pharaoh relented and let the Hebrews go, he would rid himself of the worry and humiliation he was suffering. But on the other hand he would have to face a danger more sure and certain right away. The nobles would never permit him to save his face at their expense. Even the servants who served about him personally belonged to that ruling class and so he could not even hope to escape with his life. If the house of Pharaoh had not preached and practiced hatred and vengeance for generations, he could save himself by a show of generosity and dismiss the slaves. But the intolerance of Pharaoh and his fathers was fighting

against him. Pharaoh was locked up in his own palace and inside himself. Moses walked out of the palace with a sense of power. (206–7)

Hurston has a Foucauldian appreciation of power. Power is not static. It is not centralized and is not concentrated in the hands of the so-called powerful. It does not extend itself downward from a center to the base. In *Power/Knowledge,* Foucault writes,

> Power is not to be taken to be a phenomenon of one individual's con-solidated and homogeneous domination over others, or that of one group or class over others. . . . Power must [be] analysed as something which circulates, or rather as something which only functions in the form of a chain. It is never localised here or there, never in anybody's hands, never appropriated as a commodity or piece of wealth. Power is employed and exercised through a net-like organisation. And not only do individuals circulate between its threads; they are always in the posi-tion of simultaneously undergoing and exercising this power. They are not only its inert or consenting target; they are always also the elements of its articulation. In other words, individuals are the vehicles of power, not its points of application. (98)

Moses' experiences in the palace make him understand how individ-uals circulate between the threads of power: His life endangered, Moses admits, " 'I feel the cursing thought of the law and power. I had always felt the beneficence of law and power and never stopped to consider that it had any other side. It is a sword with two edges. Never mind whether it is directed against me honestly or not. That has nothing to do with its power to injure me' " (99). The agitation stirred by the Hebrews under the Egyptians and their constant acts of rebellion against Moses clearly demonstrate that power does not necessarily extend itself from the top to the bottom of the hierarchical ladder. In Hurston's theory and formulation, power is not absolute. Pharaoh does not have absolute power, just as whites do not and gods do not. And neither is power juridical. It does not rest in the declaration of laws and prohibi-tions: Despite Pharaoh's fiat against it, boy babies continued to be born.

Moses rejects the idea of assuming the crown of Egypt and the crown of Israel. He is sorely disappointed when the people offer him a "kingly crown" they fashion from the melted-down crowns of conquered kings. Instead of sitting on a throne, Moses prefers to sit on the side of a mountain, "seeking answers to questions that Nature put to him" (144). For him power is constituted in an autonomous existence and autonomy is achieved through understanding the self in the context of the laws of nature, not through "lawing over others" or blindly following the laws and dictates of others. Moses "loved freedom and justice with a fierce love and he wanted Israel to be free and just. All that he had done to them and for them was intended to bring them to his viewpoint. And here they were wanting to be like other halted people that they touched along the way. They despised their high destiny" (327).

Through Moses, Hurston indicates her own desires for and disappointment in African Americans who, like the Hebrews, still feel the imprint of the "iron collar." The ideal political state she longs for is the same as the one Moses envisions. But the Israelites are yet beset with a self-defeating, master-slave mentality. They despise "bossmen" but they just would be "bossed." They beg for mercy but respect only force. "They didn't believe they could take on any responsibility for themselves at all. They kept clamoring for somebody to act for them" (248). " 'You done got free of Pharaoh and the Egyptian oppressors, be careful you don't raise up none among yourselves,' " Moses exhorts (327).

In the midst of his disappointment is hope and the possibility that the Israelites might one day realize their high destiny. Moses had given them what he wished for all humanity—opportunity. "He had put the future in their hands to do with it according to their hearts and their talents . . . and had given them the strife of freedom." With that, Moses satisfies himself. He had done "as much as it was possible for one man to do for another" (346). Not the Egyptians, not the Amalekites or Canaanites, *they* are all that stand in their way. The Israelites have their own songs, singers, and army, and their own God. But the Israelites also have in their midst the "sordid": "conniving politicians, stupid, but stubborn pushers and suspicions and avarice" (349). The Israelites have amongst them "My People! My People!" who just won't do. Hurston's representation of the Hebrews as "My People" reflects her belief that African Americans are often their own worst enemies, that their progress and empowerment is as often impeded by internal conflict as by external circumstances. As with the Hebrews, the divisiveness, stagnation, and halting progress are due to greed, envy, and deep-seated *ressentiment.*

When Moses ponders the fifty years he spent straining against the malcontents, he stiffens in anger and frowns and wonders what made him endure it. As Moses understands the forces of nature, he also understands the forces of human nature and the power dynamics in human relationships. He understands the "newness come to power, the cruelty and greed" of a Ta-Phar as he does the jealousy and envy of a Miriam and Aaron and the will of the downtrodden "to humble a man more powerful than themselves." As does Nietzsche's Zarathustra,

Moses can see into the mentality that acts on the principle that "many dogs are the death of the lion" (*Moses* 96).[9] Moses learns " 'the first law of Nature is that everybody likes to receive things, but nobody likes to feel grateful. And the very next law is that people talk about tenderness and mercy, but they love force' " (105). The Israelites show their ingratitude time and time again. They suspect Moses of bringing them out of Egypt only to set himself up as the "straw-boss." They question his leadership when they fear dying in the wilderness from starvation; so they long to return to Egypt and its "flesh-pots." They expect him to do everything necessary for their survival, freedom, and nationhood. Thus they resent having to do anything to help themselves. They conspire to kill him, but are too full of cowardice to do so. Yet Moses endures. He understands the effects of centuries of enslavement and the centuries necessary to shake the slave morality that resulted from it. He sympathizes with those who struggle under the weight of past years. When the "old heads" murmur their discouragement and their fear of facing Pharaoh and his army, Moses counsels Joshua against marching out of Egypt and leaving them: " 'What them old folks know is a stumbling stone to their thinking. But just for that we can't leave 'em behind. Joshua, when you find a man who has lost the way, you don't make fun of him and scorn him and leave him there. You show him the way. If you don't do that you just prove that you're sort of lost yourself. Remember that, son, if you ever get in the lead of people' " (202).

From the Exodus to the banks of the Jordan, Moses has to counsel himself with the same words he offers to Joshua. Moses' sympathy with the "stiff-necked" children of Israel bespeaks Hurston's sensitivity toward "My People" in African American society. She is not uncomprehending of their sociohistorical circumstances, their oppression, its affects on the psyche, the difficulty of moving beyond them, nor the possibility of their doing so. After a meeting with Pharaoh, one of the elders despairs, " 'No rest, no property, no babies, no gods. . . . Why would anybody want to live? Why don't we kill ourselves and be done with the thing?' " Another responds, " 'Maybe we hope we'll beat the game somehow without dying. That's human, ain't it?' " (35–36). Hurston succinctly captures the pathos of an oppressed and suffering people who stubbornly continue to exist. She puts in bas-relief the universal human will to persist, to "beat the game."

Hurston's sympathetic and "serious" portrayal of the Hebrews often gives way to burlesque. She lampoons the very aspects of their nature with which Moses sympathetically struggles. Thereby, she renders her critical interpretation and assessment of "My People" and the African

American experience. The comedy provides the balancing *countre-partie* to the serious discourse articulating a people's resistance to oppression and bid for freedom. African Americans, not quite a century out of enslavement, are paralleled with the Hebrews in the wilderness, not long out of Egypt. The Hebrews are caricatured as ungrateful, irresponsible, back-sliding individuals who continue to look to others for their welfare and protection. Concerned more about their stomachs than their status and continually complaining that " 'there ain't a thing to eat,' " they provoke Moses to a chastising anger: " 'I had the idea all along that you came out here hunting freedom. I didn't know you were hunting a barbecue' " (252). They are never satisfied and are always on the verge of revolt. If they are not plotting against Moses, they are murmuring against themselves.

"My People" consist not only of the multitudes or the masses, but of their would-be leaders as well. The parody of Aaron and Miriam as leaders is seen against the solemn characterization of Moses as the ideal leader who provides ideal leadership. Where Aaron and Miriam are motivated by desire for personal gain and recognition, Moses bears personal deprivation and loneliness. " 'Leaders have to be people who give up things. They ain't made out of people who grab things' " (263). The Hebrew leaders in *Moses* are "the laughing reflection" of the Black intelligentsia. The caricatures of Aaron and Miriam stand as correctives to the "so-called Race Leaders" whom Hurston saw as hypocritical and full of self-importance and false pride.[10] Aaron is as big as his littleness. His cunning hatred for Moses is expressed in the refrain of the blues song he sings: " 'It's your time now, be mine after while' " (293). The head priest of Israel, Aaron is more concerned with his raiments and his whiskers than his responsibilities to the people. He delays a meeting with Moses, explaining that "his beard-boy was looking after his beard so he could not come right away" (328).

Miriam is no less petty, pretentious, and power-hungry. Envious of Zipporah's "well-cared-for hands and feet" and fearing the loss of the other women's allegiance, Miriam attempts to vilify Zipporah on the basis of skin color: " 'That black Mrs. Pharaoh got to leave here right now,' " she challenges Moses (300). Miriam is stricken with leprosy for her narrowness. In this Signifying act, Hurston inverts the conceptions and connotations that have been attached to skin color. Whiteness is disease and disgust. It symbolizes putridity instead of purity, foulness instead of fairness, and an abomination instead of a blessing. Miriam is cast out. Hurston illustrates here the absurdity, divisiveness, and (self) destructiveness of racism and color consciousness. She attacks those who assume social and cultural superiority based on something as arbitrary as skin color.

In a hodgepodge of Signifying inversions throughout the text, Hurston gives her view on and interpretation of several other topical and controversial issues. She mocks the notion of the sanctity of white womanhood and the Black man as beast and rapist as she satirizes the Ethiopian princess who accuses Moses of rape—a charge based on a two-year-old treaty kiss. When Moses declares his innocence, the princess responds, " 'It is rape for you to even look at me' " (87). In another Signifying instance, Moses is accused of "passing" and the Hebrews who believe he is Hebrew stick their chests out in pride and gloat of their kinship with Pharaoh: " 'There is plenty of Hebrew blood in that family already. . . . The country can't get along without us' " (49). But Moses is no Hebrew, so the joke is on those who believe that being Hebrew—that is, white or light-skinned—signifies anything at all. Though according to the allegory the Hebrew situation parallels that of African Americans, Hurston depicts the Hebrews as white. Miriam, for instance, is described as having thick red hair and a white face (22). Moses is Egyptian and Asian, but obviously light-skinned enough to be thought a Hebrew, yet tanned enough to "pass" as an Egyptian. Hurston condemns white racists and spurious white liberals alike. Depicted as Egyptian nobles, these foes and "friends of the Negro" are unable to fathom why the Hebrews would want to be free. They label Moses a radical for demanding their complete freedom and consider bribing him to shut him up: " 'Perhaps we had better give him some sort of office to keep him quiet' " (191). If Moses could be bought, the Egyptians would effectively stem the tide of the people's discontent and anger. They would be somewhat pacified to have "one of their own" within the Egyptian power structure. Hurston decries the not-so-well-intentioned "friends of the Negro" as well as those Blacks who accept bribes and offices and sell the masses short. She is no less critical of visionless, nonproductive, though perhaps well-meaning leaders who accomplish little or nothing. Interminable protest meetings called by the Hebrew elders, in and out of bondage, make a laughingstock of protest organizers and organizations of the Renaissance period. Everything and everyone is duly Signified upon.

Comedy is indeed the *"vade mecum"* of *Moses, Man of the Mountain.* The humor in the novel is derived as much, if not more so, from the language of the characters as their actions. The story of Moses, told in Black vernacular, southern dialect, and in various modes of African American folk expression, contrasts sharply with the sacred, biblical text of Judeo-Christian tradition. And the colloquial speech of Pharaoh and the Egyptian nobles parodies the serious and solemn decorum of a royal court. Hurston's use of Black linguistic traditions throughout the novel manifests an aesthetic interpretive code that privileges the values and voice of the African American folk. Moses is not only indoctrinated with folk values through Mentu and Jethro but he also learns and adopts the language of the folk, whether he be in Midian with Jethro or among the Israelites. Though he is wont to speak in the "high-toned" language of the court, Moses finds himself speaking the "lowly" language of the Hebrews. He expresses himself in the riddles, proverbs, and stories learned from Mentu and in the Signifying language of the Hebrew folk. He is as full of braggadocio as he is of the power to back it up. To Aaron's hope that Pharaoh is vanquished and ready to comply with God's demand to let the Hebrews go, Moses responds: " 'I don't want his consent, really. It would spoil everything I planned. I mean to whip his head to the ground and then lead out with a high hand' " (185).

Hurston's use of Black folk expressions casts the story of Moses and the saga of the Hebrews in comic relief. The parody creates not only humor but also a travestying discourse that objectifies the "otherness" of the texts, the language, and the culture of those societies to which she directly and indirectly refers. Difference is foregrounded and the alienation and exclusion of one culture from another becomes salient. According to Bakhtin,

> any straightforward genre, any and every direct discourse—epic, tragic, lyric, philosophical—may and indeed must itself become the object of representation, the object of a parodic travestying "mimicry." It is as if such mimicry rips the word away from its object, disunifies the two, shows that a given straightforward generic word—epic or tragic—is one-sided, bounded, incapable of exhausting the object; the process of parodying forces us to experience those sides of the object that are not otherwise included in a given genre or a given style. (*Dialogic* 55)

The articulation of these differences through parody is realized in a resulting "double-voiced" discourse. The author appropriates the speech of another, redirecting the intention of the first voice and forcing it to serve authorial aims. Embedded in this "battlefield for opposing intentions" is a "hidden polemic." In this hidden polemic, "each assertion about . . . [an] object is constructed in such a way that, besides its referential meaning, the author's discourse brings a polemical attack to bear against another speech act, another assertion, on the same topic" ("Discourse Typology" 185, 187).

In an ironically serious turn, humor, in the form of parody, creates a dialogue from which issues multivocality, thus a multiplicity of views, in an otherwise monoglot world. Moreover, it questions received worldviews and clears space for alternative ones. The use of the language and lore of the folk as the parodying-travestying language has far-reaching sociopolitical implications. When a national or predominant language is parodied, one hears the folkloric quarrel of old and new and the "folkloric disgracing and ridiculing of the old—old authority, old truth, the old word" (*Dialogic* 81–82). The double-voiced, parodic language in *Moses* becomes a din of competing voices and views as parodic discourse is fused with the hermeneutic enterprise of allegory. What rings loud and clear through the heteroglossia is the voice of the folk. It challenges and debates the presumed truth of three assumed authorities: the Bible (as the infallible word of the Judeo-Christian God), white America, and the Black intelligentsia.

By pointing up the legends of Moses emanating from Asia and Africa, Hurston checks the biblical rendering of Moses as a Hebrew and the conventional American depiction of Moses as a white man (a persistent image continued today in the portrayal of Moses by actors such as Charlton Heston). Moses' haphazard association with the Hebrews questions his miraculous deliverance from a decreed death, as described in Exodus, as it mocks his fate as the handpicked prophet of God and savior of Israel. Although the side of the mountain got too hot for Moses as Jethro predicted, delivering Israel from bondage is described more as a mission Moses undertakes of his own accord than as a command of God. Moses is portrayed as the master of his own destiny and the destiny of Israel, which is more often determined by choices made by Moses than by God. Israel depends more on Moses' ability, power, ingenuity, and personal sagacity than on divine will. And Israel becomes for Moses an external, objective manifestation of his entrenched beliefs and aspirations for humanity. Moses confides to Joshua, " 'The lowest feeling for me in these forty-odd years was when I come down and saw *my* Israel around that golden calf' " (341; emphasis added). Moses takes his mission of emancipating Israel personally, so much so that *he,* not God, determines that Aaron must not cross over into Canaan and so kills him. Afterward, Moses looks down on Israel from the peaks of Mount Hor and contemplates: " '*I* have made a nation, but at a price' " (336; emphasis added). Moses is "willful," "egotistical," "cocky," and "belligerent" in regards to his own life and that of Israel. He will defy all for Israel, even God, even Israel itself. He determines that the slave-minded among the people will not enter the promised land. They, for whom the memory of bondage became "a hold back," will not cross over. However, Moses has hope in their posterity: " 'I can make something out of their children, but not out of them. They have the essence of greatness in them and I shall fight them and fight myself and the world and even God for them. They shall not refuse their destiny' " (315–16).

Moses' reading of the Book of Thoth redefines power as a dynamic force inherent in all nature and manifested in and accessible to those desirous of it, not a commodity located in the hands of an omnipotent god who parcels it out at will. The paradoxical coup d'etat is that Moses gets most of his power, not through the sacred, spoken Word of God, but from the written word. Mentu's knowledge of the Book of Thoth comes to him by way of oral tradition: " 'It was told by the father of the father of my father to the father of my father and the father of my father has told it to my father' " (73). Oral tradition, though travestied in this arabesque of begotten fathers, maintains, in and of itself, its credibility and revered status: Mentu speaks the truth. The book exists, and Moses is empowered by reading it, as Mentu said he would be. But the introduction of the written word as a source of power contends with the assumption that the spoken Word of the Judeo-Christian God is *the* source of all creativity, truth, meaning, and power. The spoken Word, as transcendental signified, is no longer absolute. The decentering of *the presence,* the ultimate referent, creates the possibility of a multiplicity of alternative world orders. The Presence in *Moses* is not only decentered, but is rendered questionable. Presence is described as Moses' creation.

It was Moses . . . who saw in the little puff of white smoke that rose from the incense on the altar the symbol of the Presence behind the clouds on the crest of the holy mountain and he developed the smoke into a thick white mass that hung stationary and huge above the altar for as long as the ceremony lasted. It made the voice of the unseen Moses speaking behind the altar seem like the voice of God. . . . So when Moses lifted his hand the smoke of the incense ceased to be smoke. It became the Presence. If it was not the actual Presence, then it enclosed and clothed the Presence. Finally the smoke itself was deified. It was not understood so it became divine. (150–51)

Hurston demystifies God as she demystifies religion. She triumphs over what Wole Soyinka describes as the "anti-terrestrialism" of Judeo-Christianity, which dichotomizes heaven and earth and vitiates the significance of the chthonic realm in the cosmic totality (3, 4). In her apotheosis of Moses is symbolized the unity and continuity of the upper and lower regions, the divine and mundane, the spiritual and physical, and the infinite and temporal. When Moses descends into the river at Koptos in search of the Book of Thoth, he enters the continuum of time and travels to the underworld, the chthonic realm of regeneration, transition, and transformation. Empowered to enchant the heavens, earth, and the abyss, Moses calls upon the powers he gained in the underworld to guide the Hebrews to their destiny. A human being with extraordinary powers, with one foot on a mountain and the other upon a deathless snake in the deep, Moses personifies the belief that every individual is divine and is an integral and potent factor in the cosmic totality. Hurston thus places human destiny in human hands, removing God, the Presence, from the center of human affairs.[11]

As God as Presence is decentered and questioned, the rhetoric with which racist white America buoys itself up is also deconstructed. White Americans, as a chosen people with a manifest destiny who see themselves as the image of God, grant themselves the same superior status they would grant their God. Hurston lambasts racist interpretations of biblical doctrine, characters, and stories and the application of those interpretations in modern American society. As Hurston creates Moses in her own image and endows him with an African American folk sensibility and an inner urge for self-empowerment, she questions both the concept of God and whites as ultimate referents and authorities. In fact, Hurston retells the Moses story in such a way that both God and whites are dependent upon Moses—an African Asian.

*Moses* questions the judiciousness of Blacks in embracing the Judeo-Christian God and the utility of their stooping and bowing at the foot of Anglo-American civilization and culture. It also disputes the wisdom and vision of Black organizations and their leaders. In vain, the Hebrew intelligentsia in *Moses* organize a meeting to protest Pharaoh's new decrees. Amram agrees to join the delegation formed to meet with Pharaoh, but not with any faith that the protests would do any good. He tells Caleb, " 'You all talk like somebody else made these laws and Pharaoh don't know nothing about 'em. He makes 'em his own self and he's glad when we come tell him they hurt' " (15). Negotiating with "the oppressor" is self-defeating. Begging others for just treatment is a show of weakness, and worshipping the goods and gods of the oppressor is sheer folly. Just as gods serve the people who make them, people cannot look to their oppressor for justice.

Fredric Jameson writes that literature is "a weaker form of myth or a later stage of ritual." He concludes "that in that sense all literature, no matter how weakly, must be informed by what we have called a political unconscious, that all literature must be read as a symbolic meditation on the destiny of community" (70). As such, all literature, then, is to some extent visionary and prophetic. Most critics of *Moses,* however, do not see the novel in that light. Blyden Jackson states, "If there was meant to be a lesson for the black leadership of Hurston's day in *Moses,* it is difficult to say of what that lesson was intended to consist. Hurston was no social visionary. She was neither another Percy Shelley nor another Karl Marx hypothesizing terms, loose or precise, for an earthly paradise. It was much more of the guild of Aristophanes and Gilbert and Sullivan—all, like her, conservatives—to which she belonged. Consequently, allegory though it is, *Moses* is also satire" (xvii). This passage implies that because *Moses* is satire as well as allegory, it cannot be visionary. The summoning of Shelley and Marx as social visionaries evokes the stereotypical, elitist, and masculinist image of the quintessential intellectual. Hurston is at her most visionary in *Moses.* The vision she has, though, is problematic and troublesome to many. She does not envision an earthly paradise because, according to her experience and philosophy, utopia does not nor ever will exist—not for Blacks, not for any people. Democracy, equality, and justice, like freedom, are never and will never be absolute and constant states of human existence. Human nature defies it. Through her depiction of an autonomous Moses and Moses' hope for an independent, just, and self-determining Israel, Hurston, nevertheless, gives a glimpse into the possibilities of human existence. Moses' "vision of destiny for Israel" is symbolized by the tablets he brings down from Mount Sinai. They represent freedom and self-government: "They had something of the essence of divinity expressed in order. They had the chart and compass of behavior. They need not stumble into blind ways and injure themselves. This was bigger than Israel itself. It comprehended the world. Israel could be a heaven for all men forever, by these sacred stones" (285). The Aarons and Miriams and Ta-Phars of the world, however, are a stumbling block to such a heaven, to such "an earthly paradise."

Moses sees freedom as "the biggest thing that God ever made." But he learns that it is not something one individual could give another. And it is not something that, once acquired, would maintain itself. "'This freedom is a funny thing,'" Moses concludes. "'It ain't something permanent like rocks and hills. It's like manna; you just got to keep on gathering it fresh every day. If you don't, one day you're going to find you ain't got none no more'" (327). Just as the Hebrews in Goshen awakened to find themselves under the heel of Pharaoh, Africans found themselves in strange lands under the yoke of European imperialists. They too yearned for freedom, but, like the Hebrews, were afflicted with a slave mentality that manifested itself in envy, bitterness, self-contempt, self-pity, and despair. Hurston believes that the salvation of Blacks, like the Hebrews, was not to be found in the rallying cry of unity, but in a philosophy of resistance and self-reliance.[12] Leaders could not free the masses anymore than Moses could. Like Moses, they could only help to create the opportunity for freedom.

Through a Signifying and parodic inversion of African, Eastern, and Western canonical and cultural texts, Zora Neale Hurston revises her individual experience and the collective experience of Black people. From the resulting intertextuality, Hurston creates a new myth that is transforming and empowering. In *Moses* she rejects Western epistemologies and symbologies and situates African-based cultural traditions at the center of this newly envisioned cosmology. Vehemently resisting identification of African peoples as the downtrodden of the earth, Hurston transforms a people's suffering from a potentially disabling experience to an empowering one. This reclamation and reinterpretation of the legends of Moses and the Hebrews resist and subvert conventional, Western notions of power and empowerment.[13] Told from Hurston's standpoint, the Moses legend produces new moral imperatives that speak directly to the African American masses and African American leadership: the goal is equal opportunity, not equality; and emphasis is placed on the individual as the basic social unit, not the group. If self-respect and self-reliance is cultivated in the individual, then the group will be strong and the nation will survive and continue.

# 6

## Politics of Self: Ambivalences, Paradoxes, and Ironies of Race, Color, Sex, Class, and Gender

---

I got an overwhelming complex about my looks before I was grown, and it was very hard for a long time for me to believe that any man really cared for me.

        —Letter to Burroughs Mitchell

A strong, resourceful individual, Zora Neale Hurston has become a model of resistance. She is often evoked as the exceptional Black woman who, by dint of will, transcended the barriers of economic deprivation, racial prejudice, and gender and class discrimination to become a woman of remarkable achievement. Hurston, like other "exceptional" Black women, is revered as a survivor instead of mourned as a victim. The fact that she distinguished herself in spite of her circumstances implies her adaptive capacity and her skills at coping and surviving. Assessments of Hurston's life and work sometimes explore survival strategies and coping mechanisms but seldom explore the psychological and spiritual conflicts of her interior life. The lack of attention to this facet of Black women's lives is problematic, as bell hooks observes: "I was profoundly discouraged by the many forces colluding to support the myth of the strong super-black woman, and it seemed that it would be impossible to compel recognition of black woman's exploitation and oppression. It is not that black women have not been and are not strong; it is simply that this is only a part of our story, a dimension, just as the suffering is another dimension—one that has been most unnoticed and unattended to" (*Talking Back* 152–53). Though Hurston defied Western, patriarchal hegemony and developed her own individual standpoint, it was not easy, and she was not unaffected by the struggle. She was no victim, but she suffered the African American anxiety of double consciousness and the pain of

Black womanhood. Hurston was an individual in a society that ignored and as often actively annihilated the lives of Black women. The effects of this adverse relationship with the larger society on Hurston are virtually unexplored. These effects constitute an unattended story of pain. Between the idea of "the hero" and "the victim" lies the sphere of Black women's consciousness in which strategies of survival are developed and patterns of resistance take root. Also embedded there is a cache of pained memory.

Hurston's texts raise many questions surrounding "the central conflicts" of her life as a Black woman and the lives of Black women in general. No matter how bravely and admirably one deals with the import of institutionalized marginalization, one is never unaffected by it. Hurston dealt with the central conflicts of her life masterfully, but those conflicts were never completely resolved. She survived. She soared. But she was not unscathed. The traumatic experience of negotiating a world wherein one is designated "other" is usually glossed over in examinations of Hurston's life and work. Probing analyses of Hurston's inner self could yield further knowledge useful to those who inherit and continue legacies of struggle and resistance. For, ultimately, one's self-image, self-concept, and sense of self-worth determine the nature of struggle, the vigor of resistance, and the resolve for empowerment.

• • •

Feminist and womanist scholarship emphasize and laud the mother-daughter relationship Hurston described in her autobiography.[1] Lucy Potts Hurston is seen as a nurturing, inspiring, and protective presence in Hurston's life. Lucy Hurston's oft-quoted exhortation that her children "jump at de sun" functions as an icon symbolizing the sacred union between mother and daughter. Hurston's mother can certainly be seen as one source of Hurston's self-confidence, self-determination, and achievement. But John Hurston also figures significantly in his daughter's sense of self. Depicted more as a negative force, in Hurston's life as well as in the life of Hurston's mother, John Hurston symbolizes the various faces of patriarchal oppression. Nevertheless, Hurston was greatly influenced by him—for good and ill. Her relationship with her father, as described in her autobiography, appears to be the locus from which emanates much of the conflict in Hurston's sense of self. Contradictions and ironies of race, color, and class characterize conflicts in her personal life. These conflicts are manifested in the ruptures and sutures that mark the body of Hurston's work.

Although John Hurston is recognized as the source of Hurston's portrayal of the folk preacher, this is only one aspect of his influence. Hurston's admiration of her father's gray-green eyes and light skin color is reflected in the descriptions of her characters. Her treatment of those characters can also be traced to his treatment of Hurston, particularly as seen in contradistinction to his treatment of her sister Sarah. The second daughter of a father who had eyes only for the first must have been painful enough. "A little of my sugar used to sweeten his coffee," Hurston related (*Dust Tracks* 27); so she was always threatened by how his impatience with her might express itself. (Black) feminist and womanist critics have long argued that race, sex, and class, as "interlocking systems of domination," must be considered in any analysis of the lives and works of African American women.[2] Although she agrees, bell hooks argues for the primacy of feminist movement against sexism since "it is that form of domination we are most likely to encounter in an ongoing way in everyday life" (*Talking Back* 21). Her point is well taken in light of Hurston's childhood experiences. Hurston wrote that even though her father didn't want another girl baby, at least he "didn't tie me in a sack and drop me in the lake, as he probably felt like doing" (*Dust Tracks* 28). The statement evidences recognition of a power dynamic inscribed in a relationship that is at once parent-child and male-female. Amazingly, Hurston never completely surrendered before this kind of intimidation.

Perhaps the most profound and devastating manifestation of her father's feelings was his out-and-out rejection of her in the face of his ostentatious embracing of Sarah. Alienated, an outsider inside her own family, Hurston was forced to be a spectator of, as opposed to a participant in, the father-daughter bonding she longed for, but learned to repress. Hurston wrote that Sarah was her father's favorite, his feminine ideal, and he spoiled her: "What was it Papa's girl-baby wanted to eat? She wanted two dolls instead of one? Bless her little heart! . . . Papa delighted in putting the finest and the softest shoes on her dainty feet; the fluffiest white organdy dresses with the stiffest ribbon sashes. 'Dat's a switching little gal!' He used to gloat" (98–99). She had gold rings and earrings and music lessons she did not want. "When I begged for music lessons, I was told to dry up before he bust the hide on my back" (99). Although she was the second daughter, unwanted, ill treated, even abandoned by her father, Hurston claimed it "did not matter" (100).

Such treatment of a child by a parent, of a daughter by her father, leaves its marks. Though she resembled her father, whom she described as a handsome man, Hurston thought of herself as unattractive. In describing her prep class at Morgan College, she portrayed herself as the ugly duckling: "Good-looking, well-dressed girls from Baltimore's best Negro families were classmates of mine. . . . And here I was, with my face looking like it had been chopped out of a knot of pine wood with a hatchet on somebody's off day, sitting up in the middle of all this pretty" (149–50). Even as a woman who was "by all accounts a handsome woman," writes Hemenway, Hurston did not consider herself attractive (314). In his discussion of *Seraph on the Suwanee,* he alludes to a letter Hurston wrote to her editor, explaining the psychological and emotional makeup of Arvay, the novel's protagonist. In her explanation Hurston draws on her personal experiences to demonstrate Arvay's character. The comparison indicates Hurston's problematic self-image: "Though brash enough otherwise, I got an overwhelming complex about my looks before I was grown, and it was very hard for a long time for me to believe that any man really cared for me. I set out to win my fight against this feeling, and I did. I don't care how homely I am now. I know that it doesn't really matter, and so my relations with others are easier" (310).

The inferiority complex instilled in Hurston at home, intensified by the cult of white beauty and white supremacy outside home, resulted in a variation of what might be described as the Pecola complex.[3] Made to feel ugly and valueless by the male authority in the home, the central figure of patriarchal domination through whom is sifted external ideologies of beauty and femininity as well as masculinity, Hurston was rendered vulnerable to oppressive and destructive forces in the larger society. As bell hooks argues, "experiencing exploitation and oppression in the home made one feel all the more powerless when encountering dominating forces outside the home" (*Talking Back* 21). After being told and made to feel that her absence was preferable, after suffering willful abandonment at the hands of her father, a primary caregiver, everything else that happened to her might very well have been described as "duck soup."

• • •

When she left the protective bosom of Eatonville for school in Jacksonville, Hurston had a momentous discovery: "I was now a little colored girl. I found it out in certain ways. In my heart as well as in the mirror, I became a fast brown—warranted not to rub nor run" ("How It Feels to Be Colored Me" 153). *Fast:* firmly fixed; stuck; stable; firmly loyal; tenacious; wild; "daringly unconventional, esp. in sexual matters <a ——— woman>; quickness of motion; agile of mind; *esp:* quick to learn." What did being "a fast brown" mean to "a little colored girl" who came to realize what being "a little colored girl" meant to everybody else?[4] In what "certain ways" did Hurston find out? Colored and a girl and unwanted as both, she was quick to learn of her imposed multimarginal status. Beneath her strident condemnation of systems of institutionalized oppression in the essay "Crazy for This Democracy," one hears plaintive undertones of hurt and the outrage of an adult looking back, from an emotional distance, at the scars of her child self:

> These Jim Crow laws have been put on the books for a purpose, and that purpose is psychological. It has two edges to the thing. By physical evidence, back seats in trains, back-doors of houses, exclusion from certain places and activities, to promote in the mind of the smallest white child the conviction of First by Birth, eternal and irrevocable like the place assigned to the Levites by Moses over the other tribes of the Hebrews. Talent, capabilities, nothing has anything to do with the case. Just FIRST BY BIRTH.
>
> No one of darker skin can ever be considered an equal. Seeing the daily humiliations of the darker people confirms the child in its superiority, so that it comes to feel it the arrangement of God. By the same means, the smallest dark child is to be convinced of its inferiority, so that it is to be convinced that competition is out of the question, and against all nature and God. (167–68)

Hurston was not "First by Birth," being neither male nor first-born female. And as an African American, she was not "First by Birth." Hurston, like most Black women, resisted and struggled against the negative psychological effects engendered by Black female marginalization in white and patriarchal social structures. William H. Grier and Price Cobbs comment on this deep-rooted psychic trauma, stating how external controlling images define the Black woman out of existence:

> In this country, the standard is the blonde, blue-eyed, white skinned girl with regular features. . . . The girl who is black has no option in the matter of how much she will change herself. Her blackness is the antithesis of a creamy white skin, her lips are thick, her hair is kinky and short. She is, in fact, the antithesis of American beauty. However beautiful she might be in a different setting with different standards, in this country she is ugly. However loved and prized she may be by her mother, family, and community, she has no real basis of feminine attractiveness on which to build a sound feminine narcissism. (33)

Hurston recognized the battle she had to wage to develop and protect a positive self-image. She set out to win the fight against her "overwhelming complex" about her looks. In this battle, Hurston's mother and the community played life-affirming roles. Her own resolve was also a major factor. So as an adult, Hurston, for the most part, displayed a positive, psychologically healthy sense of herself: "I do not coyly admit to a touch of the tarbrush to my Indian and white ancestry. You can consider me Old Tar-Brush in person if you want to. I am a mixed-blood, it is true, but I differ from the party line in that I neither consider it an honor nor a shame" (*Dust Tracks* 235). Zora Neale Hurston was proud of who she was, what she was, and whence she came. The nurturing bosom of Eatonville, Florida, instilled in her that sense of pride and, no doubt, was recalled countless times to reaffirm and revalidate her self-worth in the world beyond Eatonville. Writing essays such as "How It Feels to Be Colored Me" and descriptions of herself as "Old Tar-Brush in person" suggest that Hurston was comfortable in her black skin. The numerous works in which she celebrated African American culture attest to the pride she had in her folk roots and the joy she found in being Black. She considered whites colorless and pitiable. She held in contempt the "pink-toes" who felt they were owed something "just for being blond" (*Dust Tracks* 343). Light-skinned Blacks who did consider their color and ancestry as something honorable were just as contemptible in her sight.

Even though Hurston condemned color prejudice and discrimination, she practiced it. Darwin Turner is one of few critics who address this paradox:

> Upon the deformed figure of Mrs. Turner, Miss Hurston vented her disgust with middle-class Negroes who distrust or dislike their race. She ridiculed Mrs. Turner's hatred of black-skinned people, Booker T. Washington, Negro doctors and businessmen, and African features. Paradoxically, Miss Hurston was guilty of some of the very prejudices for which she condemned Mrs. Turner. In *Jonah's Gourd Vine* and in *Dust Tracks*, a reader discerns Miss Hurston's obvious admiration of her father's gray eyes and fair skin. Furthermore, she described her protagonist Janie as a fair-skinned woman with "fine hair." In short, despite her impassioned defense of African features as a matter of principle, Miss Hurston's personal biases positioned her nearer to Mrs. Turner than she admitted. (*Minor Chord* 106–7)

Vashti Lewis contends that "the mulatto female as major character" began to decline in significance in Hurston's work with the publication of *Their Eyes Were Watching God* (127). Yet, the "mulatto" female's very presence is, in and of itself, highly suspect in Hurston's work. Also suspect is the male and female "mulatto" as main figures in all of Hurston's novels except *Seraph on the Suwanee* and "Herod the Great," in which the main characters are white. In *Jonah's Gourd Vine*, Reverend John Pearson is "mulatto," as is Janie in *Their Eyes* and Moses in *Moses, Man of the Mountain*. In none of her novels does she cast an African American with typically African features as the main character. Hurston's characterizations reflect the concern over race and color that typified the Harlem Renaissance. Gloria Hull addresses these issues, with particular reference to other women writers of the period:

> Color defined the Harlem Renaissance. Philosophically and practically, it was a racial movement whose overriding preoccupation can be seen in all of its aspects and manifestations—the name of the era (where Harlem is synonymous with Black), its debates and manifestos (Locke's "The New Negro" and Hughes's "The Negro Artist and the Racial Mountain"), book titles (Georgia Johnson's *Bronze*, Cullen's *Color, The Ballad of the Brown Girl*, and *Copper Sun*), artistic illustrations (the African motifs of Aaron Douglas and Gwendolyn Bennett), and so on. Indeed, during the 1920s, Alice Dunbar-Nelson, Angelina Grimké, and Georgia Douglas Johnson were participating in a literary movement that was, by self-definition, race oriented. How they were affected by this general reality emerged from their own specific realities as black women. Racial attitudes of the larger society, Harlem Renaissance dictates, and personal experience all combined to determine the handling of color in their writings. (17)

Hurston's handling of color must be examined according to the same contexts, particularly that of personal experience. Her predilection for "the mulatto" in her writings might very well be traced to her adoration of her father. Though Hurston feigned indifference to him, she admired him—his gray-green eyes, light skin, and his strong build. She was proud that she "looked more like him than any child in the house" (*Dust Tracks* 28). She wrote that her maternal grandmother never had a good word for her or him and resented her for "being the spitting image of dat good-for-nothing yaller bastard" (72). Hurston boasted of the similarities she shared with her father, both physically and idiosyncratically. His wandering and adventuresome spirit became hers as did his genius for sermonic poetry. "Some children are just bound to take after their fathers in spite of women's prayers," she wrote decidedly (32).

Though Hurston resented and resisted her father's ideal of beauty and femininity, she internalized it. The interior space where her childhood dreams were realized was also the secret sphere where she vested herself with the "beauty" and behavior that would win her the protective love of her father, the archetypal man in her life. The mulatto image as one of beauty and privilege is a specter in many of her works. This image of the coveted, ideal woman subtly manifests itself throughout Hurston's work. As Hull emphasizes, "the matter of color has always had a heavier impact on black women. Like [Claude] McKay, men rhapsodized about their teasing browns, chocolate-to-the-bones, and lemon yellows, but many still preferred to marry the paler shades. Deep historical links between fair color and beauty, and fair color and class affiliation, are not easily broken" (17).[5] Mary Helen Washington also attests that "the color/hair problem has cut deep into the psyche of the black woman": "The subject of the black woman's physical beauty occurs with such frequency in the writing of black women that it indicates they have been deeply affected by the discrimination against the shade of their skin and the texture of their hair. In almost every novel or autobiography written by a black woman, there is at least one incident in which the dark-skinned girl wishes to be either white or light-skinned with 'good' hair" (xvii, xiv–xv). In Hurston's work, "mulatto" and white characters are usually cast in a fairy-tale-like ambience and have a spellbinding effect on those around them. Their features become fetishes as Hurston's writings reveal a fixation on light or white skin and, particularly, a fixation on "righteous moss," that is, straight or "fine" hair texture, as the short story "Muttsy" demonstrates. In this story, Pinkie Jones is compared to little Red Riding Hood and depicted as Sleeping Beauty.[6] Pinkie is described as having brown skin, but her brown skin pales in the light of her "white-folks haih" and a would-be suitor's allusion to her as a "Pink Mama," transforming Pinkie into a fairy-tale "beauty." "Pinkie had everything she needed in her face" (20). And her name is indicative of her manner: pure, innocent, delicate. That made her the envy of all women and the desire of all men. But only the man of means, Muttsy Owens, wins out. He slips a diamond ring on her finger as she sleeps, later marries her, and vows to Ma, madam of the house where Pinkie lives, " 'Ah'm gointer to treat her white too' " (34). Muttsy treasured in Pinkie what all the other men desired and what all the women resented: her assumed virginity—the men referred to her as "pig meat"—and her "white-folks haih." The revelers in Ma's house are awed when Pinkie's hair slips down as Muttsy chivalrously escorts her away from the boisterous, antagonistic company and the smoke-filled room:

> Pinkie's hair was slippin' down. She felt it, but her self-consciousness prevented her from catching it and down it fell in a heavy roll that spread out and covered her nearly to the waist. . . .
> "Phew!" cried Bluefront, "dat baby sho got some righteous moss on her keg—dass reg'lar 'nearrow mah Gawd tuh thee' stuff." He made a lengthy gesture with his arms as if combing out long, silky hair.

"Shux," sneered Ada in a moist, alcoholic voice. "Dat ain't nothin'
mah haih useter be so's ah could set on it."
      There was general laughter from the men.
      "Yas, ah know it's de truth!" shouted Shorty. "It's jes' ez close tuh yo'
head *now* ez ninety-nine is tuh uh hund'ed."
      "Ah'll call Muttsy tuh you," Ada threatened.
      "Oh, 'oman, Muttsy ain't got you tuh study 'bout no mo' 'cause he's
parkin' his heart wid dat li'l chicken wid white-folks haih. Why, dat li'l
chicken's foot would make you a Sunday face." (27–28)

Shorty fears no reprisal in maligning Ada. He knows, as does Ada,
that men protect only their heart's desire. Hurston had learned this
too. She related instances in which her father would step in to prevent
her mother from chastising Sarah. If her mother organized a "whipping
purge," her father might ignore it "until he found that Sarah was mixed
up in it. Then he would lay aside the county newspaper which he was
given to reading, and shout at Mama, 'Dat'll do! Dat'll do, Lulu! . . .' I
have seen Papa actually snatch the switch out of Mama's hand when
she got to Sarah" (99–100).
      Since intraracial color prejudice was a major issue during the Renais-
sance, it can be argued that Hurston, cultural anthropologist and ethnographic writer, simply portrayed Black self-contempt, a result of
internalized white standards of beauty. Hurston had proclaimed it her
moral duty to paint "a true picture of Negro life." "Literature and
other arts are supposed to hold up the mirror to nature" ("What White
Publishers Won't Print" 173). But all representation is still interpretation. And as Fredric Jameson suggests, "Interpretation proper . . . always
presupposes, if not a conception of the unconscious itself, then at least
some mechanism of mystification or repression" (60). In "Muttsy,"
Hurston gives an accurate depiction of negative self-images among
African Americans, but she also reveals her own repressed enthrallment
with the cult of white beauty.
      With the evocation of characters cast in the image of Snow White, a
definite equation evolves: Female beauty equals "fair" skin; long, "fine"
hair; good fortune; and privilege. All of these images and associations
are found in Hurston's roll call of her Morgan State classmates:

Ethel Cummings, the daughter of a very successful lawyer, Bernice
Naylor, whose father was a big preacher, the Hughes girls, Bernice and
Gwendolyn, who were not only beautiful, but whose family is distin-
guished in the professions all over America, Mary Jane Watkins of New
York, now a dentist, and considered the most sex-appealing thing, with
her lush figure and big eyes and soft skin—all of the girls in my class

passed for pretty. . . . Rosa Brown was in that class too. She had not only lovely eyes set in a cameo-like face, but shining, beautiful black curls that fell easily to her waist. She has done well by herself, too. She is now married to Tanner Moore, a prosperous lawyer of Philadelphia. Town house, cars and country place, and things like that. (149–50)

These prototypical "beauties" Hurston describes prefigure Janie Crawford in *Their Eyes*. Janie, a "quadroon," is considered beautiful and deserving of nothing but life's best. Her grandmother marries her off to the boorish Logan Killicks because he has a sound reputation, sixty acres, and represents protection. Killicks, deciding he has "spoilt" Janie enough, plans to put her behind a plow to help cultivate the sixty acres that symbolize middle-class security. But like deus ex machina, Jody Starks happens along to save the damsel in distress from what should never be the fate of a beauty. "He didn't look her way nor no other way except straight ahead, so Janie ran to the pump and jerked the handle hard while she pumped. It made a loud noise and also made her heavy hair fall down. So he stopped and looked hard, and then he asked her for a cool drink of water" (47). Janie runs off with Jody but finds that she has been moved from a frying pan to a better-oiled skillet as the chauvinistic, bourgeois, egotistical Jody really attempts to make of her the baby doll he takes her for, the kind that talks and walks whenever wound by its owner. But this, neither, is the fate of a beauty. Jody dies and Janie is given the opportunity to realize her true destiny in a romantic relationship with Verigible Tea Cake Woods.

Janie, like Pinkie, is the idol of men, and men know their responsibilities toward her. As Coker tells Hicks, who is smitten with Janie at first sight, " 'It takes money tuh feed pretty women. Dey gits a lavish uh talk' " (58). The men of Eatonville cannot feed Janie, but they can marvel and lust after her. Aware of their desires, Jody forces Janie to keep her hair covered.

> This business of the head-rag irked her endlessly. But Jody was set on it. Her hair was NOT going to show in the store. It didn't seem sensible at all. That was because Joe never told Janie how jealous he was. He never told her how often he had seen the other men figuratively wallowing in it as she went about things in the store. And one night he had caught Walter standing behind Janie and brushing the back of his hand back and forth across the loose end of her braid ever so lightly so as to enjoy the feel of it without Janie knowing what he was doing. . . . That night he ordered Janie to tie up her hair around the store. That was all. (86–87)

Tied though it was, Janie's "heavy hair" continually falls to the great awe and pleasure of the townsmen.

The "heavy hair" of Janie and Pinkie (like that of the Morgan State classmate) falls to their waists enough to give them both whiplash. The narrative's deep structure suggests an underlying Rapunzel complex. Hurston makes a fetish of this supposed essence of "woman's glory" as she makes it a symbol of beauty, femininity, and sexual passion. As women and their sexuality are to be controlled in patriarchal social systems, their hair, a symbol of their sexuality, is to be controlled as well. It becomes an object of desire and repression as it becomes a symbol of liberation from domination. Janie's hair in her kerchief symbolizes Jody's tyranny over her, her womanness, and her sexuality. Only at his death is she freed. It is then that Janie, recalling a childhood promise, focuses on herself and feels her freedom: "Years ago, she had told her girl self to wait for her in the looking glass. It had been a long time since she had remembered. Perhaps she'd better look. She went over to the dresser and looked hard at her skin and features. The young girl was gone, but a handsome woman had taken her place. She tore off the kerchief from her head and let down her plentiful hair. The weight, the length, the glory was there. She took careful stock of herself, then combed her hair and tied it back up again. Then she starched and ironed her face" and ceremoniously partook in mourning the source of her repressed self (134–35).[7] Hurston writes in "How It Feels to Be Colored Me" that when *she* looked in the mirror, she found a "fast brown" little colored girl. Oddly enough, through a sort of magical alchemy, the images peering out of the mirror of Hurston's women figures never look like her. Like Pecola Breedlove, something fantasized is reflected. For Pecola, it is the bluest eye; for Hurston, the heaviest hair.

The white image of female beauty is pervasive. Hurston uses a good deal of ink in drawing the presumably arresting and captivating portraits of the Meserve family and friends in *Seraph on the Suwanee*. Her fascination with the mystique of white beauty is best evidenced in the narrator's description of Felicia Corregio, Kenny Meserve's date. Everybody wanted to know, "Who is that pretty girl he's got with him?"

> The girl attracted a lot of attention first, because she had an unbelievable mass of curly black hair that poured and tumbled nearly to her waist, and glittered in the sun, in a company of almost universal bobbed heads. Men like hair and they looked. Then she was fresh and tender-looking. They noted that she was really built from her neck on down. The men looked at that and the women took in her clothes. She was dressed in a white sweater suit, topped by a perky white tam over one eye, white buckskin oxfords, and a loose-fitting light-weight white coat.

It was just the right thing for her dark hair and eyes. Brilliant big eyes, and a high natural pink in her cheeks. (207)

Felicia is "mixed"—of Portuguese and Anglo-American parentage—as is Janie and Pinkie. So she gets all the authorial attention due her. The features of Black women of dark hue, who are described as attractive but do not fit Hurston's stereotype of female beauty, are described in brief and usually only in respect to their color. Though Hurston's mother, for instance, "was considered the prettiest and the smartest black girl" on this side of the creek, Hurston paints her mother simply as "dark-brown Lucy Ann Potts" (*Dust Tracks* 14, 12). Whenever portraits of darker women are fleshed out, the details are less elaborate and effusive. Janie Kelsey in *Seraph* is figured as "a good-looking brown girl" (313). Described through Arvay's "Gulf-blue" eyes, her good looks are begrudgingly granted in a backhanded sort of way: "Janie now, that mixture of colors that she had on. Nothing that Angeline would have thought about picking out to wear at all. But strangely, they did not look funny on Janie. That cheap silk dress became her looks very well indeed. Her short hair was as straight as anybody's today and the way she had it fixed, it improved her looks. Janie was a pretty colored girl and good-hearted. . . . How did colored people get their hair straightened? There were no kinky-haired women these days" (317–18).

Due to the successful reign of Madame C. J. Walker, Black women could have straight, if not "fine," hair that had the promise of transforming the darkest Black woman into "a beauty"—almost. Hurston attempts such a transformation with one of her characters in *Their Eyes*:

> Daisy is walking a drum tune. You can almost hear it by looking at the way she walks. She is black and she knows that white clothes look good on her, so she wears them for dress up. She's got those big black eyes with plenty shiny white in them that makes them shine like brand new money and she knows what God gave women eyelashes for, too. Her hair is not what you might call straight. It's negro hair, but it's got a kind of white flavor. Like the piece of string out of a ham. It's not ham at all, but it's been around ham and got the flavor. It was spread down thick and heavy over her shoulders and looked just right under a big white hat. (105–6)

Everything black about Daisy is counterpoised and qualified by something white.[8] But it's still not enough to get her the attending "class" privileges that the genuine article is destined to receive. After all, she's not "pig meat." She has only the flavor of it. The men on Joe Starks's porch get into a lying contest about what they will all do just for Daisy. The result is Jim Weston's offer to treat Daisy to a pickled pig's foot, which he intends to purchase with a borrowed dime. But Daisy does not get even that. Lum sets out to fill the order, but discovers that " 'de pig feets is all gone!' " (109). Jim can't even provide Daisy with a dime's worth of pig meat; "uh lavish uh talk" will have to do.

Zipporah, otherwise known as the black Mrs. Moses in *Moses, Man of the Mountain,* is no exception. She is a woman of means due to her father's position as priest and due to the booty Moses seizes from various opponents. However, Moses, unlike Jody, is not interested in seeing his wife on a throne and does not go out of his way to provide her with the greater material wealth she desires. Moses does not go out of his way to provide her with even himself. Except for what "womanly comforts" she can supply him, he's not interested in her.

. . .

Hurston was at times awed by trappings of color, class, and privilege, much like Miriam before the Egyptian princess in *Moses.* In her treatment of race, color, sex, and class, what surfaces is the desire to experience, if only vicariously, the phenomenon of beauty and privilege as she fantasized it. This is not to suggest that Hurston longed "to be white" or bourgeois. These notions are not evidenced in her texts or in her life choices. But the fantasy of experiencing these phenomena is clearly projected. Hurston did not succumb to her complex about her looks, nor was she "a blind follower of that social code which approves arrogance toward one's assumed peers and inferiors but requires total psychological commitment to a subservient posture before one's supposed superiors," as Darwin Turner contends (*Minor Chord* 98). Given the ongoing battle Hurston waged against her feelings of inferiority, there could be no *total* psychological commitment to a *self-*annihilating social code.

Hurston's tendency to reject, repress, or mock the symbols or images that would negate her black, female identity testify to her struggle for self. For example, Hurston wrote that dolls caught hell around her. "They got into fights and leaked sawdust before New Year's. They jumped off the barn and tried to drown themselves in the lake. Perhaps, the dolls bought for me looked too different from the ones I made up myself. The dolls I made up in my mind, did everything. Those store-bought things had to be toted and helped around" (*Dust Tracks* 40). In rejecting the dolls, the child Zora rejected the classical symbol of female socialization in America. She refused to mother them, to sit still and make them new clothes. Young Zora, like Claudia in Toni Morrison's *Bluest Eye,* was confounded by the mystique surrounding this supposed object of beauty and adoration. Claudia recalled:

It had begun with Christmas and the gift of dolls. The big, the special, the loving gift was always a big, blue-eyed Baby Doll. From the clucking sounds of adults, I knew that the doll represented what they thought was my fondest wish. I was bemused with the thing itself, and the way it looked. What was I supposed to do with it? Pretend I was its mother?
. . . I had only one desire: to dismember it. To see of what it was made, to discover the dearness, to find the beauty, the desireability that had escaped me, but apparently only me. Adults, older girls, shops, magazines, newspapers, window signs—all the world had agreed that a blue-eyed, yellow-haired, pink-skinned doll was what every girl child treasured. "Here," they said, "this is beautiful, and if you are on this day 'worthy' you may have it." . . . I could not love it. But I could examine it to see what it was that all the world said was lovable. Break off the tiny fingers, bend the flat feet, loosen the hair, twist the head around. . . . Remove the cold and stupid eyeball, . . . take off the head, shake out the sawdust, crack the back against the brass bed rail. (19–21)

Neither Zora nor Claudia could identify with this image that reflected what they were not. Instead of love, contempt was generated. And with both children, the contempt for the dolls was transferred to contempt for the living replicas of the cold, pink plastic. Claudia confided, "I destroyed white baby dolls. But the dismembering of dolls was not the true horror. . . . The truly horrifying thing was the transference of the same impulses to little white girls. The indifference with which I could have axed them was shaken only by my desire to do so. To discover what eluded me: the secret of the magic they weaved on others. What made people look at them and say, 'Awwwww,' but not for me?" (22). In Hurston's world, her sister Sarah was the object of such adoration from her father. (Her mother, though a mere ninety pounds, was neither passive nor submissive, so did not qualify as an object of ideal beauty. She talked when she wished, not when wound.) In her narrative Hurston never directly expresses resentment nor animosity toward her sister. Yet resentment is suggested in the very denial of it: "It did not matter so much to me that Sarah was Papa's favorite" (100). And the animosity is revealed in the effort expended in dismembering Sarah's image as well as the image of feminine beauty and behavior sanctioned by her father. Hurston described the object of her father's "boundless joy" as small and undersized: "Sarah was diminutive. Even when she was small, you could tell that she never would grow much. She would be short like Papa's mother, and her own mother" (99). (By connecting Sarah with her mother, Hurston implied her own connection with her father.) Sarah was like the dolls Hurston resented and dismembered—helpless things to be "toted and helped around." They were weak, and in her arrogant defiance, Hurston developed an ideological and interpretive code that despised weakness in every form. Unlike Sarah, she did not need protection. Contrarily she would be the one to provide it.

Where Sarah is described as physically weak, John Hurston is described as morally and spiritually weak. At the instigation of his second wife, John Hurston strikes his beloved Sarah. "Neither Papa nor Sarah ever looked at each other in the same way again, nor at the world" (100). They are described as a pitiful pair. It was the strong self-dependent Zora, in Electra fashion, who, six years later, stepped in to avenge the diminutive Sarah and to protect the two-hundred-pound father, showing herself superior to both. She "paid the score off" by furiously beating her stepmother. Though she didn't ax the stepmother, Hurston "let fly" a hatchet at the neighbor who attempted to prevent the pulverizing of the (wicked) stepmother—the other object of her father's affection and generosity (102–3).

This repudiation of weakness maintained itself even in Hurston's adult life. It is especially reflected in her response to the prevailing ideology of "the Negro" as a pathological social problem. For Hurston, "the Negro," as defined by that discourse, had become a symbol of oppression and limitation, an object of scorn, one to be pitied and patronized. So everything associated with "the Negro" that smacked of helplessness, weakness, and timidity was to be likewise rejected, repressed, or mocked—slavery, Reconstruction, even *"the Negro."* Hurston asserted, "I maintain that I have been a Negro three times—a Negro baby, a Negro girl and a Negro woman," but presumed to have no idea of "what the Negro in America is like." She concluded, "There is no *The Negro* here" (*Dust Tracks* 237). Having italicized the term, Hurston implied her disassociation not from Negro people, per se, but from the concept of "the Negro." Her emphasis on the term itself suggests her rejection of the pathological stereotypes that defined Blacks as well as her refusal to acquiesce to the social construction of Blacks as a monolith.

Denial, as resistance, was born in the space where personal and familial history intersected in Hurston's life. Hurston's personal response to the pain of her father's neglect was denial, an attitude that allowed her some dignity and comfort. She utilized the same praxis of denial in responding to the pain of American racism. She defied identification as *the Negro*—a problem—just as she defied identification as *a Negro Woman*—a composite of pusillanimous identities. The received image of *the Negro,* constructed by racist America, was unacceptable. That of *a Negro Woman,* constructed by her father, was equally unacceptable. The statements Hurston made in the autobiography are, prima facie, reactionary. They erase Hurston as an African American and as an African American woman. They also point up her difficulty in dealing with issues of race, sex, and class as interlocking systems of domination. Hurston's refusal to assume these images as her identity, however, was not the ontological dilemma or nightmare it could have been, as it was for Emmaline in *Color Struck* and Emma Lou in Thurman's *The Blacker the Berry*. Emmaline and Emma Lou are tragic heroines who suffer from the Pecola complex. They both question their beauty as well as the motivations of those who are attracted to them. Though victims of color prejudice, they both practice it. Both lead confused, unfulfilled, and destructive lives. Instead of canceling herself out, as these fictional characters did, Hurston created another identity based on different criteria and definitions. If racist, patriarchal America were the truth, Hurston would be annihilated. Unlike Sarah, Pinkie, Janie Crawford, and their clones, Hurston was told in so many ways from so many sources that she did not have all she needed in her face. But in a system of individual merit, where "you got what your strengths brought you," she could then jump at the sun—and even become the sun in her own universe.

•   •   •

The ambivalences, paradoxes, and ironies that beset Hurston's standpoints on race, color, sex, and class also infuse her standpoint on gender issues. Hurston's assumptions about women and men and their respective roles in society are decidedly ambivalent. Though Hurston gloried in being a woman, she manifested a preference for attributes that are stereotypically male-identified, such as physical prowess and aggression, subdued emotion and rational thought, egotism and arrogance. Having imbibed the conventional politics that privilege male authority, Hurston acquired a predilection for stereotypically male paradigms of power that is reflected in her writings. The origin of Hurston's ambivalent stances in regard to gender construction and gender roles are traceable to the nexus of her personal, familial, and communal history. In the highly autobiographical "Isis," Grandma Potts, the voice of parental authority and tradition, tries her best to transform Isis from an "aggravatin'" "leven yeah ole gale" into a "lady." "Now there are certain things that Grandma Potts felt no one of this female persuasion should do—one was to sit with the knees separated, 'settin' brazen' she called it; another was whistling, another playing with boys. Finally, a lady must never cross her legs" (11). Isis, however, prefers to race and romp with the puppies, so defies her grandmother whenever she can. Even if she allows herself to be imposed upon and performs her "appropriate" role, she endeavors to have as much fun at it as possible. "Being the only girl in the family, of course she must wash the dishes, which she did in intervals between frolics with the dogs" (11). Young Zora in *Dust Tracks* is of like character. She is also cautioned against playing with boys and is warned to stay in a girl's place: "It was not ladylike for girls to play with boys. No matter how young you were, no good could come of the thing. . . . What was wrong with my doll-babies? Why couldn't I sit still and make my dolls some clothes?" she was asked. Hurston defiantly wrote, "I never did" (40).

Hurston rejected received ideologies of gender as they pertained to her. But at the same time, she found them acceptable for other women —an ironic but logical outcome. As he lavished attention on Sarah, treating her as though she were a baby doll, John Hurston's neglect of daughter Zora rendered her "other." Women and girls were treated like and behaved like Sarah. Zora was not her father's little doll, and her mother didn't want her to become a "mealy-mouthed rag doll." Hurston implied that her mother saw herself this way and was, therefore, also an example of what she was not and what she should not become. The distinctions John and Lucy Hurston made between their two girls engendered in Zora a polarized, gendered politics of power: girls were weak. Sarah might be cuddled and "lifted over puddles" and such. Zora would "come out more than conquer." For the child Zora, though, conquerors were male. In her community, they were men like Joe Clarke who founded a town. They were men like her legendary midwife-mentor, the old white man who defied lightning. In her childhood readings, they were Thor, Odin, Hercules, and David. "There were other thin books about this and that sweet and gentle little girl who gave up her heart to Christ and good works. Almost always they died from it, preaching as they passed. I was utterly indifferent to their deaths. . . . I didn't care how soon they rolled up their big, soulful, blue eyes and kicked the bucket. They had no meat on their bones" (*Dust Tracks* 54). She, however, had meat on her bones as did her father. She lionized his "two hundred pounds of bone and muscle." Big-boned, hale, and "extra-strong," she was like her father, the hero in her family. Hurston admittedly admired her father's physical prowess. The bigger-than-life notion she had of him as a child comes through in her portrayal of him as the strongest man in the village—"no man in the village could put my father's shoulders to the ground" (91)—and his perceived invincibility even before God. Though Hurston depicted her father as not so quick-witted as her mother, she still found and admired in him traits that characterize what she later formulated as her Dionysian ideal: adventuresomeness, physical strength, free-spiritedness, and poetical expression. Her sense of her father as the "purposeful wanderer" comes across in the romantic introduction she gave him in her autobiography: "Into this burly, boiling, hard-hitting, rugged-individualistic setting walked one day a tall, heavy-muscled mulatto who resolved to put down roots" (12).

Hurston's relationship with her father was of an oedipal nature. Though rebuffed, she longed for her father's affection. She showed resentment of her sister and jealousy toward her stepmother.[9] John Hurston's relationship with his daughter was profound and far-reaching. It significantly influenced Hurston's self-perception as it colored her relationships with other men and formed her perception of and relationship to women. In spite of his rejection of her, Hurston was still drawn to her father. She longed for her father's love and affection, however much she repressed those feelings. She loved him, identified with him, and strove to be like him. But she was a girl, and girls were not to behave like their fathers. However, the clash of parental ideologies created an aperture for her to be like her father. Having acquired the status of "other," and warned against becoming like her mother, Young Zora was more or less an androgynous agent—though not an entirely free one. Given the clearly demarcated and deeply entrenched lines between women and men and their respective roles in early twentieth-century American society, given the repressive nature of small, traditional communities, and given her own nature, Hurston's alternatives were limited. Not the ideal girl in her father's eyes, and encouraged by her mother to be aggressive, Hurston assumed a masculinist identity. She found conventionally male patterns of behavior more comfortable, more personally gratifying, and more rewarding. Boys accepted and admired her because she could "take a good pummeling" and not be a crybaby about it. And her midwife-mentor respected and praised her pluck. He would take her fishing and give her advice, talking to her as though she "were as grown as he" (*Dust Tracks* 39, 40).

Hurston could not win her father's love, so she resignedly contented herself with being like him. Refusing to settle for second place or to be second to anyone, she did her father one better. She rejected the caste of second-class daughter and resolved to become her father's equal in some ways and his superior in others. I do not assume here a love-hate relationship between Hurston and her father. What is most probable is a love-*hurt* relationship: a matter of unrequited love. The paternal influence in Hurston's politics of self has been minimized. But father-daughter relationships are as powerful and influencing as mother-daughter relationships. John Hurston's rejection of his daughter is as much a determining factor in her self-image and self-concept as her mother's nurturance. And his bigger-than-life impression on young Zora is not to be underestimated. Hurston's spurned love for her father led her to imitate the things about him she admired. In that way, she achieved a certain intimacy with him he could not deny her.

. . .

Generally speaking, Hurston's perspectives on gender were quite conventional and *du jour*. Her conceptions of women's and men's roles and her attitudes toward them, though not always transparent, are quite clear. Hurston admired women in some respects but, with few exceptions, did not hold them in high esteem. Like Maria Stewart, she criticized women for lacking an independent spirit, and she publicly railed against "the natural apathy of women, whether Negro or white, who vote as their husband do" (Hemenway 308). Women were the weaker sex and were to be validated through their relationships with (the right) men.[10] Two kinds of women are predominant in Hurston's texts: Those who are "good women" and have the good sense to know when they have a good man and those who were not good women, that is, petty, envious, and malicious. If they had a (good) man at all, they couldn't recognize it. If they could, they were candidates for possible redemption. They too could become seraphs.

In accordance with the genteel model of womanhood, women would be passive, moderately emotional, submissive—the gentler sex. In a letter that conveys her depression over the events of World War II, Hurston expressed these sentiments: "I see [hate] all around me every day. I am not talking of race hatred. Just hate. Everybody is at it. Kill, rend and tear! Women who are supposed to be the softening influence in life screaming for the kill" (Hemenway 300). That women were the "softening influence" is a pervasive truism in Hurston's work. Women are depicted as having the capacity to "forget all those things they don't want to remember, and remember everything they don't want to forget" (*Their Eyes* 9). That special capability allowed them to comfort men, who are more innately inclined to look at life matter-of-factly. Filling the young Moses with myth and lore, Mentu explains to him,

> "You see, male man was made with five strong senses to gather the truth of things and his mind is a threshing floor to clean his truth in. This is often an unhappy thing, for man sees himself as he really is. Thus he is made very miserable. But he does not destroy himself because the

female man was made with squint eyes so that she sees only those things which please her. And her threshing floor is cramped and cluttered. She cannot separate the wheat from the chaff. But she achieves a harvest that makes her happy. When she sees man fleeing from his bowl in horror of himself, she feeds him from her own dish and he is blindly and divinely happy. Ah, yes, the female companion of man has the gift of the soothing-balm of lies." (55–56)

Woman, then, is man's helpmeet. This is the conclusion Arvay Henson comes to as she recognizes and assumes her role as nurturer: "Her job was mothering. What more could any woman want and need? Hovering over her children and serving her husband Jim, was her privilege" (*Seraph* 351). "Unflattering attitudes about women occupy a more prominent position in . . . [*Seraph on the Suwanee*] than in any of the other Hurston works," remarks Lillie Howard. "The view that Hurston has her characters present is the traditional male one, and shows that women have been regarded as brainless, thoughtless, inferior, helpless wretches for many, many years" (*Zora Neale Hurston* 144). Howard takes special exception to several statements Jim Meserve makes, like the following: " 'Women folks don't have no mind to make up nohow. They wasn't made for that. Lady folks were just made to laugh and act loving and kind and have a good man to do for them all he's able, and have him as many boy-children as he figgers he'd like to have, and make him so happy that he's willing to work and fetch in every dad-blamed thing that his wife thinks she would like to have. That's what women are made for' " (*Seraph* 25).[11]

The traditional male view with which Howard takes exception is a controversial view in Hurston's work, yet it is a standpoint that is an integral part of Hurston's philosophical worldview. Hurston's fictional characters present a view of women (and men) that Hurston held herself. As I argued in chapter 5, when ego protrudes in Hurston's thought and work, it is castigated as "manliness" or "cockiness" or otherwise viewed as an eccentricity. David Headon judged Hurston's renunciation of "the dark days of slavery" and Reconstruction as rank "insensitivity," "callousness," and "cockiness," attitudes usually imputed to men. However, views and behaviors that are typically associated with men are integral components of Hurston's personality and the psychology of her characters. These attitudes evidence a patrilineal line of descent that is rarely acknowledged in Hurston and one that Hurston rarely acknowledged herself.

In *Tell My Horse*, Hurston compared the view of and treatment of women in Jamaica with those of women in the United States. Her conclusions about American women ring true with those of Jim Meserve:

It has been said that the United States is a large collection of little nations, each having its own ways, and that is right. But the thing that binds them all together is the way they look at women, and that is right, too. The majority of men in all the states are pretty much agreed that just for being born a girl-baby you ought to have laws and privileges and pay and perquisites. And so far as being allowed to voice opinions is concerned, why, they consider that you are born with the law in your mouth, and that is not a bad arrangement either. The majority of the solid citizens strain their ears trying to find out what it is that their womenfolk want so they can strain around and try to get it for them, and that is a *very* good idea and the right way to look at things. (57)

This construct of male-female relations denies Hurston's childhood experiences. Though born a girl baby, she had no such privilege. And far from being allowed to voice her opinions, she was directed to "dry up."

Hurston never questioned the chauvinistic and patriarchal values inherent in such views or what might be the consequences if womenfolk wanted something other than what is customary under patriarchal law. If such views are unflattering to women, they can well be read as unflattering to men, who are depicted as women's tools, as in the story "Spunk." There, Spunk Banks and Joe Kanty literally kill each other vying for Lena's love and avowed commitment. At Spunk's funeral, the townswomen sit wondering "who would be Lena's next" (8). An element of female power as subversion—"who's zooming who"—is suggested in "Spunk." However, this point of view is not the dominant one in Hurston's texts. More often than not, Hurston endowed women with a weak will and cast them in the stereotypical mode of emotional or financial dependents.

Men were made to protect and direct women and children. Portrayed as members of the stronger sex, they faced the world as it was and tamed it for self-aggrandizement and for the benefit of their dependents. More rational than women, they made definitive decisions with which everyone under their protection had to abide. Jody in *Their Eyes* declares, " 'Somebody got to think for women and chillun and chickens and cows' " (110). Jim throws his "long arm of protection" around Arvay, his "play-pretty," then he lays down the law: " 'Love and marry me and sleep with me. That is all I need you for. Your brains are not sufficient to help me with my work; you can't think with me. Let's get this thing straight in the beginning' " (35). When Moses decides he will lead Israel to Canaan, Zipporah's opinion is never sought. Moses tells her his plans and her role in them: " 'Per-

sonally, my carefree days are over for a long, long time. . . . And so far
as you are concerned, you have lost the husband you used to have. I'm
a leader now, and you'll have to suffer for it along with me' " (267).
Moses indulges himself in Zipporah's "little comforts and delights,"
but shares his thoughts and work with his father-in-law, Jethro. Moses,
as does Jethro, views women as bothersome, frivolous, intellectual
pygmies. When Moses summons the elders to discuss Israel's affairs,
he is "surprised to find a woman among them":

> "Who is the woman, Aaron?" Moses asked.
> "That's Miriam, my sister."
> "But what is she doing here? I have called the Elders to me on seri-
> ous business."

Aaron professes Miriam's gifts of prophecy and her usefulness to Israel's
cause. Moses resolves, " 'In that case we need her. Tell her to stay. She
would be useful in handling the women' " (171).

Only men, members of the more rational and serious-minded sex,
have the capacity to handle "serious business." Only they have the
mental stamina to remain focused on the business at hand. According
to the narrative voice in Moses, women's small-mindedness and super-
ficiality make them easily distracted. As soon as Mrs. Moses arrives on
the scene and dangles her bangles, the women "had no more interest
in prophecy and politics. They were still interested in the earrings of
Mrs. Moses and her sandals, and the way she walked and her fine-
twined colored linens" (273).

Though all men do not qualify, only men are depicted in leadership
roles. Four predominant male types emerge in Hurston's figurations
of men: those with ambitions of littleness like Aaron and Pharaoh in
Moses; self-made but humorless men like Logan Killicks and Jody Starks
in Their Eyes; hedonistic revelers of life like John Pearson in Jonah's Gourd
Vine and Tea Cake in Their Eyes; and real men who are the ideal blend-
ing of the industrious, self-made man and the hedonist: independent
and individualistic but public-spirited, responsible but visionary, and
compassionate but forceful. He is Moses in Moses, Jim Meserve in
Seraph, and Herod in "Herod the Great." Characterized by their amor
fati and their joy in the midst of challenge, these men are variations of
Hurston's Dionysian ideal.

The qualities these men possess, for Hurston, are attributes of the
ideal individual. These are the attributes that recommend Moses as a
leader and as a hero. In her discussion of Moses, Lillie Howard addresses
the Hebrews' consternation over Moses' identity and the motivation

behind his willingness to risk life and limb to help them: "The answer Hurston offers is that Moses is a MAN, a good man, who, unlike his peers, is not interested in money, position, and personal gain. Instead, he is interested in people, in human life, in justice, and he feels it his calling to help those less fortunate than he. Moses doesn't need to be a Hebrew to feel and to do all this. All he needs to be is a man" (120). Howard's description of Moses as "a man" speaks to his character as opposed to his biology. However, biology figures greatly in Moses' makeup. For the attributes inscribed in Hurston's ideal leaders and heroes are vested only in her male characters. Leader and man are conflated ideals. There are no heroic women in Hurston's novels. Janie has been accorded heroic status in *Their Eyes,* but only Jody is invested with agency and powers of leadership. In her ethnographic writings collected in *Sanctified Church,* Hurston touts Mother Catherine, a spiritual healer and leader, as one instance of an accountable woman leader. Hurston paints her portrait with majestic rhetoric and compares her to Catherine of Russia. Mother Catherine's "rod of office," a box of shaker salt, is comparable to Moses' "rod of power." As "fine" hair is, for Hurston, a feminine fetish, power, in the form of a "well-built" man, is a typically masculine one. Women whom Hurston perceives as powerful are either identified in typically masculinist terms or have attributes that are typically defined as masculine.

Big Sweet's larger-than-life depiction qualifies her for heroic status. Hurston's description of Big Sweet reads very much like a composite of Hurston's father and the legendary old white man who was her mentor: " 'Big Sweet? Humph! Tain't a man, woman nor child on this job going to tackle Big Sweet. If God send her a pistol she'll send him a man. . . . She ain't mean She don't bother nobody. She just don't stand for no foolishness, dat's all' " (*Dust Tracks* 187–88). Big Sweet is also cast in the stereotypical male role of protector. Hurston writes that what she had seen and heard in the sawmill camp made her feel "as timid as an egg without a shell" (188). So she sets out to win Big Sweet's friendship and the protection it could offer. Having been seduced and won over, Big Sweet vows to Hurston, " 'I aims to look out for you, too. Do your fighting for you' " (188). And like the men Hurston refers to in *Tell My Horse,* Big Sweet strains her ears trying to find out what Hurston wants. Hurston wants to collect folklore and Big Sweet helps in "a big way. She had no idea what I wanted with it, but if I wanted it, she meant to see to it that I got it" (188–89). Big Sweet might narrowly be conceived of as heroic because of her physical strength and her daring in protecting Hurston. But her daring is characterized more as temerity and her Signifying disposition as so much bravado. Hurston depicts Big Sweet as gullible and easily manipulated, traits unbefitting a hero(ine).

When Hurston has the opportunity to develop a female character of heroic stature, to question conventional gender roles, she does not. A novel of myth, legend, and reinterpretations of historical events, *Moses, Man of the Mountain* offered the most propitious circumstances for such characterization, and the character Miriam held the most promise. But Hurston does not take advantage of these opportunities. Miriam is ridiculed as a liar and a charlatan. Even as a leader of the Hebrew women, she is mocked. And her contribution to the Exodus, this mighty thing that had happened in the world, is trivialized as "the stumblings of a woman." Though Hurston embodies female characters like Arvay in *Seraph* with her own feelings of insecurity, she never inscribes female characters with her own notions of independence and empowerment. Because of the received notions of female identity Hurston imbibed in childhood and her resulting ambivalent attitudes toward women's roles and characters, women, as a political entity, do not explicitly figure into Hurston's individualist philosophy and worldview. Paradoxically, the agency she denies women, as individual characters or as a group, she claims for herself. Judging from the license she takes in retelling Moses' story and recasting him in her own image, Hurston could conceivably have depicted women altogether differently. That she didn't indicates the extent to which Hurston had difficulties coming to terms with conventions of (Black) female identity and the attendant socially prescribed roles.

·  ·  ·

In spite of an expressed concern with the lack of equanimity in traditional female-male relationships, Hurston never articulated a true complementary relationship of mutual respect and equal power sharing. Hurston's ability to see beyond the kind of racist, oppositional thinking that would keep her repressed as an African American did not extend itself, in any broad sense, to categories of sex and gender. Having developed a philosophy of self-empowerment through individual achievement, Hurston urged the idea of fair competition so that those who have it are distinguished from those who have not and are rewarded accordingly. This pattern of thinking does not easily lend itself to visions of complementarity and equanimity. Equal opportunity would clear the space for competition so that the better contender could rise to the top. Desiring only "free vertical movement," Hurston was interested in "nothing horizontal." The hierarchical underpinnings at the bottom of these statements also define Hurston's conception of heterosexual relationships.

Hurston identified with a politics of (benign) patriarchy, yet steadfastly refused to subordinate herself to it. Dianne Sadoff comments on the "anxiety" evident in Hurston's (mis)representations of male-female relationships: "Hurston profoundly distrusts heterosexual relationships because she thinks them based on male dominance and willing female submission; yet such inequality appears necessary to the institution of marriage. In her autobiography, for example, Hurston blames her mother for not submitting fully to her father and so robbing him of 'that conquesting feeling'" (21). In an unpublished passage from *Dust Tracks,* Hurston also blamed her father for not having the nerve to force her mother's submission. Although her mother always "worsted" her father "in a battle of wits," he never had "the nerve to console himself in a masculine way by beating her" ("Dust Tracks," sect. 5, p. 5). As Marion Kilson observes, "The quest for the ideal relationship between a man and a woman constituted a central theme in all Hurston's novels and many of her stories. While such a relationship was achieved ultimately only in *Their Eyes Were Watching God, Seraph on the Suwanee,* and perhaps *Moses,* Hurston's conception of such a relationship is clear. For her, this ideal relationship was a conjugal relationship in which the husband was dominant and which was based upon sustained physical passion and shared goals for work and play" (114). Hurston's vision of the ideal relationship evolved out of a deistic cosmology wherein *man* was not only provider and protector, but creator, the benevolent patriarch in a humanistic Eden. There were three commandments: man must bravely confront the challenge of "Dame Nature"; he must protect and provide for his dependents; and woman must understand, love, and support her mate. This vision characterizes much of Hurston's fictional representation of conjugal unions. From *Jonah's Gourd Vine* to *Seraph on the Suwanee,* Hurston's vision attains varying degrees of realization. The extent to which the characters become ideal women and men determines the degrees to which the vision is frustrated and paradise is troubled.

In *Seraph,* Hurston's Edenic vision of connubial bliss comes to fruition. After a process of "self-overcoming," Arvay understands Jim and her role in relation to him. Jim is a MAN. That is, he audaciously meets the challenge of Nature. He struggles with it, overcomes it, even defies it, and creates a space in it for his wife and children. Arvay's abiding faith and pride in Jim and recognition of and appreciation for the chances he takes to provide for and protect his family are motivations in all he does: He operates the liquor still and risks going to prison in order to provide a comfortable home for his family. His adventure in the shipping business is designed to place Arvay even "higher up" in society. His success with the Howland development is motivated by his desire to qualm Arvay's fears over the nearby swamp and to reconcile her to her daughter's elopement. Everything was done either to add to Arvay's glory or to seek her praise. "What woman wouldn't be glad to get hold of a man like that?" (339). Arvay comes to an appreciation of Jim as the ideal man. Along with appreciation and admiration, she understands also that Jim wants and deserves her submission. The weaker, inferior force must submit to the stronger, superior one. Arvay sees herself in terms of the *Arvay Henson,* her namesake: "The *Arvay Henson* rode gently on the bosom of the Atlantic. It lifted and bowed in harmony with the wind and the sea. It was acting in submission to the infinite, and Arvay felt its peace. For the first time in her life, she acknowledged that that was the only way" (349). A man's destiny was to face Nature. A woman's was to under-stand his destiny and stand by him, even as he laughed in the face of death.

Lillie Howard finds Hurston's delineation of sexual roles perplexing: "Where Hurston stands on all this is unclear. At times she does seem distantly ironic when she has Arvay ask, 'What more could a woman want?' Too, when this novel is compared with *Their Eyes Were Watching God,* contradictions are noticeable" (*Zora Neale Hurston* 146). Hazel Carby is equally baffled and concludes in her foreword to the novel, "The difficulty for a feminist reading of *Seraph on the Suwanee* is that Jim Meserve, unlike Jody Starks, does not conveniently die so that his wife can get on with her life" (xv). The difficulty for a feminist reading of *Seraph* is that *Seraph* is not a "feminist" text. Neither is *Their Eyes.* Among the differing criteria for a feminist or womanist text, woman as an autonomous, self-determining, self-defining agent is a constant. Janie finds her voice and speaks, then is slapped into a silence that continues until Jody's death. The freedom Janie gains is circumscribed by Tea Cake's desire to dominate her and have her take "things the way he wanted her to" (191–92). Actions Janie takes are never indepen-dent. She runs off from Logan only because she has Jody to run to. She is freed from Jody only because Jody dies. What if Jody had never strutted down the road that passed her yard? What if he had outlived her? Is life on the muck with a man determined to keep a woman dependent on him a feminist ideal? Is being *allowed* to play checkers and tell stories with this man a feminist ideal also? The relationship, however, was ideal for Janie, and if Janie had not been forced to shoot this man for whom she "felt a self-crushing love," she would have con-tinued living out her ideal—one that denied her complete autonomy.

Critics have begun to question the categorical and uncritical portrayal of Hurston as the quintessential feminist and womanist and *Their Eyes* as *the* feminist-womanist manifesto. In her analysis of *Their Eyes,* Jennifer Jordan finds the assessment of Janie as an integral member of the folk community and a liberating force for the womenfolk as untenable: "Janie's allegiance to other women of any class is minimal. She has not one real female friend on the muck and associates only with the racist Mrs. Turner to whom she is indifferent. She ultimately has little in common with the rest of the women around her, who remain mules of the world" (112). Unlike *Their Eyes,* however, there is little in *Seraph* that can be appropriated to the feminist-womanist discourse. So Mary Helen Washington dismisses *Seraph* as "an awkward and contrived novel, as vacuous as a soap opera" (21). Lillie Howard rationalizes Hurston's depiction of Arvay as an expression of individualism, a reading, in some respects, compatible with a feminist-womanist agenda. She contends that "Arvay's decision to serve" suggests Hurston's belief in individual choice and her paramount concern with "the happiness of the individual" (146). Also unable to find Hurston's representation of Arvay credible, Barbara Smith reasons that the novel is a satiric portrayal of white women, a reading in sync with a (Black) feminist-womanist discourse (30).

"Nevertheless," as Carby insists, "the sexual politics of *Seraph on the Suwanee* cannot be easily dismissed" (xv). If *Seraph* were analyzed in light of Hurston's ambivalent gender politics, *Seraph* might be less puzzling. Barbara Smith writes that in this novel, "Hurston appears to have abandoned her passionate advocacy of equality in marriage" (29). But just as equality is not a factor in Hurston's political philosophy, so it does not figure in her personal philosophy of the ideal marriage as represented in her fiction. Hurston envisioned an *ideal* traditional relationship of dominance and subordination. Recognition of Hurston's internalization of conventional sex roles is crucial in any analysis of Hurston's sexual politics. For not only is patriarchy represented as the ideal social structure, but violence as an expression of patriarchal power is also condoned.

Male violence in Hurston's fiction hardly receives in-depth analysis. The issue of Tea Cake's slapping of Janie in *Their Eyes* has been addressed.[12] But the focus of critical attention on Jim's rape of Arvay is negligible. Sexual violence between women and men, unmarried and married alike, is a primary concern of feminists, womanists, and humanists. But there is no alarm over Hurston's representation of such violence as harmless and natural. Some women and men like it "rough." But when looking at Hurston's sexual politics in the context of her entire work, reading physical violence in *Their Eyes* as "simply sexual foreplay," as Jennifer Jordan concludes, is extremely problematic and dangerous (110). Is the rape in *Seraph* simply foreplay? Ann Rayson, one of the few critics who addresses the issue, comments, "The emphasis on rape in *Seraph on the Suwanee* is interesting psychologically as the term is used both for the crime and for consentual copulation. . . . Sexuality is a weapon, but a welcome, desired weapon" (9).

Beneath the mulberry tree, looking into the sky while holding on to the branches,

> Arvay did not see Jim when he sprang away from the trunk of the tree. She only knew that he had moved when she felt his arms suddenly thrust beneath her, and his hands digging into her side.
>
> "Let go!" Jim commanded shortly.
>
> Arvay brought her head up shortly, and for a brief moment their eyes met and held. Arvay's eyes questioned fearfully. Instinct told Arvay something, and she held on to the limbs desperately.
>
> It was no use. Jim took one hand from under her and tore her grip from the swinging limbs. In a fraction of the second she was snatched from the sky to the ground. Her skirts were being roughly jerked upwards, and Jim was fumbling wildly at her thighs.
>
> "Jim! You—"
>
> Jim was gritting his teeth fiercely on encountering the barrier of her tight-legged drawers, seeking an opening. Finding none, Arvay felt one hand reach up and grasp the waistband. There was a "plop" and the girl knew that the button was gone. A tearing sound of starched fabric, and the garment was being dragged ruthlessly down her legs. Arvay opened her mouth to scream, but no sound emerged. Her mouth was closed by Jim's passionate kisses, and in a moment more, despite her struggles, Arvay knew a pain remorseless sweet. (51)

In *Their Eyes,* Janie also experiences "a pain remorseless sweet that left her limp and languid." Beneath the pear tree, she watches "the thousand sister-calyxes arch to meet the love embrace" of a "dust-bearing bee." "So this was a marriage!" is her epiphanic exclamation (24). There is joy in a mutual union. If the element of consent has anything to do with anything, then the act described in *Seraph* is out-and-out rape. And the passage does not read as though Arvay "asked for it." As "dumb" as she is painted to be, Arvay has enough sense to recognize the experience for what it was: " 'All I know is that I been raped' " (56). Arvay's second sexual experience with Jim, though one of consent, does not undo the initial act of rape. His later act of forcing Arvay to strip herself naked is also more than an "interesting" psychological conundrum.[13] Hurston expresses through her characters' actions a hierarchy of power wherein the lesser force knows it must surrender to the greater. When this dynamic is recognized and accepted, submission is portrayed as an experience "remorseless sweet." The use of coercive power as a male prerogative is treated as normative. As Jim rapes Arvay, Hatton likewise threatens to rape their daughter Angie. The incident is seen as comical to Jim, though not to Arvay.

The sexual violence depicted in *Moses* is also rendered uncritically. Ironically, Barbara Smith writes that "*Moses, Man of the Mountain* . . . does not provide much material for an analysis of sexual politics in her works. Moses is a true hero, his marriage to Zipporah is idyllic and calm" (27). But the phallocentric thrust in *Moses* is hardly subtle. And Moses and Zipporah's relationship, which observes Hurston's conjugal conventions, is also drawn with a violent edge. Contemplating his royal marriage, Moses determines, "He could be a lot of things to some woman when he found the right one. . . . Some day, sometime, he would find a woman and crush from her body that essence that made men live. He would rouse her tears and her tenderness and he would give her something that she could not live without" (82). That woman was Zipporah. Returning home from a local celebration, Zipporah and Moses are in the dark alone:

> "Come here, Zipporah!" Moses said tensely but in a low voice.
> . . . "What do you want with me?" she asked casually.
> "Come here to me, woman. I know exactly what to do with you."
> "Oh, you do, do you?"
> "I certainly do. Come here."
> "No."
> "Yes! I want you."
> "I don't come running like that. Even a hen must be sought after, Mister Moses, and I won't be less than a chicken."
> "Oh, you are going to be run after, young lady. Don't be so hard to get. Come farther away from that door before I come after you."
> He didn't wait. He rushed over and seized her girdle and snatched her towards him. And now that he had his hands on her, all the words that he had been preparing to say to her vanished from his tongue. He crushed her body against his and kissed her with as much energy as he needed for a cavalry charge. (130–31)

From Ninevah to Suwanee River, women are slapped and raped, girdles are seized, and drawers are left hanging from tree branches and dangling in the wind.

Sexual violence between consenting adults may be a personal, individual matter, but according to feminists and womanists, the personal is political. And given that all literary representations are interpretations that carry a particular political import, a more rigorous analysis of Hurston's (sexual) politics is in order. For power, the attainment of it and the expression of it, is at the core of Hurston's personal and political agenda. That agenda, when examined from Hurston's angle of vision on gender, reinforces and perpetuates an ideology of sexual dualism that privileges conventional conceptions of male authority. Following the trajectory of Moses' transition from dominant husband to autocratic leader, one can envision the implications of the personal as political. Just as Moses figures he knows "exactly what to do with" Zipporah, he figures he knows exactly what to do with Israel.

That Hurston was female does not make her idealization of male authority implausible. Her embracing of typically masculine paradigms of power functions, for herself, as a means of resisting dominant images of women as weak and dependent. The contradictions between Hurston's own life and the lives of her female characters are the result of Hurston's conflicting, ironic, and ambivalent sense of self as an African American woman. Because she internalized her father's ideology of the feminine and because she also had a sense of herself as an autonomous "other," Hurston displayed dualistic notions of Black womanhood. She fantasized about being the kind of woman for whom a man would do anything and the kind of woman who would submit to him. In her texts, women submit to male authority and are "loved." Arvay acquiesces and is never happier. But Hurston could not surrender her "self" to anyone in reality—not even her father.

Even though she expressed a desire to submit to patriarchal authority (an indication of her desire for her father's affection) she could not. As her representations of her first marriage and her affair with A.W.P. illustrate, submission was not an aspect of Hurston's nature. She chose her career over a married life with Herbert Sheen and found that she could not be the ideal submissive woman to her lover, A.W.P., the ideal dominant man. "He was a *man!* . . . Then too, he wanted to do all the doing, and keep me on the receiving end," Hurston wrote (*Dust Tracks* 253). A.W.P. "soared" in her respect after that perhaps because she had so longed for that kind of attention and adoration. But that kind of devotion undermined her autonomy. Although Hurston claimed such an arrangement was "a *very* good idea," it was not a really good idea for her. She would have had to give up her work. Career and wifedom were contradictory to A.W.P.: " 'You know, Zora, you've got a real man on your hands. You've got somebody to do for you. I'm tired of seeing you work so hard. I wouldn't want *my* wife to do anything but look after me. Be home looking like Snookums when I got there' " (255). As good as that sounded to her, Hurston "really wanted to conform, but it was impossible" (254).

Hurston left the relationship and resolved "to embalm all the tenderness of my passion for him in 'Their Eyes Were Watching God' " (*Dust Tracks* 260). But what describes the passion? And what does that mean in light of the fact that Tea Cake, the fictive A.W.P., is dead at the end of the novel? The violent deaths of men are not bound to *Their Eyes*. Domineering men who do not fit Hurston's stereotype of the ideal man die violent or otherwise hard deaths: John Pearson's collision with an oncoming train, Joe Starks's kidney failure, Sykes Jones's poisoning from a snake bite, Spunk Banks's "accidentally" falling onto the circular saw. One can argue fidelity to biographical facts in the case of John Pearson and literary realism in the case of the others. But why the violence Tea Cake suffers? A rabid dog viciously attacks him, then Janie shoots him.

Dianne Sadoff suggests, "Hurston has motivated her narrative, perhaps unconsciously, to act out her rage against male domination and to free Janie, a figure for herself, from all men" (22). The love-hurt relationship between Hurston and her father seems to get played out again and again in loving and in hurtful ways. I would argue further that Janie's defense of self-defense translates as a plea of self-defense for Hurston as well. With A.W.P., Hurston got a taste of the benevolent patriarchy she fantasized about in her writings. She found it to be the dehumanizing institution that it is and rebelled against it. Her rebellion against A.W.P. was simultaneously an adamant No to her father. With Tea Cake's immolation, Hurston was released from her father's sphere of control. She could become master of her own fate, as could Janie. Tea Cake's death represented the closure necessary for Janie's and Hurston's psychospiritual freedom. It also acquired an autocephalous status for Hurston: She was freed from external, patriarchal control. No longer entrapped by gender roles and expectations, she and Janie can follow wherever the inside urge leads.

# Conclusion: The Essence of
# Owning Oneself

Let me, personally and privately, be responsible for my survival or failure to survive in this man's world.

—Letter to Burton Rascoe

In her analysis of cultural integration, Ruth Benedict draws a parallel between culture and the individual. The implications are useful in assessing Zora Neale Hurston's life and works:

A culture, like an individual, is a more or less consistent pattern of thought and action. Within each culture there come into being characteristic purposes not necessarily shared by other types of society. In obedience to these purposes, each people further and further consolidates its experience, and in proportion to the urgency of these drives the heterogeneous items of behaviour take more and more congruous shape. Taken up by a well-integrated culture, the most ill-assorted acts become characteristic of its peculiar goals, often by the most unlikely metamorphoses. The form that these acts take we can understand only by understanding first the emotional and intellectual mainsprings of that society. (46)

As the passage suggests, Zora Neale Hurston's life and work manifested "a more or less consistent pattern of thought and action." And, in order to "interpret the incidents and directions" of Hurston's life, it is necessary to understand, as well as possible, "the emotional and intellectual mainsprings" of her life. Hurston was compelled by a "will-to-power" that expressed itself in a philosophy and politics of individualism. Having lived in an all-Black folk community that was self-governing and having imbibed the self-help philosophy of Booker T. Washington, which emphasized industry and individual merit, Hurston developed an attitude of self-reliance and independence. The love and encouragement Lucy Potts Hurston gave her daughter reinforced her independent spirit. Altogether, these influences nurtured in Hurston a positive sense of self, a vital asset in her struggle for emotional and psychological survival both at home and in the inimical environs beyond Eatonville.

Hurston's individualist standpoint was as much an outgrowth of resistance strategies as it was a reflection of her ideology of personal responsibility. Hurston had to resist, from childhood, negative, controlling images and ideologies of her Black female self. Neglected by her father, she experienced emotional alienation and isolation. She found refuge and comfort in self-introspection and fanciful imaginings. In this psychic, solitary space, she resisted the pain of rejection and gave herself what her father denied her: a riding horse, music lessons, love. Later orphaned by her mother, abandoned by her father, and "shifted from house to house of relatives and friends," Hurston no doubt developed a sense of insecurity that was assuaged only by an ardent sense of self-dependence and a fierce self-love. She could only have concluded that "every tub must sit on its on bottom—regardless."

Alienated in her home, Hurston was likewise marginalized in the larger society. To resist stereotypical images of her Black womanhood and to combat stereotypical notions of white superiority and Black inferiority that constantly assailed her, Hurston found recourse in the ideology of individual merit. She envisioned a world in which "you got what your strengths brought you." One's ethnicity had nothing to do with one's ability: "If you have got it, you can't hide it," she boasted. Her emphasis on individual achievement was her response to prejudiced whites who judged all Blacks as ethnically and culturally inferior. It was also her response to the exclusionary politics of an American society that denied its citizenry equal opportunity.

Hurston's studies in anthropology, history, and philosophy validated her beliefs in the genius and humanity of African Americans as they affirmed her own sense of self-worth and her individualist standpoint. The cultural relativist perspective she acquired while studying under Franz Boas confirmed her sense of the significance and value of Black cultural traditions. And Ruth Benedict's analyses of the individual and society and her impatience with American conformity and intolerance of individual differences seem to have impressed upon Hurston the imperative of accepting her own difference and encouraged her individualist politics. Spinoza's doctrine of self-preservation and self-perfection reflected the wisdom Hurston found in the lore of the folk and in the teachings of Booker T. Washington. Spinoza's belief in the divinity of humankind and the power of reason is mirrored in Hurston's thought. These philosophical tenets, as manifested in

Hurston's writings, undergirded her notions of individual responsibility and self-determination as they posited authority with the individual rather than with forces external to the individual. Her orientation toward individualism and achievement seem invigorated by the Nietzschean "will-to-power," a concept that translates in Hurston's philosophy as self-mastery and complete autonomy. Her abilities to deal with life as she found it, laugh in the face of adversity, and express her creative genius reflect the singular will of the Dionysian spirit.

Hurston's intellectual standpoints, shaped by the emotional mainsprings in her life, culminated in an uncompromising individualism. Her individualist stance, however, did not negate her identity as one of the folk just as it did not assume an insensitivity to the welfare of Blacks collectively. Statements Hurston made and actions she took that contradicted her identity as one of the folk exemplify the "illassorted acts" characteristic of Hurston's particular goal of self-empowerment. "The form these acts take" in Hurston's literary and political activity suggest the emotional turmoil Hurston experienced while struggling to assert herself in the world as a woman and an African American. As Barbara Christian states, African American women's politics of self are always "gravely affected by other complex issues":

> The development of Afro-American women's fiction is, in many instances, a mirror of the intensity of the relationship between sexism and racism in this country. And while many of us may grasp this fact in terms of economics or social status, we often forget the toll it takes in terms of self-expression and therefore self-empowerment. To be able to use the range of one's voice, to attempt to express the totality of self, is a recurring struggle in the tradition of these writers from the nineteenth century to the present. (172)

Hurston's writings testify to the difficulties Black women face in their efforts to express "the totality of self." They bear witness to the impediments faced and the frustrations incurred as Black women struggle for self-definition amidst prevailing ethnic and sexual stereotypes and conventional constructions of gender. Robert Hemenway observes that in *Seraph on the Suwanee,* "Hurston apparently created Arvay from two emotional sources: her knowledge of the inferiority she had been made to feel as a child, and her observations of the inadequacy felt by men when confronted by her own self-reliant, independent intelligence" (310). Out of those emotional sources she created Jim Meserve as well. Arvay embodies the diffident, inferior self of Hurston, and Jim Meserve embodies her brash, confident, and successful self. The novel represents a kind of battle of the sexes that is, ultimately, a matter of self seeking self. One of the conflicts most central to Hurston's life was the clash between her feminine and masculine natures. The unreconciled conflict is revealed in the power struggles between her female and male characters, and it also accounts for narrative gaps, silences, contradictions, ironies, and inconsistencies in Hurston's works.

Hurston's emphasis on strength, competition, and her own will-to-power aligned her with patriarchal authority. Her texts, in essence, reinscribe and celebrate patriarchy—another instance of an ill-assorted act. Barbara Smith writes that Hurston "did not worship male supremacy" (26). She did not. But she worshipped power and strength and that power and strength she associated with men. The current critical discourse on Hurston tends to search out the feminine principle in Hurston's texts to the exclusion of the masculine. It therefore leaves subordinated the stories that might revise or disrupt an idealized literary matriliny. Hurston's inferiority complexes, stemming from negative sex role socialization, color prejudice, racial discrimination, and social stratification, are among the unattended stories of psychological scars and emotional pain embedded in the text of Hurston's life and work. Hurston was not overwhelmed by the major conflicts in her life because she had a strong, resilient ego and an ardently individualist stance. The egotism is, necessarily, a salient feature of Hurston's personality and philosophy. An understanding of Hurston that can account for the more strident aspects of her personality and work, those traditionally viewed as eccentric or uncharacteristic, must acknowledge patrilineal lines of descent. As Toni Morrison has argued, "any model of criticism or evaluation that excludes males from it is as hampered as any model of criticism of Black literature that excludes women from it" ("Rootedness" 344).

In her struggle to overcome the adverse effects of being marginalized within her family, Hurston searched for empowering images of self. She found those empowering images in male models, which she emulated. If we compare Hurston's actual life achievements with the fictional lives she created in her texts, we see that Hurston has more in common with her male characters than with her female characters. Like them, she married, divorced, and had numerous affairs; she discovered new (literary) frontiers; she searched for lost cities; she navigated boats; and she climbed mountains. Like the men of her day, she smoked in public, wore pants, spoke her mind, and loved setting her hat at "a rakish angle"—just like her father.

Hurston's masculinist orientation combined with her sense of self as female "other" to create in her an androgynous character. Expulsed from the Eden of a father-daughter relationship and encouraged by her mother to develop a strong will, Hurston was situated as autonomous "other." She constructed for herself a character that empowered her as it flouted social convention. Yet Hurston was hampered from a full realization of an androgynous principle because of internalized notions of sexual dualism. She, nevertheless, advocated androgyny by virtue of her insistence on individual autonomy. Jacqueline de Weever's work shows that the androgyne, as creator, healer, and medium of transformation, figures significantly in Black women writers' mythic narratives. "The archetype of the androgyne, whose double life both as man and as woman provides the possibilities for achieving great wisdom, is applied mostly to women" (55). Medial, androgynous characters, "whose powers are rooted in folk traditions," function to bring others into psychic integration, self-affirmation, and self-definition. "This essence of owning oneself," Weever argues, "is the essence of androgyny" (15, 33). Quoting Carolyn Heilbrun, she explains further "that androgyny 'suggests a full range of experience open to individuals who may, as women, be aggressive, as men, tender; it suggests a spectrum upon which human beings choose their places without regard to propriety and custom'" (33). Certainly Hurston's life exemplifies the essence of androgyny. Owning herself as she did, she was able to transcend a multiplicity of obstacles to create works that affirm African American life and culture as they affirmed her own life and life itself, albeit in the form of male heroic characters. She invested her ideal male characters with this androgynous spirit, but never transferred it to her female characters.

Androgyny, as a transformative force, is an idea both ancient and mythic. Dominique Zahan expounds on the primacy of androgyny in human nature: "For certain West African peoples the union of man and woman is doubly symbolic and as such offers man another occasion for transcending himself. Above all it represents the union of the sun and the earth. It also reproduces the 'initial' human condition, androgyny, of which many African peoples seem to have retained 'recollections' in their religions. . . . The idea of androgyny, the ideal form of the human being, reflects the concern for perfect equilibrium between male and female and for their total reciprocity in equality" (11). Diedre L. Bádéjò writes in "The Goddess Ọ̀ṣun as a Paradigm for African Feminist Criticism" that Ọ̀ṣun, a Yoruba deity, "is a woman of power, femininity, and fecundity . . . of great beauty, wealth, and intelligence. She is the leader of àjẹ́, human and spiritual beings who manifest prodigious and transcendental energy. . . . Her mythical images and myriad roles as òrìṣà, àjẹ́, sister, wife, mother, lover, warrior, and worker reveal the complex nature of African womanism" (27). Òṣun symbolizes equilibrium and complementarity between the sexes. This is illustrated in a passage of Òṣun's orature. Accordingly, Olódùmarè, the supreme deity, "who often appears as an androgynous being" (28), sends various deities, including Òṣun, to "maintain the world." However, the other deities, all male, exclude Òṣun "because she is a woman." So "they were unable to complete their plans successfully" (27). "Excluding Òṣun creates an imbalance which can only be resolved by sacrifice." The male deities are duly reprimanded and are made accountable to Òṣun (28).

Balance is essential. The feminine and masculine principles must be recognized and must maintain a relation of complementarity as opposed to competition. Given Hurston's philosophy of individualism which emphasized hierarchical paradigms and competitiveness, her advocacy of sexual equality was an improbability. Hurston's work reveals the difficulty in achieving and maintaining this balance. Though essentially androgynous, Hurston was yet somewhat circumscribed by the politics of sexual dualism. She resisted external controlling images, but the struggle was never resolved. In typical Hurston bravado, she declared that she set out to win the fight against her feelings of inferiority and exclaimed, "I did." However, her battle to construct and maintain a positive self-concept as a Black woman was not as easy and as final as she represented it. Her continued search for selfhood is evident in the contradiction between her private self and public persona and in the pages of her texts.

Hurston's predilection for male paradigms of power, her extreme individualism, her egotism, her struggle for power are all aspects of who she was. But Hurston is not an anomaly. She is part of a continuum of manly women that stretches from the North American and South American continents to the African continent and extends itself from historical to mythic time. As Bádéjò writes, "it is those mythical images and myriad roles of Òṣun and countless other African deities that traversed the Atlantic. In the traumatic context of enslavement and racism, these oral literary roles, images, and voices have recurred, albeit altered and transformed, throughout the Diaspora. From what other source could first generation enslaved African women have evolved their perceptions of and survival tactics within Western captivity? Who else's worldview could they have passed along as a legacy to their generations?" (27). Hurston stands in a long line of female progenitors who were aggressive, forceful, and masculine-identified in one capacity or another. Hurston reminds us of Sojourner Truth, who "could work as much and eat as much as any man" (Truth 25); Harriet "Moses" Tubman, who dressed in men's clothing and led hundreds of enslaved Blacks to freedom; Maria Stewart, who demanded that women "possess the spirit of men, bold and enterprising, fearless and undaunted"; and the lesser-known Stage Coach Mary, who "dressed like a man" and "settled her arguments with her fists" (*Salute* 14).[1] Hurston also recalls the millions of women who assumed conventional male roles in addition to imposed female roles during enslavement and after.

Hurston's androgynous line can be traced to African warrior queens. Her belligerence and her tendency to stand and do battle likens her to Candace, Nzinga, Judith, and Yaa Asantewa. One queen to whom Hurston bears particular resemblance is Queen Hatshepsut, who "dominated the times in which she lived," ruling Egypt for twenty-one years.

> She is known as a warrior queen and it is true that she was aggressive, overpowering, a born dynast. But her battles were against her own rivals for power in the Egyptian hierarchy.... And though she trumpeted the war cry "I came as Horus, darting fire against my enemies," it is of enemies within her own camp and country that she speaks. She is the most unusual of Egyptian queens.... "She created a new science of rulership, the essence of which was the female manifesting male attributes." She donned male attire, sported a beard, even referred to herself, and insisted on being referred to, as *he*. (Sertima 7)[2]

As a woman in a patriarchal social structure, Hatshepsut, like Hurston, associated power with masculine identity, and, assuming that power, assumed that identity.

• • •

Zora Neale Hurston's politics of self were complex. An outsider inside her home, an outsider in the larger society, Hurston was continually assailed by negative images and ideologies of her Black female self. Yet she was not tragically colored, tragically poor, or tragically female. She insisted on sharpening her oyster knife and steadfastly declared that she did not "belong to the sobbing school of Negrohood." Implied in her declaration is a choice, a conscious decision, a coming to terms. But to say merely that life was a challenge Hurston met head on is a gross understatement that ignores Hurston's physical, psychological, and spiritual suffering. Hurston's battle for self was ongoing, given the sundry and unrelenting forces of domination and dehumanization. And in spite of Hurston's refrain that "it didn't really matter," it did. The discursivity of Hurston's texts exhibits a studied effort to repress the expression of feelings and stories of pain and emotional exile. It also documents the development of the kind of ego strength needed to wrest one's self from a dehumanizing social determinism and to define one's self into a dynamic existence that transcends the habit of surviving.

Zora Neale Hurston leaves us a number of empowering legacies. Her life expresses the transformative and revolutionary possibilities of an androgynous spirit as her works express the crucial need to move away from sexist dichotomies. Her emphasis on individual achievement and merit is utterly vital to our assessment of her. For Hurston knew well the inhibitions to fair and just play, but understood as well that the hindrances do not alter the fact that one must face the challenge or submit defeat. Therefore, her greatest legacy is that of resistance. This legacy declares it imperative to continually resist all that is limiting, confining, victimizing, and dehumanizing. It emphasizes the need to resist all ideologies of exclusion that vitiate the struggle for achievement and empowerment of the self.

# Notes

## Introduction

1. In *Black Feminist Consciousness*, Patricia Hill Collins articulates the link between Black women's intellectual work and the continued struggle against systems of domination. However, this link, in relation to Zora Neale Hurston, has been obscured and ignored. "Producing intellectual work is generally not attributed to Black women artists and political activists. Such women are typically thought of as nonintellectual and nonscholarly, classifications that create a false dichotomy between thinking and doing" (15). It is therefore necessary to (re)examine Black women's intellectual lives and reclaim their intellectual work as legacies vital to Black people's resistance and empowerment.

2. The concept "standpoint" is taken from Nancy Hartsock's definition of "feminist standpoint," particularly as it is described as an engaged perspective that "indicates a recognition of the power realities operative in a community, and points to the ways the ruling group's vision may be *both* perverse *and* made real by means of that group's power to define the terms of the community as a whole" (288). Further, my use of this concept is informed by Patricia Hill Collins's use of it to describe the "unique angle of vision" of African American women (25–28).

3. Filomina Steady argues that the African woman, as the "original feminist," inspires liberatory struggle. Also that one finds on the African continent "forms of social organization which approach sexual equality, in addition to matrilineal societies where women are central" (35).

## Chapter 1: Metaphors of Self, Language, and the Will-to-Power

1. I use this term, in the Nietzschean sense, to describe the psychological dynamics revealed in the submerged voice that speaks throughout Zora Neale Hurston's oeuvre. It describes an ardent desire for autonomy that compels her to construct a subjective world, an "apparent *inner world*," and a persona to mediate between that world and the *"real world."* Nietzsche writes that "one should not understand this compulsion to construct concepts, species, forms, purposes, laws . . . as if they enabled us to fix the *real world*; but as a compulsion to arrange a world for ourselves in which our existence is made

possible:—we thereby create a world which is calculable, simplified, comprehensible, etc., for us" (*Will to Power,* Book III, Sect. 521, p. 282).

2. Darwin Turner wrote that Hurston's "artful candor and coy reticence, her contradictions and silences, her irrationalities and extravagant boasts . . . plead for the world to recognize and respect her" (*Minor Chord* 91). He suggests that the work reflects Hurston's emotional as well as financial insecurities. Harold Preece, a radical white, saw *Dust Tracks* as "the tragedy of a gifted, sensitive mind, eaten up by an egocentrism fed on the patronizing admiration of the dominant white world." Describing Hurston as a conformist and her autobiography as "hollow" and "puerile," he writes, "Had Hurston been honest with herself, she would have called this book 'Dust in My Eyes' " (58–59). Hurston was accused of making public declarations in support of Jim Crow as a means to sell her autobiography, an accusation she said was untrue. Nevertheless, Roy Wilkins made a public response to the alleged statements in the *New York Amsterdam News:* "Now is not the time for Negro writers like Zora Hurston to come out with publicity wisecracks about the South being better for the Negro than the North. . . . The race is fighting a battle that may determine its status for fifty years. Those who are not for us, are against us" (7).

More recent critics of *Dust Tracks* tend to read the autobiography within culturally specific contexts. Such approaches to the text yield fuller, richer analyses that allow the multivocal, multivalent (coded) discourses within the text to speak.

3. Jacqueline de Weever notes that like most American writers, African American writers are inheritors of a "three-pronged tradition": "The first prong is the Greek or Attic tradition, the second prong the Hebraic tradition of the Bible (including the Christian tradition), and the third prong specific to an ethnic tradition, as in Attic-Hebraic-African. The triangulated tradition, moreover, testifies to the fragmented ontology of every American, for whom the main theme of existence is exile" (21–22). Weever further suggests that Black writers combine the three traditions, "and by adding to them the unique voice of the black American female, thus [enlarge] the definition of what it means to be American" (22).

Hurston draws on the Attic-Hebraic-African triangulation as do other African American women writers. Though these writers "respect the gods of the triple culture of the Americas," writes Weever, "their female voices invert and deconstruct the myths associated with them" (16).

4. I use "metaphor" both in its strict, analogical sense and in its broad sense as figurative language.

5. To name one's self is to identify with the Logos. Olney, examining the Greek philosopher Heraclitus's notion of Logos, defines it as "the principle of Harmony . . . underlying all change, [which] transforms human variability from mere chaos and disconnection into significant process" (5).

6. Hurston's rejection of the expectations of tradition constitutes a refusal to be named. Kimberly Benston explains that "the refusal to be named invokes the power of the Sublime, a transcendent impulse to undo all categories . . . and

thrust the self beyond received patterns and relationships into a stance of unchallenged authority. . . . [It] distinguish[es] the self from all else—including Eros, nature and community" (153).

7. I make use of the concept "race" because of its currency and historical implications, but with the understanding, as Hurston herself understood, that the concept of race is a fiction, a construct of seventeenth-century European anthropologists and scholars.

8. In "Multiple Jeopardy, Multiple Consciousness: The Context of a Black Feminist Ideology," Deborah King defines "multiple jeopardy" as the interdependent control systems of race, sex, and class oppression (47).

## Chapter 2: "Every Tub Must Sit on Its Own Bottom"

1. In her essay "On the Issue of Roles," Toni Cade concludes as well that change begins with(in) the individual, not the group. Cade's conclusions, like Hurston's, do not propose superficial dichotomies between the individual and the group. Rather, she suggests that the individual and the group are part of a dynamic social continuum wherein the whole cannot be greater than its parts. Cade explains it this way: "Revolution begins with the self, in the self. The individual, the basic revolutionary unit, must be purged of poison and lies that assault the ego and threaten the heart, that hazard the next larger unit—the couple or pair, that jeopardize the still larger unit—the family or cell, that put the entire movement in peril" (109).

2. In "The Transformation of Eatonville's Ethnographer," Marion Kilson discusses individualism and achievement as fundamental orientations in Hurston's work.

3. I use this concept of a Signifying relationship in accordance with the Signifying Monkey theory of African-American literary criticism as advanced by Henry Louis Gates, Jr. In this theory, Signifying refers to "how black texts 'talk' to other black texts" (*Signifying Monkey* xxvi). A Signifying relationship entails an author's repetition, in content or style, of the work of another, revising it with a "a signal difference" (xxi–xxv).

Literary Signification does not invariably denote mockery or parody. Pastiche, a type of literary Signification, is a mimetic act that is positive and affirming. Gates makes this distinction: "Literary Signification, then, is similar to parody and pastiche, wherein parody corresponds to what I am calling motivated Signification while pastiche would correspond roughly to unmotivated Signification" (xxvii). Gates, for instance, adduces Alice Walker's Signifying relationship to the texts of Zora Neale Hurston as pastiche, an act of "unmotivated Signifyin(g), by which I mean to suggest not the absence of a profound intention but the absence of a negative critique." Pastiche, rather, is "an act of homage" (xxvi–xxvii). Hurston's respect and admiration of Booker T. Washington makes her Signifying relationship to his texts one of pastiche, of homage.

4. Though critical of both industrial and classical education, Carter G. Woodson, in his philosophy on education as outlined in *The Mis-Education of the Negro*, agrees with Washington and Hurston on several points. All three share similar views on the educational and sociopolitical situation of African Americans and advocate some of the same strategies for ameliorating that situation. Woodson, like Washington and Hurston, believed it essential that African Americans become independent thinkers. Like Hurston, Woodson resisted European-American cultural hegemony, seeing the miseducation of African Americans, who are "taught to admire the Hebrew, the Greek, the Latin and the Teuton and to despise the African," as "the seat of the trouble." He believed also that African Americans should become self-dependent through personal responsibility, industry, and creativity as opposed to imitation and duplication.

5. Hurston's reductive description of African American culture reflects her absorption of Boas's notion of cultural integration. This concept views culture, more or less, as an organic whole, a gestalt. It recognizes the interdependence of cultural forms and emphasizes certain consistent and dominating features in the forms and behaviors of a culture as expressive of the identifying attitudes and "ruling motivations" of that culture. See Boas's discussion of cultural integration in "The Aims of Anthropological Research" in *Race, Language, and Culture* (243–59) and Ruth Benedict's "Integration of Culture" in *Patterns of Culture* (45–56).

6. Holloway gives a thorough exploration of what Hurston calls the "will to adorn" in *The Character of the Word*.

7. Hazel Carby notes in her foreword to *Seraph on the Suwanee* that Hurston's views concerning authentic African American folk culture were "complex and controversial." In writing to her publisher about the "Seraph" manuscript, Hurston "repudiated theories of the uniqueness of Black linguistic structures" (viii). In one letter, she declared that "what is known as Negro dialect in the South is no such thing." She attributed southern speech patterns to Elizabethan, not African, influences. Hurston stated further: "There is no more Negro music in the U.S. It has been fused and merged and become the national expression. . . . In fact, it is now denied, (and with some truth) that it never was pure Negro music, but adaptation of white music. . . . But the fact remains that what has evolved here is something American" (viii-x). A look at Hurston's work in its entirety puts such statements into perspective. Hurston was desperate to have her manuscript published and was not above flattering the ego of her white publisher to accomplish her goal. She had long anticipated discovering her lost Honduran city, as Carby states. Profits from the sale of her book were, in part, a means to that end. Hurston's desire to have African American life and culture seen as *American* and universal must also be considered. Though she may have desired to be seen in a national and universal light, Hurston gloried in being *African* American to the extent that she pitied whites, whom she considered pathological and culturally deprived. (Hurston specifically expressed her feeling of pathos for Anglo-Saxon civilization in the essay "My Most Humiliating Jim Crow Experience.")

The contradictory statements to which Carby refers must necessarily be taken with a grain of salt, especially as Hurston was an expert at "tomming" and puttin' one over on "ole massa." It was an expedient for her, and she enjoyed doing it.

8. The vestiges of traditional African thought in the worldview of the African American folk allows for the easy reception of ideas such as Spinoza's. This is understandable in light of the assimilation of aspects of African culture by the early Greeks, on whose thought Spinoza's philosophy is based. In *Black Athena: The Afroasiatic Roots of Classical Civilization,* Martin Bernal argues in his "Revised Ancient Model" of Greek history that Egyptian colonization of Greece, beginning in the first half of the second millennium B.C.E., played a major role in the foundation of Greek civilization. Early Greek linguistic, religious, philosophical, aesthetic, and political thought, he contends, were heavily indebted to Africa. The idea of individual identity with the cosmos, the divinity of nature, immortality of the soul, and "an animate universe without need for a regulator or even a creator originates in Egypt" (27).

Friedrich Nietzsche, in acknowledging the influence of Spinoza, traces his own thought back to the pre-Socratic Greek philosophers. Hellenistic thought found in Nietzsche is likewise derived from ancient Africa. Even the Dionysian spirit he valorizes so much in the Greeks has its roots there. Nietzsche bows to the Greeks, but as Martin Bernal attests, "the cult of Dionysos . . . was introduced to Greece" during the midfifteenth century B.C.E, "another high tide of Egyptian influence" (21).

These Afrocentric aspects of Greco-European philosophy are notable in that they help us to better illuminate influences in Hurston's thought and her reconciliation or, rather, her synthesis of what might otherwise be considered antipodal ideologies. Wole Soyinka's essay "The Fourth Stage" in *Myth, Literature, and the African World* attests to the similarities between African and Greco-European myth and philosophy. In his exploration of the source and meaning of Yoruba tragic art, Soyinka adopts the paradigm set forth in Nietzsche's *The Birth of Tragedy* as he places the Yoruba deities Obatala and Ogun "in a parallel evolutionary relationship to Nietzsche's Dionysos-Apollo brotherhood" (141).

9. These concepts are foreshadowed in the writings of the ancient Greek philosopher Heraclitus, a student of Egyptian priests (James 9), to whom Nietzsche attributes the "doctrine of the 'eternal recurrence,' that is, of the unconditional and infinitely repeated circular course of all things" (*Genealogy* 273–74). In his discussion, James Olney likewise traces this idea to Heraclitus. He offers the following analysis of Heraclitus's statement that "the elements are in continual flux and transformation, and so also are men": "Heraclitus argues that the variability or flux is internal as well as external, but he maintains also that there is, in both instances, a balancing opposite to this continuous changeability; there is . . . an invisible . . . harmony behind discord and an integral constancy behind flux whether in the soul or in the cosmos" (5).

10. See, for instance, Patrick Bridgwater's *Nietzsche in Anglosaxony* and John Burt Foster, Jr.'s *Heirs to Dionysus.*

11. In a letter to Margaret Mead, Ruth Benedict wrote of her enthusiasm for Nietzsche. The letter also suggests the infusion of Nietzsche's ideas in American thought: "I sent you my copy of Zarathustra to take along on the boat. . . . There's a gaiety and intoxication about it that nothing else quite achieves. It was newer to me twenty years ago when I first read it than it will be to you—it's in the air we breathe now—but when you read it in Nietzsche it's more clearly the right—poetical way of seeing it than it often is in the people who have learned so much from him" (Mead 548). I thank Marco Portales of Texas A&M for suggesting that I look closer at Ruth Benedict's work for my Nietzsche-Hurston connection.

12. In *Patterns of Culture*, Benedict writes, "The basic contrast between the Pueblos and the other cultures of North America is the contrast that is named and described by Nietzsche in his studies of Greek tragedy. He discusses two diametrically opposed ways of arriving at the values of existence. The Dionysian pursues them through 'the annihilation of the ordinary bounds and limits of existence'. . . . The Apollonian . . . 'knows but one law, measure in the Hellenic sense' " (78–79).

13. The correspondence between Hurston and Benedict to which I refer is among the restricted material of the Benedict Papers. I am thankful to Nancy S. MacKechnie, curator of Rare Books and Manuscripts at Vassar College Libraries, for information she shared with me about the Hurston correspondence. I also thank my friend and colleague Margaret M. Caffrey, who has written a biography on Ruth Benedict, for bringing the letters to my attention.

14. For example, Boas writes in *Race, Language, and Culture*, "The problems of the relation of the individual to his culture, to the society in which he lives have received too little attention. The standardized anthropological data that inform us of customary behavior, give no clue to the reaction of the individual to his culture, nor to an understanding of his influence upon it" (258). Boas also considers this issue in "Methods of Research": "Notwithstanding incongruities that are never entirely absent, each culture is a whole, and its form has a dynamic force which determines the behavior of the mass of individuals. . . . How far an individual is able to free himself from the fetters that culture lays upon him depends not only upon his individuality but equally, if not more, upon the culture imposed upon him" (673).

15. Interestingly enough, Benedict describes Western civilization as one wherein the "will-to-power" is highly rewarded, the accumulation of property is highly valued, and conformity is considered a virtue. (260, 273, 274).

16. In "Why the Negro Won't Buy Communism," Hurston offers a scathing analysis of communist doctrine, its advocates, and proselytes. Her critique of communism depicts members of the Soviet Union as self-righteous, would-be "masters" who see the "downtrodden," "pitiful" Black-American community as a "useful tool" in their bid for world power (15). Her analysis of Soviet propaganda, pointing up the irony of slave morality versus master morality, has a decidedly Nietzschean flavor: "So, without putting a name to

it, the commies went about creating a permanent lower class by dialectic persuasion. Wealthy persons *per se* were born vipers. There was a great weeping and wailing over share-croppers and the like. All unskilled labor was glorified in words, but bedded down as far as possible to form a foundation for this peasant class. The pleasures of peasantry were lauded to the skies. To make it appear inevitable, the nation was flooded with propaganda about there being no more frontiers; no more chances at all for free enterprise; not a prayer for a lone individual to rise by his own efforts. No more *nothing* but collectivism. . . . No more individuals at all. Their case was really pitiful. Nothing to do but hate bosses and work toward the day when they could do away with their hated oppressors" (56).

17. Nietzsche defines *ressentiment* as a condition of the "unfortunate and worm-eaten," who are "denied the true reaction, that of deeds, and compensate themselves with an imaginary revenge [against the fortunate and happy]" (*Genealogy,* Essay III, Sect. 14, p. 124, and Essay I, Sect. 10, pp. 36, 37).

18. The pioneering Jim Mcserve in *Seraph on the Suwanee* is infused with a Dionysian spirit. His *amor fati* finds him in a life or death struggle with Dame Nature, symbolized in the oxymoronic "awful beauty" of an eight-foot diamondback on one occasion and in the form of a tempest at sea on another. While others in the scenes are paralyzed by fear and trepidation, Jim is fearless. Innocent in his daring, he considers losing or winning inconsequential. His pleasure is "the game" of "will upon will." The gamble, the risk, is everything.

19. This third level is the synthesis or overcoming of the first two levels Nietzsche outlines: In "Of the Three Metamorphoses," Nietzsche proposes that the soul is transformed thrice. The first is symbolized by the camel, "the weight-bearing spirit" that hurries off into the desert, heavy-laden. The second is symbolized by the lion: "it wants to capture freedom and be lord of its own desert" (*Zarathustra* 54).

## Chapter 3: African American Folklore as Style, Theme, and Strategy

1. The ideas expressed here are informed in part by Nathan Huggins's discussion of the minstrelsy tradition in *Harlem Renaissance* (248–50). I should like to point out here that evaluation of Hurston's work was also complicated by gender politics as well as by the dualistic logic that says that Black affirmation is not Black protest, that there is only one mode of resistance and struggle. In "On Richard Wright and Zora Neale Hurston: Notes toward a Balancing of Love and Hatred," June Jordan addresses this "either/or system of dividing the world into unnecessary conflict," creating "the notion that *only one kind* of writing—protest writing—and that *only one kind* of protest writing deserves our support and study" (5, 7). In her comparison and assessment of Wright's *Native Son* and Hurston's *Their Eyes Were Watching God,* Jordan emphasizes the need to validate the worldviews of both authors. For "both of them bespeak

our hurt, our wished-for fulfillment and, at various times, the nature and the level of our adjustment to complete fulfillment or, on the other hand, complete frustration" (7). Because women's experiences and perspectives have been devalued, writes Jordan, and because Black affirmation has not been properly evaluated, Hurston's work has been considered unimportant, not serious in its scope, and idiosyncratic (7). "I would add that the functions of protest and affirmation are not, ultimately, distinct: that, for instance, affirmation of Black values and lifestyle within the American context is, indeed, an act of protest. Therefore, Hurston's affirmative work is profoundly defiant, just as Wright's protest unmistakably asserts our need for an alternative, benign environment" (5).

    2. The term "New Negro" more often than not referred to Blacks of social, educational, or economic privilege, and consequently, the term more often than not referred to men. The men, themselves, as well as the cultural historians of the Harlem Renaissance, conceived of the period as the time of the awakening manhood of the Black race. "Manhood," "the race," and "the Negro" are often conflated terms. As Gloria Hull puts it in *Color, Sex, and Poetry: Three Women Writers in the Harlem Renaissance,* "the Renaissance, despite its veneer of equal opportunity, was a time when not only Harlem and the Negro, but men as usual were 'in vogue' " (10). In *The Sexual Mountain and Black Women Writers: Adventures in Sex, Literature, and Real Life,* Calvin Hernton makes these observations: "Historically, the battle line of the racial struggle in the United States has been drawn exclusively as a struggle between the men of the races. Everything having to do with race has been defined and counter-defined by the men as a question of whether black people were or were not a race of Men. The central concept and the universal metaphor around which all aspects of the racial situation revolve is " 'Manhood' " (38). As Elise McDougald demonstrates in her essay "The Task of Negro Womanhood," "The Woman Question" was a part of the intellectual debate of the period. McDougald explores issues of gender in terms of Black women's lives in the spheres of home, community, and industry. McDougald also focuses on the "personal inferiority" Black women suffer because of prevailing ideologies of beauty from which they are excluded and the persistent images of Black women as servants and trollops. Sympathetically listing the adverse conditions the Black woman faces, McDougald concludes that with so many forces at work against her, "both from without and within her group," "true sex equality has not been approximated" (379, 380). Yet, McDougald allowed that women's concerns were not an integral component of African Americans' quest for equality: "On the whole the Negro woman's feminist efforts are directed chiefly toward the realization of the equality of the races, the sex struggle assuming the subordinate place" (380–81). The bulk of the novels of the period written by or about Black women reveal the gender politics McDougald expressed. The novels (e.g., Nella Larsen's *Quicksand* and *Passing,* Jessie Fauset's *Plum Bun,* and Wallace Thurman's *The Blacker the Berry* ) exhibit a preoccupation with issues

of race, class, and color, often with a "tragic (or otherwise not too happy) mulatto" as the central figure.

3. Richard Wright had little respect for the Renaissance literati. He castigated the artistic production it generated as "fruits of that foul soil which was the result of a liaison between inferiority-complexed Negro 'genuises' and burnt-out white Bohemians with money" ("Blueprint" 37). He found "the so-called Harlem school of expression" lacking in "discipline and consciousness" (47). Ideological conflicts notwithstanding, Wright's socialist vision had several goals in common with the Harlem intelligentsia: reevaluation of African American history and folk culture, embracing of African heritage, and use of art and letters to promulgate political vision.

Wright determined that the sources of Black culture were "the Negro church" and "the folklore of the Negro people" (39). Within African American folk culture was the wisdom of the race, and therein was the heritage of the Black writer whose consciousness "draws for its strength upon the fluid lore of a great people" (40, 43). As well, "Negro writers must have in their consciousness the foreshortened picture of the *whole,* nourishing culture from which they were torn in Africa, and the long, complex . . . struggle to regain . . . a *whole* culture again" (47). Wright saw the Black writer's role as a messianic one. The writer is "called upon to do no less than create values by which [the] race is to struggle, live and die" (43). To the degree that the writer creates values in accordance with Wright's Marxist vision, the writer "may expect either to be consigned to oblivion, or to be recognized" as a "valued agent" (44). Wright urged Black writers to embrace Black folk culture and to understand the nationalist implications of their lives. However, Wright urged Black writers to accept their nationalism, not in order to celebrate and encourage it, but in order to change and transcend it (42).

4. E. David Cronon assesses Garveyism as "a notable achievement" (207). He referred to correspondence from William Pickens in his efforts to estimate the UNIA membership and evaluate Garvey's leadership. Amongst others, he quotes Ralph Bunche, who concludes, "No other American Negro organization has ever been able to reach and stir the masses of Negroes to the same degree, or receive from them such generous financial support" (207).

5. Though she did not consider herself part of the Harlem establishment as such, Hurston also took part in the defamation of Garvey's character. In the unpublished essay "The Emperor Effaces Himself," Hurston penned a poignant satire mocking Garvey's taste for pageantry and parade, his leadership, and his trial for fraud. In Juvenalian style, she caricatures Garvey as a mountebank, lampooning what she perceives as his pretentiousness, false pride, egoism, dishonesty, and incompetence.

6. My discussion of Hurston's efforts as producer and dramatist is informed by Hurston's own discussion of these aspects of her career in *Dust Tracks* ("Books and Things" 206–14); Robert Hemenway's discussion in his biography of her (159–87); Warren J. Carson's "Hurston as Dramatist: The Florida

Connection"; and Maurice J. O'Sullivan, Jr., and Jack C. Lane's "Zora Neale Hurston at Rollins College." This last essay includes the programs of *From Sun to Sun* and *All De Live Long Day* in the appendixes.

7. *Nommo* is comparable to Heraclitus's theory of "logos," individual creative force, and "NTU" is comparable to "Logos," as the universal source of all "logos." Olney explains that "there is a oneness of the self, an integrity or internal harmony that holds together the multiplicity and continual transformations of being, and it is not an 'imitation' of the Logos, nor is it the individual's 'piece' of the Logos. In every individual, to the degree that he is individual, the whole principle and essence of the Logos is wholly present, so that in his integrity the whole harmony of the universe is entirely and, as it were, uniquely present and existent. What the Logos demands of the individual is that he should realize his logos, which is also more than his own or private logos—it is the Logos" (6).

8. "The Signifying Monkey" is a toast featuring the monkey as a trickster figure, a clever hero who is weak and diminutive but outsmarts stronger and larger animals, like the lion, by *signifying* (Abrahams, *Deep Down* 143). Claudia Mitchell-Kernan writes that when these toasts are interpreted as allegory, the monkey symbolizes Blacks who identify with the "wily contriving, and villainous" traits of the monkey, and the lion symbolizes whites who are portrayed as foolish, naive, and gullible. There are many variations of the toast. In some, the monkey is killed and in others, the monkey triumphs (322–23). The following are opening lines of one variation of the toast entitled "The Signifying Monkey and the Lion":

> Deep down in the jungle so they say
> There's a signifying motherfucker down the way.
> There hadn't been no disturbin' in the jungle for quite a bit,
> For up jumped the monkey in the tree one day and
> laughed,
> "I guess I'll start some shit."
>
> (Abrahams, *Deep Down* 113).

9. Adopting Mitchell-Kernan's method of distinguishing between the two uses of *signifying,* I italicize the term when I refer to the specific act of direct verbal dueling or ritual insult, and I capitalize it when I refer to the art of verbal play, generally, when the term "can mean any number of things" and indirect discourse is a key element.

## Chapter 4: The Folk Preacher and the Folk Sermon Form

1. This passage from *Dust Tracks* is comparable to the testimony of Reverend Rubin Lacy, which is couched in his "The Deck of Cards" sermon:

> I shall never forget the time
> An' I shall never forget the place

One Monday mornin'
That same God
Met me that mornin'
And said Lacy
If you don't go
If you don't go
This is your last chance
I never shall forget the word I said
I said to Him that mornin' I'll go
Where ya want me to go
If it's to California I'll go
If it's to Nebraska I'll go
All the way
Ever since that day
I been on the job.

(Rosenberg 137)

2. The "habit of survival" refers "to the external adjustments and internal adaptations that people make to economic exploitation and to racial and gender-related oppression" (Scott 10).

3. Remonstration of the congregation is part of the preacher's duty. The preacher is obliged to expose and chastise negative behavior. The narrator of *Dust Tracks* does this in "My People! My People!" as she condemns what she perceives as pretension and hypocrisy among middle- and upper-class African Americans and the Black intelligentsia. She lambasts their assumptions of racial solidarity and describes as spurious their roles as "Race Leaders." In "Religion" she reproves those believers who rely on prayer to relieve their oppressed conditions instead of being self-reliant and fighting their own battles.

## Chapter 5: Politics, Parody, Power, and *Moses, Man of the Mountain*

1. In "The Renaissance Re-examined," Warrington Hudlin describes Harlem Renaissance artists, Hurston among them, as conditional integrationists: "Whites were neither all bad nor all good, they were the people with whom you had to deal. The relationship would be based on their behavior, for the moral advantage was the black [person's]" (271). Robert Bone writes that Hurston's "experience with separate-but-equal politics ... deeply affected her outlook on racial issues, as well as her approaches to the Negro novel" (57). Larry Neal characterizes Hurston as "no political radical. She was, instead, a belligerent individualist who was decidedly unpredictable and perhaps a little inconsistent. At one moment she would sound highly nationalistic. Then at other times she might mouth statements that, in terms of the ongoing struggle for black liberation, were ill-conceived and even reactionary" (161). Robert Hemenway

describes Hurston as an accommodationist and a conservative whose "politics are typically individual." Her "concentration on the individual, in her lifelong repudiation of pathological stereotypes" led to reactionary responses that "become less and less flexible" (329, 337, 336). And in Roy Wilkins's philippic against Hurston in "The Watchtower," Hurston is charged with supporting Jim Crow and being an enemy of the race.

2. Interestingly, W. E. B. Du Bois, a staunch integrationist, reversed his position on this issue. In his January 1934 *Crisis* editorial, Du Bois made a distinction between voluntary segregation and racial segregation based on discrimination: "The opposition to racial segregation is not or should not be any distaste or unwillingness of colored people to work with each other, to co-operate with each other, to live with each other. The opposition to segregation is an opposition to discrimination" ("Postscript" 20). To his query of what can be done about insistent, unassailable, and unremitting racial segregation in the face of starvation and economic upheaval, he declares in his April 1934 editorial, "The only thing that we not only can, but must do, is voluntarily and insistently to organize our economic and social power, no matter how much segregation it involves. Learn to associate with ourselves and to train ourselves for effective association. Organize our strength as consumers; learn to co-operate and use machines and power as producers; train ourselves in methods of democratic control within our own group. Run and support our own institutions. . . . It is perfectly certain that, not only shall we be compelled to submit to much segregation, but that sometimes it will be necessary to our survival and a step toward the ultimate breaking down of barriers, to increase by voluntary action our separation from our fellowmen" (115, 117)

3. Howard writes that in *Tell My Horse*, "Hurston reports the unimportant as well as the important, the trivial as well as the significant" (*Zora Neale Hurston* 156). Her statement repeats Turner's earlier statement: "*Tell My Horse* (1938) reflects even more disastrously Miss Hurston's regrettable inability to distinguish the important from the unimportant, the significant from the trivial" (*Minor Chord* 117–18). Like Turner, Howard sees Hurston's reportage of Haitian folkloric practices as the book's merit and rejects out of hand her political views. Turner was outraged that Hurston looked favorably on the American occupation of the island. She was not a trained political scientist and therefore incapable of evaluating the situation, he wrote. He compared her stance to that of James Weldon Johnson, who vociferously opposed the occupation with denouncements of imperialism and "unwarranted cruelty" (*Minor Chord* 118). Ironically, at one point Johnson had assumed Hurston's position: "Exposer of American imperialism in Haiti, he had earlier defended the occupation as a benefit to the islanders" (D. L. Lewis 147).

4. Walker is but one of several readers, artists, and critics who assumes this position and continues a moratorium on analysis of Hurston's political thought. Mary Helen Washington's prefatory remarks on Hurston's essays and articles characterize Hurston's politics as "exasperating" at times. Reading some of her political essays today, Washington winces, "makes one's flesh crawl" (151).

Even so Karla Holloway recommends that we do not investigate too thoroughly Hurston's "accumulated layers" and "that we focus our creative efforts on assuring her the status she deserves" (117–18).

5. Here, Hurston speaks with the same mind and voice and often with the same terminology as Booker T. Washington. In *Up from Slavery,* Washington conveys his stance on the Reconstruction period and his suspicion of the North: "I felt that the Reconstruction policy, so far as it related to my race, was in a large measure on a false foundation, was artificial and forced. In many cases it seemed to me that the ignorance of my race was being used as a tool with which to help white men into office, and that there was an element in the North which wanted to punish the Southern white men by forcing the Negro into positions over the heads of the Southern whites. I felt that the Negro would be the one to suffer for this in the end" (68). Although Washington asserted that "not all the coloured people who were in office during Reconstruction were unworthy of their positions" nor were "all the class designated as carpetbaggers dishonourable men," his general conclusion is that the Reconstruction was unsuccessful: "Of course the coloured people, so largely without education, and wholly without experience in government, made tremendous mistakes" (69).

6. Du Bois held the same individualist perspective as did Hurston: "The ultimate goal of DuBois' reform was a condition of social justice in which every man would be accepted on his merits as a man. A man with ability and talent would rise, and those without it would not. Society would be color-blind; race would be of no account in the equation of human worth" (Huggins 35).

7. Social historians of the Renaissance tend to enthusiastically and delightfully convey the pernicious ridiculing and muckraking that transpired amongst the men of the period, often describing their actions in militaristic terms. Du Bois, for example, spearheaded the "anti-Washington forces" that "issued a direct challenge to the philosophy and leadership of Booker T. Washington" (Huggins 19–20). Though Du Bois and Garvey defined themselves in relation to their opposition to one another, they are not denounced for taking things personally. Du Bois's vitriolic reaction to Marcus Garvey resulted in his attempt to personally sabotage Garvey and his work: "On the eve of the third Pan-African Congress in London, Brussels, and Paris, DuBois wrote Secretary of State Charles Evans Hughes for classified information which could be used against the UNIA" (D. L. Lewis 42). Du Bois's personal vendetta is not touted as an example of irrational, extreme, or eccentric behavior. And the homosocial bonding of men in bars or bedrooms where professional and political careers were nurtured and advanced tended not to be scrutinized in terms of personal politics.

8. Describing the book as one of Hurston's two masterpieces (215), Hemenway's insightful examination of the novel concludes with a projection of what kind of book it might have been and what kind of book it did not become (269). He adjudges the book "a noble failure," "the victim of its own

aspirations, a condition that can be fairly said to characterize Zora Hurston's own life for the next decade" (270, 271). Darwin Turner declares *Moses* Hurston's master work. "If she had written nothing else, Miss Hurston would deserve recognition for this book" (109). Though entertaining, he determines that the novel "does not comment significantly on life or people"; "a good joke, at best, is merely a joke" (*Minor Chord* 111). Lillie P. Howard considers Turner's praise of the book "effusive." She deems the book worthy of recognition but that "calling it her 'most accomplished achievement in fiction,' [is] a compliment reserved for *Their Eyes Were Watching God*" (113).

9. Moses' character and spirit is like that of the Nietzschean lion. Moses describes himself in such terms and so do the Hebrews: " 'He's a fine man, a noble man! He's just like a lion,' " they agree (242). Yet, they conspire to destroy him. Hurston felt the same resentment from "the herd" that Moses describes. She believed her being fired from a teaching position stemmed from resentment of her fame as a writer: "My name as an author is too big to be tolerated, lest it gather to itself the 'glory' of the school here. I have met that before. But perhaps it is natural. The mediocre have no importance except through appointment. They feel invaded and defeated by the presence of creative folk among them" (Hicks, "Discovery" 39).

10. The historian and philosopher Carter G. Woodson also shared Hurston's discontent with "Race Leaders" and was critical of their self-serving leadership. In a rhetorical style typical of the folk preacher, Woodson states his views: "If we can finally succeed in translating the idea of leadership into that of service, we may soon find it possible to lift the Negro to a higher level. Under leadership we have come into the ghetto; by service within the ranks we may work our way out of it. Under leadership we have been constrained to do the biddings of others; by service we may work out a program in the light of our own circumstances. Under leadership we have become poverty-stricken; by service we may teach the masses how to earn a living honestly. Under leadership we have been made to despise our own possibilities and to develop into parasites; by service we may prove sufficient unto the task of self-development and contribute our part to modern culture" (118–19).

11. This project of demystification recurs in *Seraph on the Suwanee*. The narrator conveys Arvay's epiphanic meanderings and compares Arvay to Moses: "All that had happened to her, good or bad, was a part of her own self and had come out of her. Within her own flesh were many mysteries. She lifted her left hand before her eyes and studied it in every detail with wonder. With wonder and deep awe like Moses before his burning bush. What all, Arvay asked of herself, was buried and hidden in human flesh? You toted it around with you all your life time, but you couldn't know. If you just could know, it would be all the religion that anybody needed. And what was in you was bound to come out and stand" (349–50).

12. Hurston transformed her social vision into personal and public praxis. During her work on the Grant Reynolds's campaign, she "found time to do some community organizing, developing a 'block mothers' plan which resembled current day-care programs. Zora told an interviewer: 'It's the old idea,

trite but true, of helping people to help themselves that will be the only salvation of the Negro in this country'" (Hemenway 303).

13. Ideas in this paragraph are informed by Jacqueline de Weever's work, specifically chapter 1, "Mythmaking: Intertextuality, Inversion, and Metaphor" (21–59).

## Chapter 6: Politics of Self

1. The term "feminist" is used to designate those scholars who, whatever their ethnicity, identify their standpoints as feminist. As Alice Walker defines the term in *In Search of Our Mothers' Gardens,* a "womanist" is a "black feminist or feminist of color. From the black folk expression of mothers to female children, 'You acting womanish,' i.e., like a woman" (xi). The term is particularly expressive of the conditions, sensibilities, and desires of African American women.

For a cogent overview of the debate surrounding Black feminist identity and ideology, see Collins, particularly chapter 2, "Defining Black Feminist Thought" (19–40).

2. Historically, Black women such as Sojourner Truth, Frances Harper, Maria Stewart, Anna Julia Cooper, Fannie Lou Hamer, Francis Barrier Washington, March Church Terrell, Ella Baker, and Ida B. Wells have directly or indirectly addressed the multiple oppressions that qualify and delimit Black womanhood. In "A Black Feminist Statement," the Combahee River Collective expressly articulated the need for a Black feminist consciousness that systematically examined "the multilayered texture of Black women's lives" (366). Theories and analyses that address and explore the multiple jeopardies Black women face are found in the works of Black women scholars such as Pauli Murray, Angela Davis, Toni Cade Bambara, June Jordan, Barbara Smith, Frances Beale, Elsa Barkley Brown, Alice Walker, bell hooks, Audre Lorde, Hazel Carby, Darlene Clark Hine, Deborah K. King, Barbara Christian, and a host of others.

3. I created the designation the "Pecola complex" to name the kind of inferiority complex many African American females suffer and to suggest the environmental conditions that induce it. The designation describes a psychological state of self-contempt or self-hate common to African American females who internalize notions of European standards of beauty, a state of mind that results in confused and often destructive patterns of behavior. It implicates a hostile, bigoted, and ethnocentric Anglo-American society that objectifies Black women as morally debased beasts of burden and makes of Black women the antithesis of all that is considered beautiful and virtuous in white women. Further, the Pecola complex suggests how the controlling images constructed in the larger society seep into the domestic sphere of home and community, insidiously damaging a Black female's self-perception and sense of intrinsic worth. The designation is drawn from Toni Morrison's delineation of the character Pecola Breedlove in her novel *The Bluest Eye.* A

dark-eyed, dark-skinned little girl, Pecola profoundly believes that if she were not ugly, if she had white skin and the bluest of blue eyes, her parents would not fight, her brother would not run away from home, and she would bask in the goodwill of friends, teachers, and neighborhood merchants—she would enjoy a blissful existence. (Pecola's last name, Breedlove, also recalls Madame C. J. Walker, born Sarah Breedlove, whose beauty products helped Black women change their [self] image [Giddings 187].)

Color consciousness among African Americans, female and male, and the attending self-hatred are still crucial issues. Even in the 1990s, the ideal beauty is the so-called mulatto. This is evident in the figures of "mixed" Blacks paraded through the media and anointed *the* ideal beauty or *the* most sexually appealing, those figures such as the TV character Whitley Gilbert, the recording artist Mariah Carey, the actor Phillip Michael Thomas, the model Iman, Miss Americas Vanessa Williams and Suzette Charles, and, questionably, the adult Michael Jackson.

4. Fannie Barrier Harris's 1905 essay "The Colored Girl" portrays the character of Zora Neale Hurston and poignantly depicts the marginalization and devaluation of Black females in American society, even as the twenty-first century dawns: "That the term 'colored girl' is almost a term of reproach in the social life of America is all too true; she is not known and hence not believed in; she belongs to a race that is best designated by the term 'problem,' and she lives beneath the shadow of that problem which envelopes [*sic*] and obscures her. . . . It is because of this tyranny of race prejudice that the colored girl is called upon to endure and overcome more difficulties than confront any other women in our country. In law, religion and ethics, she is entitled to everything, but in practice there are always forces at work that would deny her anything. But yet, as meanly as she is thought of; hindered as she is in all directions, she is always doing something of merit and credit that is not expected of her. She is irrepressible. She is insulted, but she holds up her head; she is scorned, but she proudly demands respect. Thus has it come to pass that the most interesting girl of this country is the colored girl" (150-51).

5. Wallace Thurman examines the impact of color consciousness on African American women in his novel *The Blacker the Berry*. Thurman was a very dark-skinned man who had a complex about his color. Ironically, the novel illustrates the effect of color consciousness on a female protagonist.

6. Another example of the fantasy element in Hurston's stories is seen in Jim Meserve's perception of Arvay in *Seraph:* " 'I never have seen you as a teppentime Cracker like you have thrown in my face time and again. I saw you like a king's daughter out of a story-book with your long, soft golden hair. You were deserving, and noble, and all I ever wanted to do was to have the chance to do for you and protect you' " (263).

7. This passage recalls one in *Dust Tracks* in which Hurston depicts Mrs. Alice, an employer for whom she babysat, in an atmosphere of Alice-in-Wonderland enchantment. Holding the hands of her two charges with "gray-blue" eyes, Hurston awaited instructions from Mrs. Alice. "She was a very beautiful

woman in her middle twenties and she was combing out her magnificent hair. She looked at me through the looking-glass, and we both started to grin for some reason or another" (119, 120).

8. This counterbalancing of black with white images is persistent in Hurston's writing. It is seen, for instance, in Hurston's vision of her ideal Christmas gift: "a fine black riding horse with white leather saddle and bridles" (*Dust Tracks* 38).

9. Dianne Sadoff also detects the oedipal nature of Hurston's relationship with her father: "Hurston also evades knowledge of her oedipal jealousy of her stepmother, her anger so extreme that the sequence about this 'skunk' who needed her 'behind . . . kicked' gets narrated early and out of sequence. . . . But the jealous and solitary girl must not surface in the successful woman writer's autobiography—the acceptable story of black girlhood and womanhood—and so she gets repressed" (19).

10. Janie Crawford Starks Woods is alone at the end of *Their Eyes*. She has also acquired a certain autonomy, a sense of her "somebodiness." I question, though, given Janie's history of staying with one man until the next one comes along, where Janie might have been had she not killed Tea Cake. I wonder, as well, how steadfast her commitment to her autonomous self might be should another Jody or Tea Cake come along. Janie seems to be a woman who depends on the kindness of strange men. She has experienced love as she dreamed it should be, but that kind of love casts Janie in a subordinate, dependent position. For even though she is a woman of means, she allows Tea Cake to render her economic independence null and void. She allows him to put her in a position in which she must depend on him for her welfare, in a position in which she has no agency: " 'Put dat two hundred back wid de rest, Janie. Mah dice. Ah no need no assistance tuh help me feed mah woman. From now on, you gointuh eat whutever mah money can buy yuh and wear de same. When Ah ain't got nothin' you don't git nothin',' " Janie's meek response is, " 'Dat's all right wid me' " (191).

11. Like Jim Meserve, John Hurston had plenty of boy children and did just about everything his wife told him to do. John Hurston "not only boasted among other men about 'his house full of young'uns' but he boasted that he never allowed his wife to go out and hit a lick of work for anybody a day in her life" (*Dust Tracks* 16).

12. Jennifer Jordan's "Feminist Fantasies: Zora Neale Hurston's *Their Eyes Were Watching God*" is a good overview of the debate on these issues.

13. Comparably, Moses demands that Aaron strip before him. Then Moses kills him (333–34). Both acts uncritically represent male domination in terms of control, moral degradation, and physical violence.

## Conclusion

1. Mary Fields (1832–1914), also known as "Black Mary," escaped enslavement and ran to Toledo, Ohio, where she worked in a convent. When the

nuns moved to Montana, Mary followed. She helped the nuns build a school and served as their protector. One can see Big Sweet in this description of Mary Fields: "In all the west, Mary Fields had no equal. She was a 6-foot, 200-pound, cigar-smoking, gun-totin' pioneer who settled her arguments with her fists, and once in a while with her six-shooter. The folks around Cascade, Montana, knew her as a freight hauler, laundress, restaurant owner, and the second female ever to drive a United States mail coach. . . . Because of the extreme cold, Mary dressed like a man, except for a long dress and apron she wore over a pair of men's pants" (*Black Pioneers* 14).

2. Sertima cites from Diedre Wimby's essay "The Female Horuses and Great Wives of Kemet," which is also included in *Black Women in Antiquity* (36–48). See also John Henrik Clarke's "African Warrior Queens" in the same volume.

# Works Cited

Abrahams, Roger D. *Deep Down in the Jungle: Negro Narrative Folklore from the Streets of Philadelphia.* Chicago: Aldine, 1970.
————. "Negotiating Respect: Patterns of Presentation among Black Women." *Journal of American Folklore* 88 (Jan.-Mar. 1975): 58–80.
Bádéjò, Diedre L. "The Goddess Òsun as a Paradigm for African Feminist Criticism." *Sage: A Scholarly Journal on Black Women* 6, no. 1 (Summer 1989): 27–32.
Baker, Houston A., Jr. *Modernism and the Harlem Renaissance.* Chicago: University of Chicago Press, 1987.
Bakhtin, Mikhail. *The Dialogic Imagination: Four Essays by M. M. Bakhtin.* Ed. Michael Holquist. Trans. Caryl Emerson and Michael Holquist. Austin: University of Texas Press, 1981.
————. "Discourse Typology in Prose." In *Readings in Russian Poetics.* Ed. Ladislav Matejka and Krystyna Pomorska. Cambridge: MIT Press, 1971. 176–96.
Benedict, Ruth. *Patterns of Culture.* Sentry Edition. Boston: Houghton Mifflin, 1959.
Benston, Kimberly W. "I Yam What I Am: The Topos of Un(naming) in Afro-American Literature." *Black American Literature Forum* 16, no. 1 (1982): 151–72. Reprinted in *Black Literature and Literary Theory.* Ed. Henry L. Gates, Jr. New York: Methuen, 1984. 153–72.
Bernal, Martin. *Black Athena: The Afroasiatic Roots of Classical Civilization.* Vol 1: *The Fabrication of Ancient Greece, 1785–1985.* New Brunswick: Rutgers University Press, 1987.
Boas, Franz. "Language." In *General Anthropology.* 1938. Ed. Franz Boas. Boston: Heath, 1965. 124–45.
————. "Methods of Research." In *General Anthropology.* 1938. Ed. Franz Boas. Boston: Heath, 1965. 666–86.
————. *Race, Language, and Culture.* New York: Macmillan, 1940.
Bone, Robert. "Zora Neale Hurston." In *The Black Novelist.* Ed. Robert Hemenway. Columbus: Charles E. Merrill, 1970. 55–61.
Bridgwater, Patrick. *Nietzsche in Anglosaxony: A Study of Nietzsche's Impact on English and American Literature.* Leicester, England: Leicester University Press, 1972.

Cade, Toni. "On the Issue of Roles." In *The Black Woman: An Anthology.* Ed. Toni Cade. New York: New American Library, 1970. 101–10.

Carby, Hazel. Foreword to *Seraph on the Suwanee* by Zora Neale Hurston. 1948. New York: Harper, 1991. vii–xviii.

Carson, Warren J. "Hurston as Dramatist: The Florida Connection." In *Zora in Florida.* Ed. Steve Glassman and Kathryn Lee Seidel. Orlando: University of Central Florida Press, 1991. 121–29.

Christian, Barbara. *Black Feminist Criticism : Perspectives on Black Women Writers.* New York: Pergamon, 1985.

Clarke, John Henrik. "African Warrior Queens." In *Black Women in Antiquity.* Ed. Ivan Van Sertima. New Brunswick: Transaction Books, 1988. 123–34.

Collins, Patricia Hill. *Black Feminist Thought: Knowledge, Consciousness, and the Politics of Empowerment.* Vol. 2 of *Perspectives on Gender.* Boston: Unwin Hyman, 1990.

Combahee River Collective. "A Black Feminist Statement." In *Capitalist Patriarchy and the Case for Socialist Feminism.* Ed. Zillah R. Eisenstein. New York: Monthly Review Press, 1979. 362–72.

Cronon, E. David. *Black Moses: The Story of Marcus Garvey and the Universal Negro Improvement Association.* Madison: University of Wisconsin Press, 1969.

Cross, Paulette. "Jokes and Black Consciousness: A Collection with Interviews." In *Mother Wit from the Laughing Barrel: Readings in the Interpretations of Afro-American Folklore.* Ed. Alan Dundes. Englewood Cliffs: Prentice-Hall, 1973. 649–69.

Daniel, Walter C. *Images of the Preacher in Afro-American Literature.* Washington, D.C.: University Press of America, 1981.

Du Bois, W. E. B. "Criteria of Negro Art." *Crisis* 32 (Oct. 1926): 290–97.

———. "Postscript." *Crisis* 41 (Jan. 1934): 20–21.

———. "Postscript." *Crisis* 41 (Apr. 1934): 115–17.

———. *The Souls of Black Folk.* 1903. New York: New American Library, 1969.

Dundes, Alan, ed. *Mother Wit from the Laughing Barrel: Readings in the Interpretations of Afro-American Folklore.* Englewood Cliffs: Prentice-Hall, 1973.

Fauset, Arthur Huff. "Intelligentsia." *Fire!!* 1, no. 1 (Nov. 1926): 45–46.

Fauset, Jesse. *Plum Bun: A Novel without a Moral.* 1928. Boston: Beacon, 1990.

Finnegan, Ruth. *Oral Literature in Africa.* Oxford: Clarendon Press, 1970.

Ford, Nick A. *The Contemporary Negro Novel: A Study in Race Relations.* College Park: McGrath, 1968.

Foster, John Burt, Jr. *Heirs to Dionysus: A Nietzschean Current in Literary Modernism.* Princeton: Princeton University Press, 1981.

Foucault, Michel. *Power/Knowledge: Selected Interviews and Other Writings, 1972–1977.* Ed. Colin Gordon. New York: Pantheon, 1980.

Garvey, Marcus M. "Marcus Garvey, Foremost Negro Leader, Condemns Harmful Trend of Books of a New Group of Race Writers." *Negro World* (Sept. 29, 1928): 1.

Gates, Henry Louis, Jr. "The Blackness of Blackness: A Critique of the Sign and the Signifying Monkey." In *Black Literature and Literary Theory*. Ed. Henry Louis Gates, Jr. New York: Methuen, 1984. 285–321.

———. *The Signifying Monkey: A Theory of Afro-American Literary Criticism*. New York: Oxford University Press, 1988.

Giddings, Paula. *When and Where I Enter: The Impact of Black Women on Race and Sex in America*. New York: Bantam, 1984.

Glassman, Steve, and Kathryn Lee Seidel, eds. *Zora in Florida*. Orlando: University of Central Florida Press, 1991.

Grant, Jacquelyn. "Black Women and the Church." In *All the Women Are White, All the Blacks Are Men, but Some of Us Are Brave: Black Women's Studies*. Ed. Gloria T. Hull, Patricia Bell Scott, and Barbara Smith. Old Westbury: Feminist Press, 1982. 141–52.

Grier, William H., and Price M. Cobbs. *Black Rage*. New York: Bantam, 1968.

Harding, Vincent. *There Is a River: The Black Struggle for Freedom in America*. New York: Vintage, 1983.

Harris, Fannie Barrier. "The Colored Girl." 1905. In *Invented Lives: Narratives of Black Women, 1860–1960*. Ed. Mary Helen Washington. Garden City: Anchor Press, 1987.

Hartsock, Nancy C. M. "The Feminist Standpoint: Developing the Ground for a Specifically Feminist Historical Materialism." In *Discovering Reality: Feminist Perspectives on Epistemology, Metaphysics, Methodology, and Philosophy of Science*. Ed. Sandra Harding and Merrill B. Hintikka. Dordrecht, Holland: D. Reidel, 1983. 283–310.

Headon, David. "'Beginning to See Things Really': The Politics of Zora Neale Hurston." In *Zora in Florida*. Ed. Steve Glassman and Kathryn Lee Seidel. Orlando: University of Central Florida Press, 1991. 28–37.

Hemenway, Robert E. "That Which the Soul Lives By." Introduction to *Mules and Men* by Zora Neale Hurston. Bloomington: Indiana University Press, 1978. xi–xxviii.

———. *Zora Neale Hurston: A Literary Biography*. Urbana: University of Illinois Press, 1977.

Hernton, Calvin C. *The Sexual Mountain and Black Women Writers: Adventures in Sex, Literature, and Real Life*. New York: Anchor, 1987.

Hicks, John. "Discovery." In *Zora! Zora Neale Hurston: A Woman and Her Community*. Ed. N. Y. Nathiri. Orlando, Fla.: Sentinel Communications Company, 1991. 17–50.

Hine, Darlene C. "Rape and the Inner Lives of Black Women in the Middle West: Preliminary Thoughts on the Culture of Dissemblance." *Signs: Journal of Women in Culture and Society* 14, no. 4 (Summer 1989): 912–20.

Holloway, Karla F. C. *The Character of the Word: The Texts of Zora Neale Hurston*. New York: Greenwood Press, 1987.

hooks, bell. *Talking Back, Thinking Feminist, Thinking Black*. Boston: South End Press, 1989.

Howard, Lillie P. "Marriage: Zora Neale Hurston's System of Values." *College Language Association Journal* 21 (1977): 256–68.

———. *Zora Neale Hurston.* Boston: Twayne, 1980.

Hudlin, Warrington. "The Renaissance Re-examined." In *The Harlem Renaissance Remembered.* Ed. Arna Bontemps. New York: Dodd, Mead, 1972. 268–77.

Huggins, Nathan I. *Harlem Renaissance.* New York: Oxford University Press, 1971.

Hughes, Langston. *The Big Sea: An Autobiography.* 1963. New York: Thunder's Mouth Press, 1986.

———. "Jokes Negroes Tell on Themselves." In *Mother Wit from the Laughing Barrel: Readings in the Interpretations of Afro-American Folklore.* Ed. Alan Dundes. Englewood Cliffs: Prentice-Hall, 1973. 637–41.

———. "The Negro Artist and the Racial Mountain." *The Nation,* June 28, 1926. 692–94.

Hughes, Langston, and Arna Bontemps, eds. *The Book of Negro Folklore.* 1958. New York: Dodd, Mead, 1983.

Hull, Gloria T. *Color, Sex, and Poetry: Three Women Writers of the Harlem Renaissance.* Bloomington: Indiana University Press, 1987.

Hurston, Zora Neale. "Book of Harlem." In *Spunk: The Selected Short Stories of Zora Neale Hurston.* Berkeley: Turtle Island, 1985. 75–81.

———. "Characteristics of Negro Expression." In *The Sanctified Church.* Berkeley: Turtle Island, 1983. 49–68. Orig. pub. in *Negro: An Anthology.* Ed. Nancy Cunard. London: Wishart, 1934. 39–46.

———. "Cock Robin on Beale Street." In *Spunk: The Selected Short Stories of Zora Neale Hurston.* Berkeley: Turtle Island, 1985. 69–74. Orig. pub. in *Southern Literary Messenger* 3 (July 1941): 321–23.

———. *Color Struck: A Play. Fire!!* 1, no. 1 (Nov. 1926): 7–15.

———. "Conversions and Visions." In *The Sanctified Church.* Berkeley: Turtle Island, 1983. 85–90. Orig. pub. in *Negro: An Anthology.* Ed. Nancy Cunard. London: Wishart, 1934. 47–49.

———. "Crazy for This Democracy." In *I Love Myself when I'm Laughing and Then Again when I'm Looking Mean and Impressive: A Zora Neale Hurston Reader.* Ed. Alice Walker. Old Westbury: Feminist Press, 1979. 165–68. Orig. pub. in *Negro Digest* 4 (Dec. 1945): 45–48.

———. *Dust Tracks on a Road: An Autobiography.* 1942. 2d ed. Ed. Robert E. Hemenway. Urbana: University of Illinois Press, 1984.

———. "Dust Tracks on a Road." Manuscript. James Weldon Johnson Memorial Collection, Box 1, Folders 10–15, Beinecke Rare Book and Manuscript Library, Yale University Library.

———. "The Emperor Effaces Himself." Manuscript. James Weldon Johnson Memorial Collection, Box 1, Folder 16, Beinecke Rare Book and Manuscript Library, Yale University Library.

———. "The Fire and the Cloud." *Challenge* 1 (Sept. 1934): 10–14.

———. "Herod on Trial." In *Spunk: The Selected Short Stories of Zora Neale Hurston*. Berkeley: Turtle Island, 1985. 99–106.

———. "High John de Conquer." In *The Sanctified Church*. Berkeley: Turtle Island, 1983. 69–78. Orig. pub. in *American Mercury* 57 (Oct 1943): 450–58. Reprinted in *The Book of Negro Folklore*. 1958. Ed. Langston Hughes and Arna Bontemps. New York: Dodd, Mead, 1983. 93–102.

———. "How It Feels to Be Colored Me." In *I Love Myself when I'm Laughing and Then Again when I'm Looking Mean and Impressive: A Zora Neale Hurston Reader*. Ed. Alice Walker. Old Westbury: Feminist Press, 1979. 152–55. Orig. pub. in *World Tomorrow* 11 (May 1928): 215–16.

———. "The Hue and Cry about Howard University." *Messenger* 7 (Sept. 1925): 315–19, 338.

———. *I Love Myself when I'm Laughing and Then Again when I'm Looking Mean and Impressive: A Zora Neale Hurston Reader*. Ed. Alice Walker. Old Westbury: Feminist Press, 1979.

———. "I Saw Negro Votes Peddled." *American Legion Magazine* 49 (Nov. 1950): 12–13, 54–57, 59–60.

———. "Isis." In *Spunk: The Selected Short Stories of Zora Neale Hurston*. Berkeley: Turtle Island, 1985. 9–18. Orig. pub. as "Drenched in Light" in *Opportunity* 2 (Dec. 1924): 371–74.

———. *Jonah's Gourd Vine*. 1934. New York: Harper and Row, 1990.

———. "The Life of Herod the Great." Manuscript. Hurston Collection, Rare Books and Manuscripts, University of Florida.

———. *Moses, Man of the Mountain*. 1939. Urbana: University of Illinois Press, 1984.

———. *Mules and Men* 1935. Bloomington: Indiana University Press, 1978.

———. "Muttsy." In *Spunk: The Selected Short Stories of Zora Neale Hurston*. Berkeley: Turtle Island, 1985. 19–37. Orig. pub. in *Opportunity* 4 (Aug. 1926): 246–50.

———. "My Most Humiliating Jim Crow Experience." In *I Love Myself when I'm Laughing and Then Again when I'm Looking Mean and Impressive: A Zora Neale Hurston Reader*. Ed. Alice Walker. Old Westbury: Feminist Press, 1979. 163–64. Orig. pub. in *Negro Digest* 2 (June 1944): 25–26.

———. "My People! My People!" Manuscript. James Weldon Johnson Memorial Collection, Box 1, Folder 11, Beinecke Rare Book and Manuscript Library, Yale University Library.

———. "Negroes without Self-Pity." *American Mercury* 57 (Nov. 1943): 601–3.

———. "The 'Pet' Negro System." In *I Love Myself when I'm Laughing and Then Again when I'm Looking Mean and Impressive: A Zora Neale Hurston Reader*. Ed. Alice Walker. Old Westbury: Feminist Press, 1979. 156–62. Orig. pub. in *American Mercury* 56 (May 1943): 593–600.

———. "The Race Cannot Become Great until It Recognizes Its Talent." *Washington Tribune*, 29 December 1934. 3.

———. "Rural Schools for Negroes." Rev. of *The Jeanes Teacher in the United States* by Lance G. E. Jones. *New York Herald Tribune Books,* 20 Feb. 1938. 24.

———. *The Sanctified Church.* Berkeley: Turtle Island, 1983.

———. "The Sanctified Church." In *The Sanctified Church.* Berkeley: Turtle Island, 1983. 103–7.

———. "The Sermon." In *The Sanctified Church.* Berkeley: Turtle Island, 1983. 95–102. Orig. pub. in *Negro: An Anthology.* Ed. Nancy Cunard. London: Wishart, 1934. 50–54.

———. *Seraph on the Suwanee.* 1948. New York: Harper, 1991.

———. "Shouting." In *The Sanctified Church.* Berkeley: Turtle Island, 1983. 91–94. Orig. pub. in *Negro: An Anthology.* Ed. Nancy Cunard. London: Wishart, 1934. 49–50.

———. "Spirituals and Neo-Spirituals." In *The Sanctified Church.* Berkeley: Turtle Island, 1983. 79–84. Orig. pub. in *Negro: An Anthology.* Ed. Nancy Cunard. London: Wishart, 1934. 359–61.

———. *Spunk: The Selected Short Stories of Zora Neale Hurston.* Berkeley: Turtle Island, 1985.

———. "Spunk." In *Spunk: The Selected Short Stories of Zora Neale Hurston.* Berkeley: Turtle Island, 1985. 1–8. Orig. pub. in *Opportunity* 3 (June 1925): 171–73.

———. "Story in Harlem Slang." In *Spunk: The Selected Short Stories of Zora Neale Hurston.* Berkeley: Turtle Island, 1985. 82–85. Orig. pub. in *American Mercury* 55 (July 1942): 84–96.

———. *Tell My Horse.* 1938. New York: Harper, 1990.

———. *Their Eyes Were Watching God.* 1937. Urbana: University of Illinois Press, 1978.

———. "What White Publishers Won't Print." In *I Love Myself when I'm Laughing and Then Again when I'm Looking Mean and Impressive: A Zora Neale Hurston Reader.* Ed. Alice Walker. Old Westbury: Feminist Press, 1979. 169–173. Orig. pub. in *Negro Digest* 8 (April 1950): 85–89.

———. "Why the Negro Won't Buy Communism." *American Legion Magazine* 50 (June 1951): 13–15, 55–60.

Jackson, Blyden. Introduction to *Moses, Man of the Mountain* by Zora Neale Hurston. Urbana: University of Illinois Press, 1984. vii-xix.

Jahn, Janheinz. *Muntu: An Outline of the New African Culture.* 1958. Trans. Margorie Grene. New York: Grove Press, 1961.

James, George G. M. *Stolen Legacy: The Greeks Were Not the Authors of Greek Philosophy, but the People of North Africa, Commonly Called the Egyptians.* 1954. San Francisco: Julian Richardson Associates, 1988.

Jameson, Fredric. *The Political Unconscious: Narrative as a Symbolic Act.* Ithaca: Cornell University Press, 1981.

Johnson, Charles. "Editorials." *Opportunity* 2, no. 21 (Sept. 1924): 258–60.

———. "The New Frontage on American Life." In *The New Negro: An Interpretation.* 1925. Ed. Alain Locke. New York: Arno Press and the New York Times, 1968. 278–98.

Johnson, James Weldon. *Along This Way: The Autobiography of James Weldon Johnson.* 1933. New York: Penguin, 1990.

———. *God's Trombones: Seven Negro Sermons in Verse.* New York: Viking, 1927.

———. "A Negro Looks at Race Prejudice." *American Mercury* 14 (May 1928): 52–56.

Jordan, Jennifer. "Feminist Fantasies: Zora Neale Hurston's *Their Eyes Were Watching God.* " *Tulsa Studies in Women's Literature* 7, no. 1 (Spring 1988): 105–17.

Jordan, June. "On Richard Wright and Zora Neale Hurston: Notes toward a Balancing of Love and Hatred." *Black World* (Aug. 1974): 4–8.

Kilson, Marion. "The Transformation of Eatonville's Ethnographer." *Phylon* 33 (Summer 1972): 112–19.

King, Deborah K. "Multiple Jeopardy, Multiple Consciousness: The Context of a Black Feminist Ideology." *Signs: Journal of Women in Culture and Society* 14, no. 11 (Autumn 1988): 42–72.

Larsen, Nella. *Quicksand and Passing.* 1928 and 1929. Ed. Deborah E. McDowell. New Brunswick, N.J.: Rutgers University Press, 1986.

Lewis, David L. *When Harlem Was in Vogue.* New York: Vintage, 1982.

Lewis, Vashti. "The Declining Significance of the Mulatto Female as a Major Character in the Novels of Zora Neale Hurston." *College Language Association Journal* 28 (1984): 127–49.

Lillios, Anna. "Excursions into Zora Neale Hurston's Eatonville." In *Zora in Florida.* Ed. Steve Glassman and Kathryn Lee Seidel. Orlando: University of Central Florida Press, 1991. 13–27.

Locke, Alain. " 'Deep River, Deeper Sea': Retrospective Review of the Literature of the Negro for 1935." *Opportunity* 14, no. 1 (Jan. 1936): 6–10.

———. " 'Jingo, Counter-Jingo, and Us—Part 1' Retrospective Review of the Literature of the Negro: 1937." *Opportunity* 16, no. 1 (Jan. 1938): 7–11, 27.

———. "The Legacy of the Ancestral Arts." In *The New Negro: An Interpretation.* 1925. Ed. Alain Locke. New York: Arno Press and the New York Times, 1968. 254–67.

———. "The New Negro." In *The New Negro: An Interpretation.* 1925. Ed. Alain Locke. New York: Arno Press and the New York Times, 1968. 3–16.

Lomax, Louis. Introduction to *Up from Slavery* by Booker T. Washington. 1901. New York: Dell, 1965. 8–15.

McDougald, Elise. "The Task of Negro Womanhood." In *The New Negro: An Interpretation.* 1925. Ed. Alain Locke. New York: Arno Press and the New York Times, 1968. 369–82.

McKay, Claude. *Home to Harlem.* 1928. Boston: Northeastern University Press, 1987.

Martin, Tony. *Literary Garveyism: Garvey, Black Arts, and the Harlem Renaissance.* Dover: Majority Press, 1983.

Mead, Margaret, ed. *Anthropologist at Work: Writings of Ruth Benedict.* Boston: Houghton Mifflin, 1959.

———. Preface to *Patterns of Culture* by Ruth Benedict. Sentry Edition. Boston: Houghton Mifflin, 1959. vii–x.

Mitchell-Kernan, Claudia. "Signifying." In *Mother Wit from the Laughing Barrel: Readings in the Interpretations of Afro-American Folklore*. Ed. Alan Dundes. Englewood Cliffs: Prentice-Hall, 1973. 310–28.

Morrison, Toni. *The Bluest Eye*. New York: Pocket Books, 1970.

———. "Rootedness: The Ancestor as Foundation." In *Black Women Writers (1950–1980): A Critical Evaluation*. Ed. Mari Evans. Garden City: Anchor, 1984. 339–45.

Nathiri, N. Y. "Reunion." In *Zora! Zora Neale Hurston: A Woman and Her Community*. Ed. N. Y. Nathiri. Orlando: Sentinel Communications, 1991. 59–75.

Neal, Larry. "A Profile: Zora Neale Hurston." *Southern Exposure* 1 (Winter 1974): 160–68.

Ngugi wa Thiong'o. *Barrel of a Pen: Resistance to Repression in Neo-Colonial Kenya*. Trenton: Africa World Press, 1983.

Nietzsche, Friedrich. *Beyond Good and Evil: Prelude to a Philosophy of the Future*. 1886. Trans. R. J. Hollingdale. Middlesex: Penguin Books, 1973.

———. *The Birth of Tragedy and the Case of Wagner*. 1872 and 1888. Trans. Walter Kaufmann. New York: Vintage, 1967.

———. *The Gay Science with a Prelude in Rhymes and an Appendix of Songs*. 1887. Trans. Walter Kaufmann. New York: Vintage, 1974.

———. *On the Genealogy of Morals and Ecce Homo*. 1887. Trans. of *On the Genealogy of Morals* by Walter Kaufmann and R. J. Hollingdale. Trans. and ed. of *Ecce Homo* by Walter Kaufmann. New York: Random House, 1969.

———. *Thus Spoke Zarathustra*. 1883. Trans. R. J. Hollingdale. London: Penguin, 1961.

———. *The Will to Power*. 1901. Trans. and ed. Walter Kaufmann and R. J. Hollingdale. New York: Random House, 1968.

Olney, James. *Metaphors of Self: The Meaning of Autobiography*. Princeton: Princeton University Press, 1972.

O'Sullivan, Maurice J., Jr., and Jack C. Lane. "Zora Neale Hurston at Rollins College." In *Zora in Florida*. Ed. Steve Glassman and Kathryn Lee Seidel. Orlando: University of Central Florida Press, 1991. 130–45.

Owomoyela, Oyekan. "Proverbs—Exploration of an African Philosophy of Social Communication." *Ba Shiru* 12, no. 1 (1981): 3–16.

Preece, Harold. "Dust Tracks on a Road." *Tomorrow* 1 (Feb. 1943): 58–59.

Ramsey, Eleanor, and Everett Fly. "Understanding." In *Zora! Zora Neale Hurston: A Woman and Her Community*. Ed. N. Y. Nathiri. Orlando, Fla.: Sentinel Communications Company, 1991. 105–30.

Rayson, Ann. "The Novels of Zora Neale Hurston." *Studies in Black Literature* 5, no. 3 (Winter 1974): 1–10.

Richardson, Marilyn. *Maria Stewart: America's First Black Woman Political Writer*. Bloomington: Indiana University Press, 1987.

Rosenberg, Bruce. *The Art of the American Folk Preacher.* New York: Oxford University Press, 1970.

Ruhl, Arthur. Review of *The Great Day* by Zora Neale Hurston. *New York Herald Tribune,* 17 January 1932. 1, 11.

Sadoff, Dianne. "Black Matrilineage: The Case of Alice Walker and Zora Neale Hurston." *Signs: A Journal of Women in Culture and Society* 11, no. 1 (1985): 4–26.

*A Salute to Black Pioneers.* Vol. 3. Chicago: Empak Publishing Company, 1986.

Scott, Kesho Y. *The Habit of Surviving.* New York: Ballantine, 1991.

Sertima, Ivan Van. "The African Eve: Introduction and Summary." In *Black Women in Antiquity.* Ed. Ivan Van Sertima. New Brunswick: Transaction Books, 1988. 5–11.

Sheffey, Ruthe T. "Zora Neale Hurston's *Moses, Man of the Mountain:* A Fictionalized Manifesto on the Imperatives of Black Leadership." *College Language Association* 29, no. 2 (1985): 206–21.

Smith, Barbara. "Sexual Politics and the Fiction of Zora Neale Hurston." *Radical Teacher* (May 1978): 26–30.

Smitherman, Geneva. *Talkin and Testifyin: The Language of Black America.* Detroit: Wayne State University Press, 1977.

Soyinka, Wole. *Myth, Literature, and the African World.* Cambridge: Cambridge University Press, 1976.

Spinoza, Benedict de. *"On the Improvement of the Understanding," The Ethics, and Correspondence.* 1883. Trans. R. H. M. Elwes. Mineola, N.Y.: Dover, 1955.

Steady, Filomina Chioma. "The Black Woman Cross-Culturally: An Overview." In *The Black Woman Cross-Culturally.* Ed. Filomina Chioma Steady. 1981. Rochester: Schenkman, 1985. 7–41.

Thurman, Wallace. *The Blacker the Berry.* 1929. New York: Collier. 1970.

———. "Negro Artists and the Negro." *New Republic,* Aug. 31, 1927, 37–39.

Truth, Sojourner. "Ain't I a Woman." In *Black Sister: Poetry by Black American Women, 1746–1980.* Ed. Erlene Stetson. Bloomington: Indiana University Press, 1981. 24–25.

Turner, Darwin T. Foreword to *Dust Tracks on a Road* by Zora Neale Hurston. New York: Arno Press and the New York Times, 1969. i–v.

———. *In a Minor Chord: Three Afro-American Writers and Their Search for Identity.* Carbondale: Southern Illinois University Press, 1971.

Tutuola, Amos. *Palm-Wine Drinkard.* 1952. New York: Grove Press, 1953.

Walker, Alice. "Dedication." In *I Love Myself when I'm Laughing and Then again when I'm Looking Mean and Impressive: A Zora Neale Hurston Reader.* Ed. Alice Walker. Old Westbury: Feminist Press, 1979. 1–5.

———. Foreword to *Zora Neale Hurston: A Literary Biography* by Robert Hemenway. Urbana: University of Illinois Press, 1977. xi–xviii.

Washington, Booker T. *Up from Slavery.* 1901. New York: Dell, 1965.

Washington, Joseph R., Jr. *Black Religion: The Negro and Christianity in the United States.* Boston: Beacon, 1964.

Washington, Mary Helen. Introduction to *I Love Myself when I'm Laughing and Then Again when I'm Looking Mean and Impressive: A Zora Neale Hurston Reader*. Ed. Alice Walker. Old Westbury: Feminist Press, 1979. 7–25.

Weever, Jacqueline de. *Mythmaking and Metaphor in Black Women's Fiction*. New York: St. Martin's, 1991.

Wilkins, Roy. "The Watchtower." *New York Amsterdam News*, 27 Feb. 1943. 7.

Williams, Fannie Barrier. "The Colored Girl." In *Invented Lives*. Ed. Mary Helen Washington. Garden City: Anchor, 1987. 150–56.

Wilmore, Gayraud S. *Black Religion and Black Radicalism*. Garden City: Doubleday, 1972.

Wimby, Diedre. "The Female Horuses and Great Wives of Kemet." In *Black Women in Antiquity*. Ed. Ivan Van Sertima. New Brunswick: Transaction Books, 1988. 36–48.

Woodson, Carter G. *The Mis-Education of the Negro*. Philadelphia: Hakim's Publications, 1933.

Wright, Richard. "Between Laughter and Tears." Review of *Their Eyes Were Watching God* by Zora Neale Hurston. *New Masses*, 5 Oct. 1937. 22–23.

———. "Blueprint for Negro Writing." *New Challenge* 2 (Fall 1937). 53–65. Reprinted in *Richard Wright Reader*. Ed. Ellen Wright and Michel Fabre. New York: Harper and Row, 1978. 36–49.

Zahan, Dominique. *The Religion, Spirituality, and Thought of Traditional Africa*. Trans. Kate Ezra and Lawrence M. Martin. Chicago: University of Chicago Press, 1983.

# Index